Impossible Refuge

Impossible Refuge brings the perspectives of refugees into rapidly emerging dialogues about contemporary situations of mass forced migration, asking, "What does it mean to be displaced?" Based on multi-sited ethnographic research conducted with refugees from Central Africa living in situations of protracted asylum in Uganda and resettlement in Australia, the book provides a unique comparative analysis of global humanitarian systems and the experiences of refugees whose lives are interwoven with them. The book problematises the solutions that are currently in place to resolve the displacement of refugees, considering that since displacement cannot be reduced to a politico-legal problem but is an experience that resonates at an existential level, it cannot be assumed that politico-legal solutions to displacement automatically resolve what is, fundamentally, an existential state of being. *Impossible Refuge* therefore offers a new theoretical foundation through which to think about the experiences of refugees as well as the systems in place to manage and resolve their displacement. The book argues that the refuge provided to refugees through international humanitarian systems is conditional, requiring that they conform to lifestyles that benefit the hegemonic future horizons of the societies that host and receive them. *Impossible Refuge* calls for new ways of approaching displacement that go beyond the exceptionality of refugee experience to consider instead how the contestation and control of possible futures makes displacement a general condition of our time. As such, it will appeal to scholars across the social sciences with interests in migration and refugees, humanitarianism and violence, sovereignty and citizenship, cosmology and temporality, and African studies, broadly.

Georgina Ramsay is a sociocultural anthropologist at the University of Delaware, USA. She has conducted research with refugees from Burundi, Rwanda, Liberia, and the Democratic Republic of the Congo across settings of asylum in Uganda and resettlement in Australia. She has a professional background of working with resettled refugees in Australia and has also published opinion pieces on topics related to forced migration in public media outlets.

On Edge: Ethnographies and Theories of Threshold Phenomena

https://www.routledge.com/On-Edge-Ethnographies-and-Theories-of-Threshold-Phenomena/book-series/ASHSER1447

This series seeks to explore the circumstances that compel subjects, life-forms, and material things to reimagine, redefine and reorder their existence at the edge of experience and social orders. Concerned with the ever-present but often unarticulated doubt embedded in everyday life and based on a metaphysics of emergence, novelty and creativity as forces in their own right, it welcomes anthropological and trans-disciplinary studies of transformations and threshold phenomena, such as crises, disasters and catastrophes, deaths and births, sexualities, rituals of transition, and social movements.

With attention to phenomena that lie beyond the reach of everyday experience, whether these be life forms such as bacteria, material processes such as rusting, or the uncanny dimensions of the cultural and social, On Edge: Ethnographies and Theories of Threshold Phenomena encourages studies that develop innovative methodologies, including those informed by post-humanist perspectives, and seeks to make space for inventive and experimental projects.

Series Editors

Mark Graham is Head of the Department of Social Anthropology at the University of Stockholm, Sweden. He is the author of Anthropological Explorations in Queer Theory.

Elisabeth Lund Engebretsen is Senior Lecturer at the Centre for Gender Research, University of Oslo, Norway. She is the author of Queer Women in Urban China: An Ethnography and co-editor of Queer/Tongzhi China: New Perspectives on Research, Activism and Media Cultures.

Titles in the Series

Impossible Refuge
The Control and Constraint of Refugee Futures
Georgina Ramsay

Impossible Refuge

The Control and Constraint of Refugee Futures

Georgina Ramsay

Routledge
Taylor & Francis Group
LONDON AND NEW YORK

First published 2018 by Routledge

2 Park Square, Milton Park, Abingdon, Oxfordshire OX14 4RN
52 Vanderbilt Avenue, New York, NY 10017

Routledge is an imprint of the Taylor & Francis Group, an informa business

First issued in paperback 2019

British Library Cataloguing-in-Publication Data
A catalogue record for this book is available from the British Library

Library of Congress Cataloging-in-Publication Data
A catalog record for this book has been requested.

ISBN: 978-1-138-63334-6 (hbk)
ISBN: 978-0-367-22963-4 (pbk)

Typeset in Times New Roman
by codeMantra

Contents

Acknowledgments

On an unseasonably warm August afternoon in 2012, I was invited to visit a Congolese woman after beginning the recruitment process for my doctoral research. She welcomed me into her home and life with characteristic warmth, along with a meal that we shared with her family whilst sitting outside on the veranda of her house in a suburban Australian neighbourhood. Since that afternoon, and especially for the 18 months of ethnographic fieldwork that followed, I have been deeply interwoven in her life and the lives of many other Central African women. In their particular ways, each has taught me much: not only about their experiences of refugee settlement but also about life itself. I am eternally indebted to all of the women and their families for sharing their lives, stories, and food with me. The meaning of sharing food together is not lost on me. No matter what happens in my future, I will always be, to them, a "daughter."

Although I cannot acknowledge them by their real names, special thanks must be given to two of the women I conducted fieldwork with. Firstly, to "Nyomanda" for her deep and unfaltering investment in this project. My family and I are eternally grateful to you for being another "mother" to me when I needed it most. And to "Camille," I cannot adequately express how deeply sorry I am for what you have experienced in Australia. I have put your story into these pages as you asked me to. I am sorry I could not do more.

Funding for this research was provided as an Australian Postgraduate Award through the University of Newcastle. I also want to acknowledge my funded participation through Duke University to participate in the Futures and Ruins workshops held there in 2016. The discussions held during those workshops, and the friends I made there, have in large part inspired the direction of this book.

I completed the doctoral research that this book is based on with supervision from three remarkable academics at the University of Newcastle: Daniela Heil, Hedda Askland, and Barry Morris. Each has provided inspiring insights over the years, which have now been layered into this book. Thanks must also go to Dianna Shandy for her thoughtful engagement with this work in dissertation form as an external examiner and for her continuing encouragement of my research as a mentor. For providing me with a space to write, intellectual stimulation, endless encouragement, and especially a home away from home, I must thank Elizabeth Dunn and the Department of Geography at Indiana University Bloomington. I also want to thank Susan Seizer and Jeanne Sept from the Department of Anthropology at Indiana University Bloomington for allowing a rogue anthropologist to become part of their intellectual community.

To all of my Newcastle friends and colleagues who have supported me over the last few years: You are layered into this book too. Thanks must go to Sarah Kabanoff, Sally Baker, Matt Bunn, Nathan Morris, Jo Hiles, Dena Sharrock, Debbi Long, Vanessa Bowden (and Mana), Ann Taylor, Emma Quilty, Joel McGregor, and all the others I have missed. To all of my colleagues at the Centre of Excellence for Equity in Higher Education, and especially to Penny Jane Burke, thank you for understanding my need to pursue this possibility while supporting the good work of the centre. Thanks must especially go to Kiri Hata for being a mentor, colleague, and friend to me in the darkest times. To all of my Bloomington friends and colleagues: you may not have realised it, but I was working (sometimes). Thanks must go especially to Uri Eran, Clemence Pinaud, Oliver Shao, Elena Popa, Kurt Baer, and all the others. Special thanks must also go to Zandro Pleimann and Fiona Taggart for being the most generous people I know.

Thank you to Chris Upton for being my intellectual companion over the growth of this work from dissertation to book and for being there to work through all the ruptures and impossible possibilities that accompany that kind of growth. Many chapters are inspired by our meanders and conversations. Thank you to Jen and Callan for watching me grow and loving me in spite of my wildness. Special thanks must go to Victoria Jack, a truly wonderful human being and an absolute inspiration in all ways.

Thanks must be given to Nate O'Sullivan for being my constant and unconditional friend. Our friendship is one of the best and most unexpected surprises I have known. Your encouragement and belief has helped me to recognise and seize possibilities I did not know existed. You will always be the longest.

To my family: Lisa, Paul, Mathew, Brian, and Sylvia. Thanks is not enough. Your endless support and belief is the basis of this book.

List of terms and abbreviations

ABC	Australian Broadcasting Corporation
AHRC	Australian Human Rights Commission
AIHW	Australian Institute of Health and Welfare
BBC	British Broadcasting Corporation
DIBP	Department of Immigration and Border Protection
DRC	Democratic Republic of the Congo
DSS	Department of Social Services
HRW	Human Rights Watch
LGBTQI	Lesbian, Gay, Bisexual, Transgender, Queer, Intersex
M23	March 23 Movement, a rebel military group based in DRC
NGOs	Non-government Organisations
UK	United Kingdom
UN	United Nations
UNHCR	United Nations High Commissioner for Refugees
US	United States

Figure 1 Uganda: Sarah embodies the cosmology of regeneration through fertility and the preparation of plant foods to distribute to family. Source: Photograph: Author.

Introduction

"This is violence. What they are doing to us here, now. This is violence."

Helen spoke these words during a conversation with me in March 2014.[1] At that time, I had known Helen for almost two years and was familiar with her background and experiences. In 1998, she had fled the DRC after militia broke into her home and tortured her husband, threatening to murder him. Fleeing to Uganda with her husband and their then small children, the family initially lived in the urban sprawl of the capital city, Kampala. At that time, in Uganda, legal recognition of refugee status was only available to peoples living in designated camps. Those people who, like Helen and her family, sought asylum in the country but lived outside of camps, such as in Kampala, were considered illegal residents. They did not have a right to work, rent housing, access health care services, or seek humanitarian relief. For a couple of years, Helen and her family lived a precarious existence in those conditions, earning a small living from informal entrepreneurial ventures in a textile business. Eventually, however, the strain of surviving as illegal residents became too difficult. The family relocated to a camp where they were registered as refugees, but they were far from safe. In the camp, they became the targets of ongoing persecution. Helen claims that her entire family was poisoned in the camp and that, as a result, her children almost died. Soon after that incident, Helen and her family began the application process to be resettled in a country outside of Uganda. Because of their continuing vulnerability to violence, their application for resettlement was accelerated. Eventually, they were selected for resettlement to Australia.

When recounted in this way, as a linear trajectory from exodus to exile and eventual resettlement, Helen's story evokes the conventional refugee narrative of moving from a distinct point of displacement to a distinct point of refuge (Ramsay 2017a). But it was not the hardships of life as a refugee in Uganda that Helen was describing when she referred to violence. Rather, she was referring to the violences of resettlement in Australia.

What is the meaning of displacement for those who experience it? This is a seemingly obvious question through which to enter into a dialogue about the experiences of refugees and from which to develop strategies to resolve their displacement. Yet it is this question that is typically absent from humanitarian responses to refugees, public and political imaginaries of refugees, and scholarly research about refugees. It is this question, of what it means to experience displacement, which is the focus of this book.

The experiences of refugees are often approached in humanitarian institutions similarly to the way in which I recount the experiences of Helen above, that is, as a linear trajectory from a distinct point of displacement to a distinct point of refuge. In humanitarian institutions, this assumption of temporal linearity is expressed through responses to refugees that implicitly conflate their experiences of displacement with a politico-legal condition of being stripped of civic rights and protections. In scholarly research, this assumption of temporal linearity is expressed through a dominant characterisation of displacement as an experience of liminality: that is, of being betwixt and between categories of social recognition, in which progressing from a condition of displacement to an experience of refuge is inadvertently implicated within processes that resolve the politico-legal ambiguity of refugee status and restore civic rights and protections. Both approaches apply an assumption of temporal linearity to the experiences of refugees and conflate the experience of displacement with a condition of statelessness.

I began the research for this book wanting to explore how refugees themselves understand what it means to experience refuge, particularly in the context of resettlement. Between August 2012 and March 2014, I conducted in-depth ethnographic research with approximately 35 women from a refugee background, as well as other members of their families, who had been resettled in Australia from the DRC, Burundi, and Rwanda. I reasoned, however, that in order to examine what it means to experience refuge, it is also necessary to explore what it means to experience displacement. And so, when I was invited by a resettled refugee to journey with her back to Uganda, where she had previously lived after fleeing the DRC, I agreed. Together, Nyomanda and I moved to Kampala, the capital city of Uganda, where we lived in a two-room apartment in a 12-unit apartment complex in Namasuba, an outer suburb of the city. Between January and March 2013, I conducted research in Kampala, living not only with Nyomanda and members of her family but amongst five other families of refugees, approximately 35 people, from the DRC exclusively.

As one of few researchers who has conducted research with refugees in both a context of asylum and a context of resettlement, I positioned this book to explore how refugees experience displacement and refuge in ways that transcend the dominant assumption that these are discrete domains of experience. For the women whose stories are recounted in this book, being displaced or in refuge are not exclusive experiences and are certainly not able to be mapped onto a linear trajectory that corresponds to politico-legal status. By opening up new ways to think about displacement and refuge, this book critically unsettles the assumption that the resettlement of refugees is an automatic solution to displacement. I argue that not only is the resettlement of refugees not a durable solution to displacement; for some, it is not a solution at all.

Seeking solutions to the refugee "crisis"

In 2016, the UNHCR estimated that up to 65 million people across the world were dislocated from their homes, unable to return. This mass movement of refugees has been referred to in international media as a "crisis" (Holmes and Casteñada 2016). But the term "crisis" implies eventfulness (Roitman 2013; Vigh 2008): a distinct problem that can be solved. In this period of mass migration, however, it seems that conventional responses to movements of refugees and other populations of displaced peoples and irregular migrants are failing.

It is not only the number of peoples who have been forced to flee their homes that has escalated in recent years. Conventional pathways of seeking asylum, temporary protection, and refuge have also changed. Typically, refugees were people who had been forced to flee their home, had entered a country neighbouring that which they were fleeing, had sought asylum and refugee status there, and had generally then been contained in a camp or designated settlement area: that is, set aside and away from civilian populations to make the policing of refugee populations and the provision of humanitarian relief to them more efficient. The experiences of Helen, and many other refugees I came to know during my research, reflect this supposedly typical trajectory of forced migration. Today, however, more than half of the world's refugees have self-selected to live in urban areas, often illegally (UNHCR 2017c). In addition, many asylum seekers have eschewed the traditional process of applying for refugee status in the country they first arrive in after fleeing, choosing instead to journey further to nations in Europe or elsewhere in an attempt to independently select where to seek asylum. The figure of the "refugee" in public and political imaginaries has long represented inherent otherness: a category of person who is "matter out of place" (Douglas 1966; Malkki 1992: 34). In recent years, this characterisation has persisted and indeed been bolstered by media dialogues that represent refugees as potential security threats and link them to the potential to commit terrorist acts (Cannizzaro and Gholami 2016; Walsh 2016). Global responses to increasing populations of asylum seekers and refugees, especially to those seeking to enter Europe and other Western nations, have been almost universal, comprising increased and enhanced modes of policing, detainment, and the fortification of national borders (Fassin 2011). The refugee is no longer simply objectified through a humanitarian gaze as a passive victim but is now also objectified through a criminal lens as a potential threat.

Recognising that such responses are neither sustainable nor humanitarian, governments and international organisations are seeking new ways to manage populations of displaced peoples. In 2016, this culminated in the development of the New York Declaration for Refugees and Migrants (UN General Assembly 2016), the outcome of a global summit of worldwide governments and the UN in which responsibility to protect the rights and lives of refugees and migrants at a global scale was announced, with the intent to create a global compact to achieve this goal in 2018. One centrepiece of the New York Declaration for Refugees and Migrants was a commitment to changing the conventional model of containing refugees in countries of first asylum by providing increased opportunities for the resettlement of refugees to a third country.

Resettlement is a programme of migration that is administered by the UNHCR in partnership with participating countries that agree to resettle refugees each year. As set out in the Resettlement Handbook (UNHCR 2011a), the process of applying for refugee resettlement is as follows: in camps and other sites, refugees apply for resettlement, have their applications for resettlement assessed by UN officials, and are either denied or waitlisted, and then representatives of individual nations select refugees for resettlement based on country-specific criteria. The three countries which have, at least in recent years, accepted the most refugees for resettlement have been the US, Canada, and Australia.

Resettlement is assumed to be an automatic solution to the displacement of refugees. The UNHCR puts forward resettlement as one of the three durable solutions to protracted refugee situations (UNHCR 2017a, 2011b). In academic literature, the assumption of resettlement as refuge is rarely problematised. For refugees themselves, resettlement is often mythologised: longed for in a way that means "many people in refugee camps think of resettlement as akin to winning the lottery" (Jacobsen 2005: 55). But, currently, the number of refugees who have applied for resettlement through the UNHCR vastly exceeds the number of resettlement placements that are made available to refugees. Generally, as was seen in 2016 and previous years, less than 1 per cent of refugees in need of resettlement actually have the opportunity to resettle each year (UNHCR 2017a). Given how exclusive this programme is, it is perhaps not surprising that it has come to be assumed in dominant humanitarian, political, and scholarly dialogues that resettlement is an automatic source of refuge that resolves the displacement of refugees. It is such taken-for-granted logics, which conflate resettlement with refuge, that have informed recent commitments to increase the number of refugees resettled each year, especially those put forward by the UN and other global actors who are in the process of developing a global compact in 2018 that is dedicated to providing more effective protection for refugees and migrants (UN General Assembly 2016). One of the goals of that global compact is to increase and enhance programmes of refugee resettlement.

It seems counter-intuitive to the goal of protecting refugees to critically examine resettlement because resettlement is, ostensibly, one of the most obvious methods of resolving displacement, identified as such by humanitarian institutions, scholars, and even refugees themselves. However, analysing solutions to displacement from the perspectives of refugees who have actually experienced resettlement opens up new ways to think about displacement and the solutions that are proposed to resolve it. In this book,

I put forward an analysis of asylum and resettlement based on the ways in which refugees themselves understand and experience displacement. In doing so, the experiences recounted in this book complicate conventional assumptions about where, when, and how displacement and refuge are constituted for refugees. By collapsing the idea of displacement and refuge as discrete categories of experience, I consider that, without seeking to understand how refugees themselves understand and experience displacement, the so-called solutions that are designed to resolve that condition can only ever be based on assumptions of benevolence. Such assumptions conceal that a sense of displacement can endure even after refugees have, ostensibly, been provided with a solution to resolve it. As I describe in this book, displacement can also itself be a product of those solutions. This analysis brings up a question to contemplate in future work with refugees: who does the resettlement of refugees serve, if not themselves?

The displacement of refugees is predominantly understood in humanitarian contexts and scholarly research as a problem of refugees being out of place: both in a spatial sense, by being dislocated physically from their homes, and in a politico-legal sense, by being dislocated from frameworks of civic rights and protections that are tied to national identification. The particular theoretical focus of this book is to explore how displacement can be understood in terms of time and temporality. I consider time to be contextual and variable. I describe how, for the refugees I conducted fieldwork with, time is experienced and understood as circular: trajectories of life and projections of the future are understood in relation to a view of time as cyclic, involving a cosmological dynamic of stagnation and regeneration. I also focus on how the organisation of refugee lives through bureaucratic models of asylum and resettlement imposes assumptions of linear time on these refugees, rupturing their sense of existential continuity and inflicting new forms of violence. Through this theoretical approach, I consider how time itself is implicated in the production of displacement. Just as Johannes Fabian (1983) pointed to the ways in which the subject of anthropological inquiry is so often understood through ethnographic engagement as existing in and of another time, so too do assumptions of temporal alterity characterise and conceal how refugees, and particularly refugees from continental Africa, experience both displacement and refuge across contexts of asylum and resettlement.

Temporary asylum in Uganda

The technical purpose of a country of asylum is to provide refugees with temporary protection after fleeing their country of origin. Uganda has one of the most "favourable refugee protection environments in the world," according to the UNHCR (2017b). Uganda is one of few countries, especially in continental Africa, which does not enforce a containment policy toward refugees: such containment policies would require refugees to live in designated camps, or otherwise be considered illegal residents. The Ugandan government has passed the Refugees Act of 2006 and Refugee Regulations of 2010, which allow refugees to have freedom of movement (meaning they can choose where to live), rights to work, and rights to use land for farming and settlement. Refugees can choose to live in an urban area or to live in a designated refugee settlement, where they are provided with a plot of land and tools to farm for their own use and to create agricultural trade opportunities (Sharpe and Naumsobya 2012). Refugees are encouraged to create sustainable livelihoods, independent from humanitarian relief, by becoming involved in trade economies with local Uganda peoples, gaining employment, or engaging in entrepreneurial activities.

But the lived experience of asylum in Uganda is, at least for the refugees I came to know there, not as "favourable" as it is popularly portrayed. Although refugees do have a legal right to freedom of movement, it is generally required that refugees who choose to live outside of a designated refugee settlement be granted permission to take up the right (Sharpe and Naumsobya 2012: 569) and, in doing so, declare themselves as self-sufficient and relinquish any claim to humanitarian relief. This means that refugees who live outside of designated settlements must be wholly self-reliant. Many, however, are not equipped to be so.

The refugees I met had decided to live outside of the settlements for many reasons. Some were not familiar with farming and did not see how they could sustain an adequate livelihood through agricultural practices alone. Others feared that the close proximity to other refugees in the settlements meant that they were less anonymous there and could be identified by peoples of the same groups who had threatened, or practiced, violence toward them in the DRC. And so many refugees chose to live in Kampala, but without a specific means to create self-reliant livelihoods. In Kampala, they were faced with the necessity of creating a self-sustaining livelihood, but in attempting to do so they were often not treated equitably. Rather, they were confronted with an often hostile employment market in which many were funnelled into low-paying and precarious work. They were vulnerable to exploitation. Some of the women I spoke with had been forced into situations of survival sex more than once since living in the city. These are the "favourable" conditions of asylum that are provided to refugees in Uganda. Every refugee I met there told me that they wished for resettlement.

For these refugees, asylum in Uganda is not a context of "temporary" protection. Indeed, this assumed temporariness of asylum is another layer of insecurity in their already insecure lives. It calls their futures into crisis: should they build roots in Uganda or seek a new life elsewhere? As such, these refugees experience life in Uganda as a temporal paradox: as a permanent temporariness, a continual stagnation that makes regenerating life and rejuvenating the circular cycle of time impossible. Their desire for resettlement was based on the seemingly obvious premise that life in resettlement is better than life as a refugee in Uganda. Resettlement was imagined by many to be a context in which it is possible to create, in their words, a "new life." For many refugees I worked with in Australia, however, this premise is false.

Permanent resettlement in Australia

Australia has an international reputation for cruelty towards refugees. This reputation has been constructed particularly in relation to the regime of mandatory detention that is imposed on refugees who seek asylum in Australia by boat. Although international attention has been focused on the detainment of asylum seekers in Australia in recent years, the mandatory detention of people seeking asylum was first introduced in 1992 (Fleay and Briskman 2013). The policy set out that any person who arrived undocumented in Australia to seek refugee status would be detained until their claim was processed and finalised. Especially since 2001, however, following the September 11 attacks in the US, the policies of detaining asylum seekers have been expanded (Triggs 2016). Since then, and under successive governments from competing political parties, these containment policies have also periodically included the excision of asylum seekers on islands surrounding mainland Australia and eventually other countries in the Pacific region, including Papua New Guinea and Nauru (Fleay and Briskman 2013).

These centres are colloquially termed in Australian media as "detention centres" because asylum seekers housed within them are, effectively, being detained. A report into the conditions of children being detained in facilities on Christmas Island, which have now been closed, describes how asylum seekers were forced to live in overcrowded prison-like structures, with concrete floors and high wire fences (AHRC 2014). Recent commissioned reports and leaked information describing the experiences of asylum seekers on Christmas Island (AHRC 2014), as well as Nauru (Farrell, Evershed, and Davidson 2016), attest to the pervasive problem of detainees, and especially children, being made vulnerable to physical, sexual, and psychological abuse in detention.

In 2013, the Australian government announced that it would no longer resettle any person who seeks asylum in Australia by boat, even if their refugee status is found to be valid (ABC 2013), a stance that has been continued by successive governments from competing parties (ABC 2016). In 2016, the Australian Prime Minister, Malcolm Turnbull, announced an intention to extend the ban on resettling asylum seekers who arrive by boat in Australia, proposing to introduce legislation that would not only block their resettlement as refugees, but which would be a "lifetime ban" that would block them from obtaining any visa to Australia in the future, including business and tourist visas. Turnbull claimed:

> This will send the strongest possible signal to the people smugglers … They must know that the door to Australia is closed to those who seek

> to come here by boat with a people smuggler. It is closed. Those passengers will never settle in this country.
>
> (ABC 2016)

Historically and contemporaneously, Australian policies of detaining asylum seekers have, as Turnbull's comments suggest, been based on the idea that imprisoning those who seek to settle in Australia by boat will deter them from making the dangerous sea passage (Fleay and Briskman 2013). Detaining asylum seekers is, and has historically been, projected by the government not only as a way to protect the Australian population from security threats but as a way to protect refugees themselves.

The decision, from 2013, to not resettle those refugees who seek asylum by boat left thousands of people indefinitely detained in regional processing centres. To date, most of those asylum seekers and recognised refugees remain in those conditions. They have been stranded for years, unable to return to their country of origin for fear of death, unable or unwilling to be settled in the local nations they are being warehoused in, and unable to be settled in Australia. International and national organisations have repeatedly investigated the policies and conditions of offshore processing and mandatory detainment of asylum seekers and refugees and have deemed that such practices contravene international conventions on human rights and seeking asylum (AHRC 2014; HRW 2016). Australia is the only nation in the world that has in a place a policy of the mandatory and indefinite detention of asylum seekers as a first action that indiscriminately applies to all, including children (AHRC 2014: 19).

This regime of mandatory detention seems worlds apart from the formal programme of refugee resettlement that the Australian government operates, which is, perhaps ironically, called the Humanitarian Programme (DIBP 2017). This programme includes a generous quota of migration placements that are specifically intended for refugees seeking to be resettled in Australia from offshore contexts. Usually, these are refugees who have applied for resettlement through the UNHCR and who have then been selected, and deemed suitable for resettlement, by representatives of the Australian government (UNHCR 2016). Even though these two streams of refugee and asylum seeker immigration—one policy that selects refugees from offshore contexts and another policy that rejects them when they seek asylum in onshore contexts—seem separate, each programme reinforces the logics of the other.

The Australian government considers the regime of mandatory detention of asylum seekers to be necessary "to ensure that those arriving by boat do not get an unfair advantage over others" (Karlsen 2016). This advantage is, ostensibly, over those "others" who wait for resettlement from camps and other protracted refugee situations, that is, those who the government themselves can select for migration to Australia. What this means is that the migration of refugees to Australia is deeply dichotomised between the "good" refugees who wait for resettlement and the "bad" refugees who attempt to be settled in Australia by directly seeking asylum. But the offshore component of the Humanitarian Programme of resettling "good" refugees that is operated through the Australian government is not as humanitarian as it is portrayed to be through government and popular representations. Rather, refugees who are resettled through the Humanitarian Programme continue to be made into problems: only, their problematisation is realised through expectations that, as "good" refugees, they will comply with a trajectory of integration that follows a linear timescale. Over time, the benefits that support resettled refugees are reduced and expectations that they will join education and labour market activities in order to become self-reliant are increased. It is assumed that, over time, they will become "good" citizens who demonstrate their integration through neoliberal indicators of value and worth. The many refugees who fail to conform to such expectations within the limited time frame become marked and encoded as problems.

The Australian programme of resettlement is one of the most extensive in the world. In the first six months of settlement, refugees are provided with access to intensive specialist support services, government benefits, long-term housing, educational (including English language tuition) enrolment, and health care services (UNHCR 2016). This intensive support for new arrivals is replaced from six months with refugee-specific casework services and broader public institutions that provide assistance with general employment, housing, educational, heath, and family services as requested. But, as Fozdar and Hartley (2013) have argued, providing refugees with civic recognition and rights upon resettlement does not equate to social belonging. Rather, this programme of resettlement reduces refuge to a linear trajectory of neoliberal markers of integration: beginning at English language proficiency, moving into self-sufficiency from social welfare support services, and eventually being evidenced through independence from government financial benefits by being employed. If refugees fail to conform to these expectations of resettlement, they are made into problems that require fixing: usually through punitive institutional interventions. But refugees often fail to conform to these expectations through no intrinsic deficiency of their own. Instead, assumptions of difference, deficiency, and inferiority that are attached to them in resettlement can set them up to fail.

In Australia, refugees who are resettled from Africa are able to access extensive services that support their material welfare, but they are also being resettled into a social context that, on the basis of the blackness of their skin colour, already encodes them with assumptions of difference (Colic-Peisker 2005; Hanson-Easey and Augoustinos 2010; Ramsay 2017a, 2017b). These assumptions of difference are lived and negotiated by refugees from Africa on a daily basis, at least according to what I observed while I conducted fieldwork with them. At best, these are expressed as micro-aggressions: an occasional comment referring to Africa as a single country or ignorant remarks about the assumed savagery of peoples from Africa who are imagined to be non-literate, uneducated, and untouched by civilisation. Then, there are direct insults: calls for refugees to "Go back to Africa" abused from the windows of passing cars, among others. But there are also more subtle but deeply damaging, institutional interventions: hospital staff who are unwilling to respect the wishes of refugees under their care, police officers who refuse to recognise contextual factors that surround offences, and child welfare institutions that read the caregiving practices of refugees from Africa as child abuse. I witnessed all of these examples, and many others, while conducting fieldwork with resettled refugees in Australia.

It is not, therefore, just the idea that refugees from Africa bring with them different cultural practices that leads to their being made into a problem in resettlement. The specific kind of otherness that is attached to Africa, and those peoples and practices associated with it, stems from a constructed idea of temporal incommensurability (Ramsay 2017a), that is, the association of Africa with violence, primitivism, and a static temporality of pre-civilisation ways of living (Apter 1999; Mbembe 2001). For many refugees, resettlement to Australia is not the permanent refuge that was hoped for. Rather, by constructing refugees as problems and continuously re-problematising them, resettlement in Australia emerges for these refugees as a context in which new, and in some cases previously unimaginable, experiences of displacement are made possible.

Terms and concepts

Refugee

The most common and internationally recognised definition of a refugee comes from the UNHCR 1951 Convention and 1967 Protocol relating to the status of refugees. This document defines a refugee as a person who:

> Owing to well founded fear of being persecuted for reasons of race, religion, nationality, membership of a particular social group or political opinion, is outside the country of his nationality or is unable or, owing to such fear, is unwilling to avail himself of the protection that country.
> (UNHCR 2011c: 3)

This definition dominates how refugees are identified and categorised across international contexts. But, under this definition, the status of refugee can only be applied to peoples who are not able to seek protection from persecution from the government in their country of origin and who, as a result, have crossed a national border to seek asylum elsewhere. Refugee status is, fundamentally, a category of statelessness.

The term statelessness refers to a person who has no claim to national protection. Technically, then, the category of the refugee is not legally synonymous with that of a stateless person because it is possible to be stateless without being a refugee: many peoples who do not have a formal nationality maintain a living residence within a country without persecution. Nonetheless, refugees are treated, analytically and empirically, as paradigmatic figures of statelessness (Agamben 1998). When seeking asylum in a country outside their nation of origin, refugees are political aliens who are generally not protected by the rule of law in that country but are still subject to possible persecution by it. This vulnerability of statelessness is supposed to be mediated by international conventions on inalienable human rights. But, in responding to populations of refugees seeking asylum, individual states are often not equipped to mandate inalienable rights and protections whilst at the same time provide specific rights and protections to the citizens under sovereign rule. As such, it is often transnational humanitarian organisations that are tasked with responding to the needs of refugee populations. Being structured into relationships of dependency with international relief organisations is an empirical marker of the statelessness of the refugee, who has no state from which to seek aid or protection (Dunn forthcoming; Harrell-Bond 1987; Hyndman 2000). As such, refugees are defined and treated as a problem.

Contrary to the dominant representation of refugees as passive victims, refugees are not a problem because they are peoples whose national context has rendered them subjects of extreme violence. Rather, they are a problem because, having been ejected from a national context, they complicate how global populations are organised and ruled according to national boundaries (Malkki 1992). In the wake of the Second World War, Hannah Arendt, who had herself fled Europe as a refugee, pointed out that the discourse of shared humanity and inalienable rights that had emerged since the end of the war, particularly through international institutions like the UN, is based on a fallacy. This is because, according to Arendt (1967), the universal human at the centre of the inalienable human rights discourse cannot be understood except in relation to their national identity: birth itself is the catalyst of acquiring citizenship. The refugee, whose connection between national identity and human being is ambiguous, throws this assumed conflation between human and citizen into question, meaning that refugees become populations to be governed as much as populations to protect.

The intimate connection between protection and policing of refugees endures in contemporary contexts precisely because refugees continue to represent a fundamental category of otherness to a global system of organising political, economic, and social networks according to national identification. The persistence of the nation as an organising category can appear to be paradoxical in a contemporary context because the increasing intensification of global connectedness over recent decades has destabilised the idea of the nation state as the fundamental platform of geopolitical governance (Appadurai 1996; Glick-Schiller 1997). But even before technology and other modes of globalisation enabled new possibilities for transnational connectedness, Hannah Arendt (1967) argued that the decentralisation of nation state power is, and will continue to be, expressed through processes that concentrate rights and protections into categories of national identification. These categories, according to Arendt (1967), become increasingly tightened and exclusive during periods in which national governments wrestle over, and seek to affirm, sovereignty: that is, the political organisation of control over individual autonomy. The shrinking of rights-based protection to citizens has shifted and intensified in recent years, morphed into what Aihwa Ong (1999, 2006) identifies as a kind of flexible regime of citizenship that includes and excludes depending on the needs of market logics and neoliberal agendas, which now seem to be inextricably intertwined with the sovereignty of nation states. The state is no longer considered to be an absolute locus of political governance: transnational corporations have challenged the authority of national economies; political formations that transcend distinct national boundaries, such as the EU, have been constructed (and now contested); and the idea of the "civil war" has become increasingly redundant as supposedly intra-national conflicts across countries in Africa, Latin America, and Asia have been overtly fuelled by international interests and transnational war economies (Aretxaga 2003). Refugees and asylum seekers are another layer of insecurity within this shifting regime of nation-based sovereignty. Ghassan Hage (2016) has described how the increasing numbers of asylum seekers in Europe since 2014, during what has been termed the "European Refugee Crisis" in popular international media accounts, have evoked a "siege" mentality response. Marked as inherently threatening to the political and social life of European nations, this normalisation of the would-be refugee as a person who embodies inherent otherness is, according to Hage (2016), an attempt to reinforce a "dying" national order.

The normalisation of the refugee category as a political and legal condition defined by externality to the nation state positions refugees as a problem. However, it also forecloses the possibility of re-imagining the displacement of refugees outside of a seemingly fundamental condition of statelessness, thereby developing new, and possibly more effective, solutions to their experiences of insecurity. The terminology and categories through which humanitarian programmes support refugees and resolve their displacement serve, despite being applied with ostensibly benevolent intentions, to normalise the objectification of refugees as stateless peoples. With the lives of displaced peoples continuing to be organised through terminology, politico-legal categories, and structural interventions that can only understand their displacement through their ability (or not) to seek protection from a nation state, it remains difficult to analyse and imagine solutions to displacement that can consider that category more expansively: that is, beyond a conflation of displacement with statelessness.

Displacement

Displacement is a concept that is often used to describe the experiences of refugees but is rarely defined. Most frequently, however, displacement is conflated with a condition of statelessness, based on dominant understandings of refugees as stateless peoples. This conflation between displacement and statelessness is generally not directly stated but is reproduced when the solutions that are proposed to resolve displacement invariably seek to re-insert refugees back into a category of national identification.

The UNHCR has devised three "durable solutions" to resolve the problem of refugees who live in what is termed a "protracted refugee situation." Some deciphering of this humanitarian language reveals, again, how the problem of refugees is as much about their inability to be ruled through a national order as it is about the vulnerability of their persecution. The UNHCR (2006) defines a "protracted refugee situation" as:

> [O]ne in which refugees find themselves in a long-lasting and intractable state of limbo. Their lives may not be at risk but their basic rights and essential economic, social and psychological needs remain unfulfilled after years in exile. A refugee in this situation is often unable to break free from enforced reliance on external assistance.
>
> (UNHCR 2006: 106)

This characterisation of a protracted refugee situation recognises that the displacement experienced by refugees is not reducible to a political and legal category of exclusion but is also experienced as a state of existential "limbo." However, the so-called durable solutions that have been devised by the UNHCR to resolve the displacement of refugees who live in protracted refugee situations reduce such existential aspects of displacement to a product of being outside of a national order. The three durable solutions put forward by the UNHCR to resolve the displacement of refugees include the following: the repatriation of a refugee back to their country of origin, if and when it is safe; the local integration of a refugee into a host country of asylum, including the right to their eventual citizenship in that nation; and the resettlement of refugees to a third nation, including the provision of permanent residency and the right to eventual citizenship in that nation. Each of these three solutions requires re-inserting the refugee into a category of national identification and proection.

In assuming that the re-insertion of the refugee into a national order resolves the problem of displacement, however, these solutions also imply that the experience of being displaced is a linear trajectory: from exodus, to exile, to eventual solution. The ways in which displacement endures, and is reproduced, even after these solutions have been provided to refugees is overlooked and concealed by such assumptions. Not only are the so-called solutions that are proposed to resolve displacement based on a fundamental misreading of displacement as a politico-legal category of statelessness rather than an existential condition that is defined and experienced by refugees themselves, the global programmes that are in place to respond to and resolve the displacement of refugees are also based on an assumption of linear time.

Time and temporality

Time is not a universal experience. Indeed, it is difficult to assign a general meaning through which to conceptualise and define what is meant by the term. Attempts to define time can often reify what are implicitly taken-for-granted assumptions about temporality (Koselleck 1985). For example, time is often characterised as a passage of events that signal the change and vacillation of social and material existence, and yet terms like "passage" and "event" themselves reflect a culturally specific claim to time as a linear and cumulative trajectory. Rather than try to specifically define time, it can be more productive, as Nancy Munn (1992) puts forward, to recognise that social life and human experience are inherently temporalised, that is, made meaningful in relation to subjective understandings and experiences of time. Time seems to be an intangible, and yet fundamental, logic through which humans attach meaning to existence.

There are a myriad of ways through which lived experiences are temporalised. This heterogeneity of time has long been a focal point of social science and humanities research. From the perspectives of early functionalist theorists, time was put forward as a method of organising human existence in meaningful, and collectively recognisable, ways. Emile Durkheim (1976), for example, described time as a set of categories, both collectively and personally constituted, through which activities of life become segmented in ways that follow a seemingly natural rhythm. Bronislaw Malinowski (1927) put forward a view of what he termed "time-reckoning," in which ideas of time were considered units of measurement through which activities of daily life are coordinated. Based on fieldwork with the Nuer, E.E. Evans-Pritchard (1939, 1969) wrote about the possibility of dual and concurrent modalities of time. Evans-Pritchard (1939) theorised two modes of time: "oecological time," which was used to describe the processual creation of temporal rhythms through immersion in everyday activity, and "structural time," which was used to describe the quantification of time through the social distance attached to intergenerational descent. These ways of recognising the temporalisation of experience as fundamentally grounded in social and cultural understandings pointed to the heterogeneous and multi-modal ways through which time is experienced.

From the 1970s, the temporalisation of experience began to be understood as a process that reflects not only social and cultural contexts but also systems of political and economic domination (Munn 1992). When developing his theory of practice as a process through which modes of social differentiation are reproduced, Pierre Bourdieu (1977), for example, recognised that the regularisation of practice has a tempo. Bourdieu (1977: 9) described practice as being "inscribed in the current of time." Eric Wolf (1982) brought a temporal lens to what were then emerging theorisations of core/periphery relations, describing how those peoples enmeshed in imperialist forms of capitalist production have historically, and contemporaneously, been silenced by assumptions about whose history, and indeed whose time, is significant. Reinhart Koselleck (1985), a philosophical historian, described how the temporalisation of history as "past" and the future as "new" is a way to capture a particularly modern condition of seemingly accelerated time. Koselleck (1985) described how assumptions embedded in the semantic representation of time can lead subjects to feel that their sense of existing in the present is oriented towards progress, freedom, and infinite improvement, thereby maximising and accelerating their temporal experience but foreclosing the opportunity for focus on the present and critical reflection. Johannes Fabian (1983) turned the critical lens of differential temporalisations to the discipline of anthropology itself, pointing out that anthropologists had long used assumptions of incommensurable time to deny coevalness with those amongst whom they conducted fieldwork. According to Fabian (1983), this implicit process of representing the ethnographic subject as existing in and of another time is a way to solidify and naturalise hierarchical assumptions of innate and incommensurable difference. Recognising that assumptions about time are crucial to the reproduction of power in ethnographic encounters, this work by Fabian (1983) formed part of what was to become a critical turn in anthropology more broadly to examine how methods of ethnographic fieldwork and conventions on writing culture embed seemingly taken-for-granted structures of power in the discipline (Abu-Lughod 1996; Behar 1996; Clifford and Marcus 1986).

The idea of a "bounded" culture became the central problem in this critical reflective turn in the discipline. Previously, subjects of anthropological inquiry had been primarily understood as members of a distinct social group and often conceptualised as a bounded, stable, and mappable community (Malkki 1992), often termed as a village, tribe, ethnic group, or national collective. But the emergence of disciplinary debates in the 1980s and early 1990s on the reproduction of power through anthropological inquiry emerged at a point in which it seemed that global interconnectedness had become especially intensified (Abu-Lughod 1996; Clifford and Marcus 1986; Gupta and Ferguson 1992; Ingold 1996). As such, this seemingly conventional way of approaching groups and cultures as bounded and stable entities became a specific point of contention. Collectivising peoples by seemingly arbitrary and bounded categorisations was identified as a way to reify and reproduce an idea of the "other" by essentialising the relationship between people, place, and culture.

As a result of these dialogues, the focus on anthropological inquiry in the 1990s reflected what has been termed a "spatial turn" (Warf and Arias 2009). Researchers like Arjun Appadurai (1988, 1996), Akhil Gupta and James Ferguson (1992, 1997), Liisa Malkki (1992, 1995a, 1995b), and others (Castells 1996; Olwig and Hastrup 1997) heralded a new approach to examining lived experiences without essentialising peoples or culture to distinct and mappable places. Indeed, the idea of "culture" itself became a point of disciplinary contention, with researchers like Lila Abu-Lughod (1996) describing how the concept of culture attaches a false sense of innate difference and staticity to what are inherently contingent and processual lived experiences. Instead, Abu-Lughod (1996) argued for an "anthropology of the particular," in which practices and beliefs become known and analysed as actions that reflect and reproduce specificities of context. Those previous theorisations of time as heterogeneous became incorporated into this turn towards the contingency of unbounded experience, with temporal ontologies increasingly, but somewhat vaguely, being recognised as "flows," in line with the fluidity of peoples, materialities, and cultural forms across space (Hodges 2008).

However, the spatial turn somewhat relegated a focus on time to the theoretical backburner in anthropology. It was not until the mid-2000s that temporality once again emerged as a major topic in anthropology: a turn that, it seems, the discipline is still in the midst of grappling with as a major and as yet emergent theoretical lens through which to analyse and comprehend contemporary events (Bear 2014; Rabinow 2008). Indeed, this renewed focus on time emerged in significant part as a response to the idea of the "event" as a crucial organiser of experience in the 21st century. The idea of the event has long been a focus of anthropological inquiry (Kapferer 2010; Vigh 2008) but has gained recent momentum, especially following the 2008 global financial crisis (Rotiman 2013) and subsequent austerity measures (Knight and Stewart 2016), the refugee "crisis" in Europe (Kallius, Monterescu, and Rajaram 2016), and now, most likely, the political events of 2016, including Brexit and the outcome of the US election. Concurrently, anthropologists have begun to consider how experiences of time are formed through specific modes of neoliberal capitalism and economic production that intersect both local and global scales (Bear 2014; Guyer 2007; Hodges 2014; Millar 2014). These dialogues have, to an extent, coalesced into a general concern regarding time in anthropology in which it is the idea of the "future," as both an object and imaginary, that has become a broad focus of disciplinary inquiry (Allison and Piot 2014; Hankins 2015; Piot 2010; Vigh 2009a). Perhaps this disciplinary turn towards the future reflects broader public and popular concerns over similar questions.

Displacement is a critical entry point through which to consider the temporalisation of experience, especially in regard to this new turn towards theorising futures. Predictions and projections of the future have long been recognised as an orienting point of experience in the present. Indeed, this future orientation is considered, particularly in phenomenological philosophy and in the work of social scientists whose research is informed by phenomenology, to be crucial to the ways in which the present is, for most, experienced as mundane and unremarkable (Desjarlais and Throop 2011): because expectations of the future—be that the future that will unfold in the next minute or the future that will unfold in the next year—is generally assumed to be a consistent and knowable object based on expectations of the world and lived experience within it that have become regularised and been reproduced through past experiences. Referring to the ways in which the surroundings of a person are generally perceived as coherent, Maurice Merleau-Ponty (1962), for example, describes how:

> There is vision only through anticipation and intention, and since no intention could be a true intention if the object towards which it tends were given to it ready made and with no motivation, it is true that all vision assumes in the last resort, at the core of subjectivity, a total project or a logic of the world which empirical perceptions endow with specific form, but to which they cannot give rise.
>
> (Merleau-Ponty 1962: 713)

For most, life is experienced, as Merleau-Ponty (1962) suggests, with a certain "givenness," that is, with a projected sense of coherency and continuity. But a sense of displacement arises when this expectation of the future, this givenness of the world, is disrupted by processes and events that make those expectations uncertain. Displacement, according to Michael Jackson (2013b: 257), is a process through which a person is unexpectedly ejected from their habitual routines of thought and behaviour and is required to radically rethink themselves in relation to a new, uncertain, and often disconcerting projection of the world and future possibilities within it.

In recent years, anthropologists have increasingly focused on the ways in which people reconcile what seem to be inherently uncertain futures into a sense of certainty in everyday life (Allison 2012; James 2010; Millar 2014). Future uncertainty, it seems, is a new state of normal everywhere. Perhaps, then, displacement is not an exceptional experience but is, in fact, a defining condition of existence in the contemporary period?

This is a question that was poised more than two decades ago by Liisa Malkki (1992) who described how the "refugee" category is only exceptional because it represents a fundamental exclusion from a national order of things: a national order that is, nonetheless, being undermined everywhere by the unboundedness of social, political, and economic life across the globe. Indeed, Annika Lems (2016) has described how displacement has come to hold a certain symbolic power in the discipline of anthropology as a concept that exemplifies what is considered to be a fundamental condition of spatial uprooting. Urging for a return to recognising the significance of place in the process through which a sense of being displaced is constituted, Lems (2016) draws on the work of Edward Casey (1997) to emphasise that humans are always already occupying the materiality and surroundings of being in place, even if that place is not immediately familiar to them. This turn that Lems (2016) encourages towards recognising that displacement is both a phenomenological experience of ontological discontinuity and an empirical experience of occupying an unfamiliar place pushes forward a new way to think about displacement as a broadly existential condition. What Edward Casey (1993: xiv) pointed to, however, was not just that displacement is the "loss of a vital connection with place itself" but that being displaced involves loss of the "permanence of place." The ways in which the temporalisation of experience are implicated in the ways in which people live and understand displacement have been largely absent in these theoretical dialogues.

If the temporalisation of experience is crucial to the ways in which peoples come to attach coherency and continuity to their lives, then a fundamental rupture of the ways in which people experience time can also be considered as a basis of displacement. It is not only the impermanence of place but the inability to project and envision the permanence of a future which I contend is central to the ways in which refugees experience what it means to be displaced. Displacement is not simply an experience of being disconnected from place, then, but is also an experience of being disconnected from temporal rhythms of ordinary life.

This temporal dynamic of displacement has become a focus of recent research in anthropology (Brun 2015, 2016; El-Shaarawi 2015; Griffiths 2014; Horst and Grabska 2015; Rotter 2016). In these emerging dialogues, however, displacement is often theorised as a juncture in time, that is, as a condition of temporal liminality in which refugees and other kinds of irregular migrants are seemingly permanently suspended in the immediacy of the present (Agier 2002; Bauman 2002). The domination through which the displacement of refugees and other kinds of irregular migrants is produced is described as intertwined with the refugees' temporal suspension in spaces of asylum and immigration detention, in which they are unable to or restricted from actively working towards futures of their own imagining (Rotter 2016). And, certainly, elements of temporal domination emerged in the experiences of the refugees I conducted fieldwork with, whose lives I trace throughout this book.

Reifying the temporality of displacement to a condition of liminality, however, embeds an assumption of linearity onto the experiences of refugees and those whose lives are labelled as displaced. More perniciously, describing displacement as a liminal condition that is temporally linear implies that this condition of indefinite indeterminacy can be resolved if the foundational cause of the ambiguity of refugee status is also resolved. It is as if the temporality of displacement as a condition of protracted impermanence begins at exodus, when refugees lose the national identity of their origin country, and is resolved when the refugee is once again re-inserted into a context of national identification, whether that be through repatriation, local integration, or resettlement.

In this book, I trace the experiences of refugees across diverse contexts, tracing their lives in the seemingly protracted indeterminacy of asylum in Uganda and their lives in the supposedly permanent refuge of resettlement. But this distinction is one that is rendered meaningful by political and legal differences between the assumed temporariness of asylum and the assumed permanence of resettlement and is not a distinction that is rendered meaningful in the ways that refugees themselves experience displacement. The uncertainty of their futures and the disruption to their temporal rhythms are not automatically solved upon being provided with a supposedly permanent politico-legal solution to their displacement. Indeed, these processes themselves can embed new ways to control and constrain the lives and futures of refugees, protracting their displacement well beyond the political and legal categories through which it is conventionally defined.

Note

1 Names used throughout are pseudonyms. Identifying details of each participant have been obscured.

References

ABC. 2013. Kevin Rudd Announces New Asylum Seeker Processing and Refugee Settlement Deal with Nauru. Available at: www.abc.net.au/news/2013-08-03/rudd-announces-asylum-policy/4863226 (Accessed 22 January 2017).

ABC. 2016. Manus Island, Nauru Refugees to Be Banned from Entering Australia, Malcolm Turnbull Says. Available at: www.abc.net.au/news/2016-10-30/manus-nauru-refugees-asylum-seekers-to-be-banned-turnbull-says/7978228 (Accessed 22 January 2017).

Abu-Lughod, L. 1996. Writing against Culture. In *Recapturing Anthropology: Working in the Present*. R.G. Fox (Ed.), pp. 137–162. Santa Fe, NM: School of American Research Press.

Agamben, G. 1998. *Homo Sacer: Sovereign Power and Bare Life*. Translated by Daniel Heller-Roazen. Stanford, CA: Stanford University Press.

Agier, M. 2002. Between War and City: Towards an Urban Anthropology of Refugee Camps. *Ethnography* 3(3): 317–341.

AHRC. 2014. The Forgotten Children: National Inquiry into Children in Immigration Detention. Available at: www.humanrights.gov.au/sites/default/files/document/publication/forgotten_children_2014.pdf (Accessed 3 October 2016).

Allison, A. 2012. Ordinary Refugees: Social Precarity and Soul in 21st Century Japan. *Anthropological Quarterly* 85(2): 345–370.

Allison, A. and Piot, C. 2014. Editor's Note on Neoliberal Futures. *Cultural Anthropology* 29(1): 3–7.

Appadurai, A. (Ed.). 1988. *The Social Life of Things: Commodities in Cultural Perspective*. Cambridge; New York: Cambridge University Press.

Appadurai, A. 1996. *Modernity at Large: Cultural Dimensions of Globalization*. Minneapolis: University of Minnesota Press.

Apter, A. 1999. Africa, Empire, and Anthropology: A Philological Exploration of Anthropology's Heart of Darkness. *Annual Review of Anthropology* 28: 577–598.

Arendt, H. 1967. *The Origins of Totalitarianism*. London: Allen & Unwin.

Aretxaga, B. 2003. Maddening States. *Annual Review of Anthropology* 32: 393–410.

Bauman, Z. 2002. In the Lowly Nowherevilles of Liquid Modernity: Comments on and Around Agier. *Ethnography* 3(3): 343–349.

Bear, L. 2014. Doubt, Conflict, Mediation: The Anthropology of Modern Time. *Journal of the Royal Anthropological Institute* 20(S1): 3–30.

Behar, R. 1996. *Women Writing Culture*. Berkeley: University of California Press.

Bourdieu, P. 1977. *Outline of a Theory of Practice.* Translated by R. Nice. Cambridge; New York: Cambridge University Press.Brun, C. 2015. Active Waiting and Changing Hopes: Toward a Time Perspective on Protracted Displacement. *Social Analysis* 59(1): 19–37.

Brun, C. 2016. There is No Future in Humanitarianism: Emergency, Temporality, and Protracted Displacement. *History and Anthropology* 27(4): 393–410.

Cannizzaro, S. and Gholami, R. 2016. The Devil Is *Not* in the Detail: Representational Absence and Stereotyping in the "Trojan Horse" News Story. *Race Ethnicity and Education.* doi:10.1080/13613324.2016.1195350.

Casey, E. 1993. *Getting Back into Place: Toward a Renewed Understanding of the Place-World.* Bloomington; Indianapolis: Indiana University Press.

Casey, E. 1997. Smooth Spaces and Rough-Edged Places: The Hidden History of Place. *The Review of Metaphysics* 51(2): 267–296.

Castells, M. 1996. *The Network Society.* Oxford: Blackwell.

Clifford, J. and Marcus, G.E. 1986. *Writing Culture: The Poetics and Politics of Ethnography.* Berkeley: University of California Press.

Colic-Peisker, V. 2005. "At Least You're the Right Colour": Identity and Social Inclusion of Bosnian Refugees in Australia. *Journal of Ethnic and Migration Studies* 31(4): 615–638.

Desjarlais, R. and Throop, C.J. 2011. Phenomenological Approaches in Anthropology. *Annual Review of Anthropology* 40: 87–102.

DIBP. 2017. Fact Sheet—Australia's Refugee and Humanitarian Programme. Available at: www.border.gov.au/about/corporate/information/fact-sheets/60refugee (Accessed 20 January 2017).

Douglas, M. 1966. *Purity and Danger: An Analysis of the Concepts of Pollution and Taboo.* London; New York: Routledge.

Dunn, E. forthcoming. *No Path Home: Humanitarian Camps and the Grief of Displacement.* Ithaca, NY: Cornell University Press.

Durkheim, E 1976. *The Elementary Forms of Religious Life.* 2nd edition. Translated by J.W. Swain. London: Allen & Unwin.

El-Shaarawi, N. 2015. Living in an Uncertain Future: Temporality, Uncertainty, and Well-Being among Iraqi Refugees in Egypt. *Social Analysis* 59(1): 38–56.

Evans-Pritchard, E.E. 1939. Nuer Time Reckoning. *Africa* 12: 189–216.

Evans-Pritchard, E.E. 1969. *The Nuer: A Description of the Modes of Livelihood and Political Institutions of a Nilotic People.* New York; Oxford: Oxford University Press.

Fabian, J. 1983. *Time and the Other: How Anthropology Makes Its Object.* New York: Columbia University Press.

Farrell, P., Evershed, N., and Davidson, H. 2016. The Nauru Files: Cache of 2,000 leaked reports reveals scale of abuse of children in Australian offshore detention. Available at: https://www.theguardian.com/australia-news/2016/aug/10/the-nauru-files-2000-leaked-reports-reveal-scale-of-abuse-of-children-in-australian-offshore-detention (Accessed 12 January 2017).

Fassin, D. 2011. Policing Borders, Producing Boundaries: The Governmentality of Immigration in Dark Times. *Annual Review of Anthropology* 40: 213–226.

Fleay, C. and Briskman, L. 2013. Hidden Men: Bearing Witness to Mandatory Detention in Australia. *Refugee Survey Quarterly* 32(3): 112–129.

Fozdar, F. and Hartley, L. 2013. Civic and Ethno Belonging among Recent Refugees to Australia. *Journal of Refugee Studies* 27(1): 126–144.

Glick-Schiller, N. 1997. The Situation of Transnational Studies. *Identities: Global Studies in Culture and Power* 4(2): 155–166.

Griffiths, M. 2014. Out of Time: the Temporal Uncertainties of Refused Asylum Seekers and Immigration Detainees. *Journal of Ethnic and Migration Studies* 40(12): 1991–2009.

Gupta, A. and Ferguson, J. 1992. Beyond "Culture": Space, Identity, and the Politics of Difference. *Cultural Anthropology* 7(1): 6–23.

Gupta, A. and Ferguson, J. (Eds.). 1997. *Anthropological Locations: Boundaries and Grounds of a Field Science*. Berkeley: University of California Press.

Guyer, J. 2007. Prophecy and the Near Future: Thoughts on Macroeconomic, Evangelical, and Punctuated Time. *American Ethnologist* 34(3): 409–421.

Hage, G. 2016. *Etat de siege*: A Dying Domesticating Colonialism? *American Ethnologist* 43(1): 38–49.

Hankins, J.D. 2015. The Ends of Anthropology: 2014 in U.S. Sociocultural Anthropology. *American Anthropologist* 117(3): 553–564.

Hanson-Easey, S. and Augoustinos, M. 2010. Out of Africa: Accounting for Refugee Policy and the Language of Casual Attribution. *Discourse & Society* 21(3): 295–323.

Harrell-Bond, B. 1986. *Imposing Aid: Emergency Assistance to Refugees*. Oxford: Oxford University Press.

Hodges, M. 2008. Rethinking Time's Arrow: Bergson, Deleuze and the Anthropology of Time. *Anthropological Theory* 8(4): 399–429.

Hodges, M. 2014. Immanent Anthropology: A Comparative Study of "Process" in Contemporary France. *Journal of the Royal Anthropological Institute* 20(S1): 33–51.

Holmes, S.M. and Casteñada, H. 2016. Representing the "European Refugee Crisis" in Germany and Beyond: Deservingness and Difference, Life and Death. *American Ethnologist* 43(1): 12–24.

Horst, C. and Grabska, K. 2015. Flight and Exile—Uncertainty in the Context of Conflict-Induced Displacement. *Social Analysis* 59(1): 1–18.

HRW. 2016. World Report 2016: Australia. Available at: www.hrw.org/world-report/2016/country-chapters/australia (Accessed 13 February 2017).

Hyndman, J. 2000. *Managing Displacement: Refugees and the Politics of Humanitarianism*. Minneapolis: University of Minnesota Press.

Ingold, T. (Ed.). 1996. *Key Debates in Anthropology*. London; New York: Routledge.

Jacobsen, K. 2005. *The Economic Life of Refugees*. Bloomfield, CT: Kumarian Press.

Jackson, M. 2013b. *The Politics of Storytelling: Variations on a Theme by Hannah Arendt*. 2nd Edition. Copenhagen: Museum Tusculanum Press.

James, E. 2010. *Democratic Insecurities: Violence, Trauma, and Intervention in Haiti*. Berkeley: University of California Press.

Kallius, A., Monterescu, D., and Rajaram, P. 2016. Immobilizing Mobility: Border Ethnograpy, Illiberal Democracy, and the Politics of the "Refugee Crisis" in Hungary. *American Ethnologist* 43(1): 25–37.

Kapferer, B. 2010. In the Event—Toward an Anthropology of Generic Moments. *Social Analysis* 54(3): 1–27.

Karlsen, E. 2016. Australia's Offshore Processing of Asylum Seekers in Nauru and PNG: A Quick Guide to Statistics and Resources. Available at: www.aph.gov.au/About_Parliament/Parliamentary_Departments/Parliamentary_Library/pubs/rp/rp1617/Quick_Guides/Offshore (Accessed 2 November 2016).

Knight, D.M. and Stewart, C. 2016. Ethnographies of Austerity: Temporality, Crisis and Affect in Southern Europe. *History and Anthropology* 27(1): 1–18.

Koselleck, R. 1985. *Futures Past: On the Semantics of Historical Time*. Cambridge, MA: MIT Press.

Lems, A. 2016. Placing Displacement: Place-Making in a World of Movement. *Ethnos* 81(2): 315–337.

Malinowski, B. 1927. Lunar and Seasonal Calendar in the Trobriands. *Journal of the Royal Anthropological Institute of Great Britain and Ireland* 57: 203–215.

Malkki, L. 1992. National Geographic: The Rooting of Peoples and the Territorialization of National Identity among Scholars and Refugees. *Cultural Anthropology* 7(1): 24–44.

Malkki, L 1995a. *Purity and Exile: Violence, Memory, and National Cosmology among Hutu Refugees in Tanzania*. Chicago, IL: University of Chicago Press.

Malkki, L. 1995b. Refugees and Exile: From "Refugee Studies" to the National Order of Things. *Annual Review of Anthropology* 24: 495–523.

Mbembe, A. 2001. *On the Postcolony*. Berkeley: University of California Press.

Merleau-Ponty, M. 1962. *Phenomenology of Perception*. Translated by C. Smith. New York: Humanities Press.

Millar, K. 2014. The Precarious Present: Wageless Labor and Disrupted Life in Rio de Janeiro, Brazil. *Cultural Anthropology* 29(1): 32–53.

Munn, N. 1992. The Cultural Anthropology of Time: A Critical Essay. *Annual Review of Anthropology* 21: 93–123.

Olwig, K.F. and Hastrup, K. 1997. *Siting Culture: The Shifting Anthropological Object*. New York; London: Routledge.

Ong, A. 1999. *Flexible Citizenship: The Cultural Logics of Transnationality*. Durham, NC: Duke University Press.

Ong, A. 2006. *Neoliberalism as Exception: Mutations in Citizenship and Sovereignty*. Durham, NC: Duke University Press.

Piot, C. 2010. *Nostalgia for the Future: West Africa after the Cold War*. Chicago, IL: University of Chicago Press.

Rabinow, P. 2008. *Marking Time: On the Anthropology of the Contemporary*. Princeton, NJ: Princeton University Press.

Ramsay, G. 2017a. Incommensurable Futures and Displaced Lives: Sovereignty as Control over Time. *Public Culture* 29(3): 515–538.

Ramsay, G. 2017b. A Civilising Process: Colonial Legacies of Racism toward Central African Refugee Women Resettled in Australia. *Journal of Intercultural Studies*. 38(2): 170–188.

Roitman, J. 2013. *Anti-Crisis*. Durham, NC: Duke University Press.

Rotter, R. 2016. Waiting in the Asylum Determination Process: Just an Empty Interlude? *Time & Society* 25(1): 80–101.

Sharpe, M. and Naumsobya, S. 2012. Refugee Status Determination and the Rights of Recognized Refugees under Uganda's Refugees Act 2006. *International Journal of Refugee Law* 24(3): 561–578.

Triggs, G. 2016. Human Rights and the Overreach of Executive Discretion: Citizenship, Asylum Seekers, and Whistleblowers. *Macquarie Law Journal* 16(3): 3–16.

UN General Assembly. 2016. New York Declaration for Refugees and Migrants. Available at: www.un.org/ga/search/view_doc.asp?symbol=A/71/L.1 (Accessed 12 January 2017).

UNHCR. 2006. Protracted Refugee Situations: the Search for Practical Solutions. In The State of the World's Refugees 2006: Human Displacement in the New Millennium. Available at: www.unhcr.org/4444afcb0.html (Accessed 29 November 2016).

UNHCR. 2011a. UNHCR Resettlement Handbook. Available at: www.unhcr.org/46f7c0ee2.html (Accessed 12 November 2016).

UNCHR. 2011b. Refugee Protection and Mixed Migration: The 10-Point Plan in Action. Available at: www.unhcr.org/50a4c2b09.pdf (Accessed 12 November 2016).

UNHCR. 2011c. The 1951 Convention Relating to the Status of Refugees and Its 1967 Protocol. Available at: www.unhcr.org/en-us/about-us/background/4ec262df9/1951-convention-relating-status-refugees-its-1967-protocol.html (Accessed 5 January 2017).

UNHCR. 2016. Australia: Country Chapter—UNHCR Resettlement Handbook. Available at: www.unhcr.org/en-au/protection/resettlement/3c5e542d4/unhcr-resettlement-handbook-country-chapter-australia.html (Accessed 2 February 2017).

UNHCR. 2017a. Resettlement. Available at: www.unhcr.org/en-au/resettlement.html (Accessed 12 January 2017).

UNHCR. 2017b. Uganda. Available at: www.unhcr.org/afr/uganda (Accessed 12 January 2017).

UNHCR. 2017c. Urban Refugees. Available at: www.unhcr.org/en-us/urban-refugees.html (Accessed 7 January 2017).

Vigh, H. 2008. Crisis and Chronicity: Anthropological Perspectives on Continuous Conflict and Decline. *Ethnos* 73(1): 5–24.

Vigh, H. 2009a. Wayward Migration: On Imagined Futures and Technological Voids. *Ethnos: Journal of Anthropology* 74(1): 91–109.

Walsh, J.P. 2016. Moral Panics by Design: The Case of Terrorism. *Current Sociology* doi:10.1177/0011392116633257.

Warf, B. and Arias, S. (Eds.). 2009. *The Spatial Turn: Interdisciplinary Perspectives.* London: Routledge.

Wolf, E. 1982. *Europe and the People without History.* Berkeley: University of California Press.

Part I

Exodus

1 Cosmology and futurity

Chaos. Pacing. Doors slammed as people file in, and then back out, of the house. Hushed voices speaking Swahili softly but forcefully over intercontinental phone calls. Cups of forgotten tea left in inconvenient places. More pacing. Small children whimpering, sensing the anxiety but only partially understanding the cause. We circulate around the television set. The television broadcasts a running loop of news headlines about the unfolding "situation" in Goma: footage of tanks, indistinguishable men dressed in camouflage gear, and the occasional blue flash of a UN Peacekeeper.

That morning I had turned up to visit Nyomanda at her home feeling confident that the day would unfold as any other ordinary day in a regional Australian city would. For people in the cluster of suburban houses around us, mostly oblivious to the politics and conditions of nations in Africa, it probably did. But that November morning in 2012 was far from ordinary for my friends from the DRC who had been resettled in Australia. Arriving, I had been dramatically rushed into the house and swept into a tense flurry of activity. I barely saw Nyomanda, who I had intended to visit, as she weaved in and out of family members and friends who, also from the DRC, had made her home the central vantage point to an unfolding crisis in the eastern states of their origin country. I was told, in whispers, "They have taken Goma."

On November 20, 2012, a militia group called the M23, which had formed to rebel against the government of the DRC, took control of Goma, the capital city of the North Kivu province in the eastern region of the DRC. In the few weeks before the M23 militia withdrew from Goma, tens of thousands of people fled from the region (Jones and Smith 2012). This included relatives of the resettled refugees I had come to know in Australia.

From the sitting room of a house in a suburban Australian neighbourhood, phone calls were being made to connect with relatives in the DRC and to establish their safety in, and in some cases passage from, the city. Snatches of one-sided phone conversations emphasised the crucial role played by resettled refugees in protecting relatives in situations of conflict violence. "Stay with Rebecca, for now..." I heard, then "Meet Moise at..." followed by "It is not safe to leave now, maybe tomorrow..." I was not only witnessing how conflicts in Africa reverberate across transnational contexts of asylum and resettlement. I was also witnessing how these transnational circuits of support historicise and particularise the experiences of refugees.

Resettled refugees are not neutral subjects whose opportunities to create new lives in Australia mean the evisceration of their pasts. This transnational network of support, so readily activated across numerous nodes of social relations whilst evidently responsive to specific instances of need, reflects existing structures of sociality that have persisted for these refugees across experiences of exodus, asylum, and eventual resettlement.

Dominant representations of refugees too often, however, de-historicise and decontextualise their experiences (Malkki 1996). Indeed, the humanitarian system of responding to refugees is broadly organised through processes that coach refugees into positions of passive victimhood, whereby the particularities of their social, cultural, and political worlds are obliterated.

Through the process of acquiring refugee status determination and applying for resettlement, refugees must tell "their story" of persecution numerous times: recounting their experiences as a linear narrative, recalling specific details of traumatic events, and carefully maintaining consistency upon each re-telling in order to affirm the veracity of their own lived experiences (Jansen 2008). The system of humanitarian governance through which the lives of refugees are structured often work to discredit them based on an assumption that they are deceptive (Thomson 2012: 198), a popular characterisation that Cindy Horst (2006a) refers to as the portrayal of refugees as "cunning crooks." Proving the veracity of a claim to refugee status requires that refugees differentiate themselves from this stereotype of the "cunning crook" and instead embody a status of "vulnerable victim," which nonetheless similarly erases personal characteristics and experiences. This trope of the refugee as victim has infiltrated dominant representations of refugee lives, so that even in academic scholarship it is common to recount the experiences of peoples who have become refugees as if their lives begin at exodus.

But the lives of refugees do not begin at exodus. They begin where most other lives begin. In the arms of family members, in a house that makes up part of a larger neighbourhood or village, and in particular social and cultural contexts that, eventually, shape how peoples who become refugees come to conceptualise and experience what it means to be displaced. In this chapter, I depart from the typical de-historicising structure of recounting refugee experiences in which analytical inquiry begins at exodus. Instead, I trace the personalised logics from which refugees constitute and experience what it means to be displaced and through which they attempt to reconcile their contemporary existences into a sense of refuge.

Cosmology of regeneration

I spent a lot of time in the kitchens of women I conducted fieldwork with. Over long afternoons spent discussing cooking techniques and sharing recipes, I was often confronted with a question that seemed, at first, to be unrelated to preparing meals, that is, "How many babies will you have?" As an unmarried woman with no children, then in my early twenties, my reproductive status was, to the refugees I came to know, a topic of public consternation. "To my people," I was told once through a fit of giggling by a woman my own age who already had one child, "you are a husk of maize." After this comment, we could not contain our shared laughter over the apparent absurdity of this cooking and plant metaphor being applied to me. When we finally recovered from our amusement, my friend added an offhand comment, however, that finally enabled me to put together what had seemed to be an irrelevant, and yet pervasive, connection between the activity of cooking and the experience of motherhood. "You are eating for free," she told me.

I was to hear this idiom, "eating for free," many more times during fieldwork, spoken always in reference to women that did not have children. This metaphor of infertility as a state of "eating" suggests an inverse metaphor between fertility and a state of "cooking." Indeed, soon after being referred to as a "husk of maize," I began to pick up on other metaphors that directly linked fertility to the processual trajectory of cooking and the cyclic growth and degeneration of subsistence plant foods, such as references to pregnancy as "cooking," procreative sexuality as "mixing," the womb as a "field" and the baby as a "plant," and the practice of birth spacing as a cycle of "growth" and "rest." But such expressions of human reproduction, the growth of plants, and the cooking and eating of plant foods as interwoven cycles of regeneration were not just metaphorical. These parallels between activities of cyclic regeneration express a whole cosmology of existential being.

The concept of a cosmology, broadly, refers to the implicit expectations that inform how people perceive and experience the world. The term is used to describe culturally specific patterns through which people categorise, and make sense of, their worlds (Douglas 1973) and the underlying premises that order how human experience is understood in relation to what is perceived to be an extrinsic structuring of events, objects, and time (Tambiah 1985). Cosmologies are those seemingly self-evident laws and logics of human existence and the universe that make some ways of being seem natural. An especially pervasive cosmological logic, which manifests across numerous cultural, religious, and historical contexts, is that which attaches assumptions of reproductive potentiality to female bodies and links human fertility to the fecundity of nature (Delaney 1991).

In anthropological work with peoples in equatorial Africa, broadly, and the region of Central Africa, specifically, this cosmological intertwining of gendered existential purpose and seemingly natural cycles of regeneration is well documented. Both Audrey Richards (1956) and Victor Turner (1967) describe how initiation rituals for young women in Central African groups involve specific acts of eating plant foods. These kinds of ritual activities are of cosmological significance for the involved women because, according to Turner (1967: 24), "the food stands for her reproductive power and her role as cultivator and cook." More recently, anthropologists who have conducted research with groups in Central and Southern Africa have similarly recognised this link between social reproduction and biological reproduction as related to seemingly natural cycles of growth and continuity (Devisch 1993; Feldman-Savelsberg 1999, 2016; Kaspin 1996; Silva 2009). The work of Christopher Taylor (1988, 1990, 1992, 1999a, 1999b) is especially significant. Based on extensive research in Rwanda, Taylor (1988: 1343) describes how "patterns which are implicit and pervasive in Rwandan culture" centre on assumptions of existence as a trajectory of blockage and flow, which is symbolised in the organisation of everyday life through the fluidity and stagnation of liquids that are crucial to maintaining human existence, that is, those liquids associated with food, drink, and sexual exchange. Though it pertains to diverse ethnographic contexts, this corpus of research points to the circulation of similar cosmological logics amongst groups in equatorial Africa and Central Africa, specifically in which existence is understood through a dialectic of reproductive potentiality and stagnation: that is, a cosmology of regeneration.

When referring to me as a person who is "eating for free" and using other metaphors linking fertility and regeneration, the refugees I conducted fieldwork with were expressing what I had otherwise only observed as an implicit, but nonetheless pervasive, pattern of cosmological logics. Their lives were often structured around an imperative to regenerate life, in terms of both biological and social reproduction. Seemingly separate domains of fertility, subsistence gardening, and cooking were, in fact, intimately interwoven as a cosmology of regeneration. It was apparently expected that my own reproduction trajectory and the activity of cooking would be brought up in the same context because neither is separate: questions and discussions about fertility, cooking, and plants are, to these refugees, as much existential as they are practical.

An ontology of "feeding"

I arrived to visit Nyomanda one morning around 10 a.m. to find the curtains drawn and the house unusually quiet. I knocked loudly, twice, on the front door but received no response. Going to the back door of the house, which was kept unlocked for close friends of Nyomanda and her family to enter, I made my way into the house, calling out to see if she was there. Eventually, I heard muffled movements from her bedroom. Nyomanda emerged, still in her pyjamas, and apologised for not being up to greet me. I, in turn, apologised profusely. After we both finished laughing at our shared awkwardness, Nyomanda explained why she had woken up so unusually late. She had been on the phone with "her boy," she said, "my sister's son, Richard."

Twelve months previously, Nyomanda's sister, who had remained in the DRC despite the conflicts of the past years, died unexpectedly. She left behind many children with no father. Despite her physical distance from the children, Nyomanda provided care for them. She told me, "I am their mother, now."

After the death of his mother, 14-year-old Richard had remained in the DRC, but his younger siblings had been sent into Uganda to live with relations in a refugee camp. Richard lived in Goma in a room shared with other young men employed as garment makers. I asked Nyomanda if something had happened to him. "Oh, no," she told me quickly, "Richard is fine, now. But he needed someone to talk to ... even though it was 3am in the morning here. I knew he had to talk with me. It is hard for him there." Again, Nyomanda emphasised that she does this because she is a "mother."

Motherhood is not, for these Central African refugees, able to be singularly understood as a social role of bearing and rearing offspring. Motherhood, to them, is an ontology: that is, a way of being. In recent years, the concept of ontology has been especially problematised in anthropological debates in regard to what is called an "ontological turn," in which anthropologists have sought to challenge previously held assumptions of ontology as a universal basis of experiential being (Holbraad and Pederson 2014). Within this context of increasing recognition of multiple modalities of being, Marilyn Strathern (2012) has characterised "eating" as a particular ontology of being. Based on a re-working of ethnographic material from Melanesia in relation to recent theorisations of ontology from anthropological work in Amazonian contexts, Strathern (2012) writes:

> What difference would it make to our apprehension of relations if the activity for (in place of) describing states of being were Eating?... Across Amazonia (the act of) eating is a fundamental classificatory or logical operator. And there are countless instances of the very being deployed in ways outsiders often take as metaphorical, as is true in Melanesia. These instances do not simply concern rules about eating food, though such rules are part of it; "eating" is applied to actions that from an English-speaking perspective do not involve taking in food in any immediate sense.
>
> (Strathern 2012: 1–2)

The ontology of "eating" that Strathern (2012) describes refers to a way of being that is characterised by consuming productive resources, such as food, material objects, and people, without replenishing those stocks. The "eating" ontology is a mode of parasitism that recalls the ways in which I, and other women who did not have children, were referred to as people who were "eating for free." That is, people who consume worldly resources without actively regenerating life.

In contrast to the ontology of "eating" that Strathern (2012) puts forward, the existential imperative to become a mother can be conceptualised as an ontology of "feeding." By "feeding" as a way of being, women who become mothers not only embody relations of care to their biological offspring. They also embody a whole mode of being that requires them to stimulate, more expansively, the regenerative potential of existence.

It is upon giving birth to a first child that this ontology of "feeding" is triggered. Women who, like myself, had not given birth to a child, were implicitly excluded from a number of activities that symbolise regeneration. For example, when helping to prepare for social events, I and other non-mothers were allowed to help with preparing food for cooking but were rarely invited to support in the process of cooking itself. When gardening, I was allowed to provide ancillary assistance, but it was mothers who oversaw that seeds and plants were nourished through watering. Upon giving birth, the status of a woman changes: she is trusted and tasked with activities that, more broadly, stimulate the regenerative potential of existence. These activities of providing care to children, nourishing the plant foods that sustain human life, and preparing and cooking foods that, when eaten, affirm survival are interwoven into a "feeding" ontology that is associated with motherhood, which reflects a cosmological imperative centred on regeneration.

The existential imperative of motherhood

The cosmology of regeneration I describe here is an analytical platform from which to characterise the existential premise of life as understood by the Central African refugees I got to know during fieldwork. However, this rendering of a cosmological imperative to regenerate life through reproduction, subsistence agriculture, and cooking and eating food is clearly based on assumptions about, as well as culturally specific readings of, gender. As I observed during fieldwork, this cosmology of regeneration is at once expansive, in that procreative sexuality is a dominant expectation for both women and men, and particularised, in that this expectation is experienced differently by peoples depending on whether their bodies are coded as male or female.

To experience personhood, a concept that refers to social recognition of an individual as a whole and actualised person, both men and women were required, it seemed, to have a child. Upon the birth of a first child, for example, the individual birth names of both biological parents would be dropped from common vernacular amongst family and close friends to be replaced with "Mama-" or "Papa-" followed by the individual birth name of the first child. Personhood, usually a concept that is applied to the realisation of the individual person, appeared, for these refugees, to signal the realisation of new and shifted forms of relatedness between peoples: between new parent and child, mother and father, and parent and wider relations. Becoming recognised as a parent, however, was not gender neutral. Motherhood and fatherhood are distinctly gendered roles within this shared constituting of personhood.

"The daddy gives the seed," I was told by one woman, Rachael, once again while standing in front of a stove. "And I grow the baby, here, in my stomach." By that stage of my life, I was already keenly aware of the biological processes through which human reproduction is achieved, but as a woman who had not yet borne a child, I was often brought into discussions about babies and children with my refugee friends as if I had no knowledge of these processes. What surprised me on this particular day was that I had been asking Rachael how she felt about her husband being away from the house most days to study and work. She understood this interpersonal dynamic between herself and her husband, which manifested in the practical organisation of everyday life, as related to broader gender differences, with the seemingly complementary but distinct roles that men and women play in reproduction being a basis from which other differences in everyday life are solidified. "Men bring the food for the family," Rachael went on, "... and wives cook it."

What Rachael is describing appears to be an understanding of gender as a set of binaries in which the coding of bodies as biologically male or female corresponds to distinct spheres of influence: men being associated with externality and public domains, and women being associated with internality and domestic domains. Anthropological inquiry has historically sought to identify universal aspects of human experience and complicate these universals by documenting cultural specificity, and one dynamic that has been put forward as universal is the tendency for people to dichotomise: to understand the world through dual categories of experience, whereby objects and processes that are not able to be categorised into binaries become labelled as potentially dangerous (Douglas 1966). There are, however, numerous problems with taking biological sex to be a basis of seemingly inherent gender distinction, which have been comprehensively analysed in feminist debates, especially from the 1970s onwards (MacCormack and Strathern 1980; Moore 1988; Ortner 1972, 1990; Ortner and Whitehead 1981). Primarily, when taken uncritically, gender binaries reflect a structural–functionalist rendering of human existence in which the reproduction of cultural and human life requires that biological sex differences map onto seemingly natural asymmetrical gender pairings that then guarantee procreative reproduction and compulsory heterosexuality (Butler 1988).

Even though the cosmology of regeneration that I describe here appears to be based on, and indeed implicated in the reproduction of, such limited gender binaries and assumptions of compulsory, procreative heterosexuality, this particular reading of gender cosmology is, ironically, premised on Eurocentric categories of analysis that give primacy to the individual subject as a vector through which gender inferiority or superiority is experienced. Regarding the pervasiveness of male dominance as a seemingly universal basis of human experience, Sherry Ortner (1990) considers that the making of gender difference into a supposedly natural dichotomy of existence is a hegemonic logic: that is, not an explicit dimension of culture or ideology but, drawing on Raymond Williams (1977), the result of a conflation of biological sex differences with gender distinctions that are implicitly reproduced and naturalised in the social ordering of everyday life. The general assumption that biological sex maps onto distinct ways of living that are known as gender differences continues to be a problem, according to Ortner (1990), precisely because it is reproduced implicitly across all societal contexts and cannot, therefore, be extensively challenged and contested by targeting explicit examples of dominance. Writing in regard to gender in Africa specifically, however, both Ifi Amadiume (1987) and Oyeronke Oyewumi (1997, 2000, 2002) complicate this position of gender difference as a kind of globalised, hegemonic logic by pointing out that such an understanding is also premised on the Eurocentric privileging of the individual subject as the basis of analytic inquiry.

A problem with much feminist analysis is that the "woman" category is primarily only understood in relation to a "man" category. According to Oyewumi (1997, 2000), such approaches implicitly privilege conjugal relations as the basis of societal organisation and, subsequently, as the nucleus of patriarchy. But in many African contexts, it is cosanguineal, and not conjugal, relations that are of most importance (Amadiume 1987; Oyewumi 2000). These are relations based on "blood" or genetic ties, such as between parent and child or brother and sister, rather than the relation between husband and wife. As Oyewumi (2000) describes:

> In all African family arrangements, the most important ties within the family flow from the mother, whatever the norms of marriage residence. These ties link the mother to the child and connect all children of the same mother in bonds that are conceived as natural and unbreakable. It is not surprising, then, that the most important and enduring identity and name that African women claim for themselves is "mother." However, motherhood is not constructed in tandem with fatherhood. The idea that mothers are powerful is very much a defining characteristic of the institution and its place in society.
>
> (Oyewumi 2000: 1097)

Motherhood was, as Oyewumi (2000) also suggests, the primary basis of identity for the refugee women I conducted fieldwork with. The majority of women I got to know in depth over the course of my fieldwork were mothers. Some had become mothers as wives, some were in informal partnerships with men, and many others were single mothers. All, however, expressed to me views about motherhood as an expectation, rather than an option, of female existence. Relations with men were not the dominant organising factor of their lives but were, rather, a transitional phase on a trajectory of motherhood.

At an event held to celebrate the birth of a new baby in Australia, the significance of motherhood was made clear to me. The event was being held to celebrate the birth of the first child of a couple from the DRC who had been married the previous year. Unlike other events that I had previously attended with Central African refugees, this was an unusually small celebration. Only the immediate family of the mother and father of the child, one other close friend, and myself were in attendance. The wedding of this couple the previous year had, in contrast, been widely attended by family members and friends from across the country. Struck by the disjuncture of size and scale between the two events, I asked the grandmother of the new baby, the mother's mother, who I was especially close to, why the celebration of the birth was a smaller and more intimate event. "It is time to become family," I was told.

For these refugees, the marriage of a couple only signals the possibility of sociality: it is the birth of a child that solidifies social recognition. As such, it is consanguinity, and not conjugality, that structures how gender is understood and experienced. Even when refugees I knew would reference the complementary roles played by male and female bodies in cycles of biological reproduction, such as referring to men as those who give "seed" and women as those who "grow" a child, these gender relations were never reducible to a binary between categories of man and woman but were always understood more expansively in relation to the potential for creating sociality through childbearing. It is the reproduction of children that is the central existential problem of being for these refugees, both men and women.

From problem to power

Motherhood is primarily approached as a problem in feminist analysis (Rich 1977). This is because motherhood is so often conflated with womanhood in hegemonic social terms, which leads to a false, but nonetheless pervasive, idea that women must become mothers if they are to experience existential completeness (Chodorow 1999). Motherhood as an essential basis of womanhood also perpetuates other damaging hegemonic logics, including the normalisation of heterosexuality as the exclusive basis of reproduction and family life (Lewin 1993). And, because it has historically and contemporaneously been mothers who provide the bulk of care work for children after they are born, motherhood has also been seen as a form of normalised gender subjugation that ejects women who are engaged in caring for children from education, employment, and leisure activities through which they could more expansively form their sense of identity, social recognition, and interpersonal value. However, as Oyewumi (1997, 2000) suggests, such readings of motherhood as a self-evident problem of female subjugation often derive from the assumption that women are individualised subjects, whose corporeal and social connectedness to children can potentially limit how their individualisation is realised when compared with those opportunities afforded to men.

But what if this scenario was reversed, and it was the ability to create corporeal and social connectedness to children that was seen as an opportunity to enhance existential purpose, rather than limit it? This is the perspective put forward by Amadiume (1987) and Oyewumi (1997, 2000, 2002), who consider that, because it is relational, rather than individualistic, aspects of personhood that are rewarded in many African contexts, motherhood is not a disadvantageous potentiality of female existence. Rather, motherhood is a salient means through which to create and solidify power.

Refugees I conducted fieldwork with expressed similar sentiments. I was told explicitly, for example, "For us, a big family, it is power." When I asked why having children created power, I was told that, in the DRC and other areas of Africa, it is typical for a woman to have ten children, maybe more. Having more children makes a family "strong," I was told, because "when there are more children, there is more life."

Taking seriously this claim to power requires, as Oyewumi (1997, 2000, 2002) suggests, recognising that, in many African contexts, it is not necessarily through individual acts that recognition is gained, but through social connectedness. This can carry through to how power is conceptualised and recognised. Jane Guyer (1993) has described how, across many equatorial African contexts, wealth is established through the accumulation of people as much as, and in some cases with more significance than, accumulating material goods and financial gains. Since it is through people that the refugees I conducted fieldwork with similarly locate power, their emphasis on motherhood cannot be singularly understood as a category of experience in relation to men and fatherhood. Rather, these refugees attach special significance to being and becoming a mother because it is through their bodies that biological, familial, and social life—indeed, the future itself—is regenerated.

Securing futures through transnational circuits of care

Shortly after the brief, but nonetheless troubling, seizure of Goma in 2012, Nyomanda began to plan a return visit to Africa. Because it was too unsafe for her to visit Goma itself, she planned instead to travel to Uganda, where many of her family members lived in Kampala and in refugee settlements, and where she too had lived as a refugee before being resettled in Australia. Nyomanda invited me to accompany her on this journey and, when I agreed, we began preparations together. Packing for the trip became an increasingly difficult task as Nyomanda and I struggled to determine how best to fill our available baggage quota with items for family members. Every item we chose to bring with us had a specific recipient and purpose. Many had the names of intended recipients already written on them. "I hope there is enough," Nyomanda told me, referring to the goods she aimed to distribute to her family in Uganda. "For the children. I am their mother." Not referring to motherhood in the sense of her direct offspring, Nyomanda was referencing a more expansive sense of motherhood: that of "feeding" peoples in her kinship group despite geographic distance and politico-legal borders through transnational circuits of care.

"Affective circuits" is the term used by Jennifer Cole and Christian Groes (2016) to describe the webs of reciprocity that are constructed by migrants from Africa across transnational contexts. Exchanges between migrants and homeland have been explored extensively in terms of global money transfers (De Haas 2007; Horst 2006a, 2008; Horst and van Hear 2002; Lindley 2009, 2010) and what is termed as social remittances (Levitt 1998; Levitt and Lamba-Nieves 2011). As Cole and Groes (2016) emphasise, however, such transnational exchanges between migrants from Africa and their relations within Africa are often characterised as unidirectional flows, in which the transfer of goods between peoples only travels from those migrants in so-called developed countries to their kin who remain in Africa. Even when the social aspects of migrant exchanges are recognised, these "social remittances" are primarily understood in terms of migrants from a developed country influencing change in their country of origin by importing ideas and practices from the new country of residence (Levitt 1998; Levitt and Lamba-Nieves 2011). Recent work by Pamela Feldman-Savelsberg (2016) draws on the idea of "affective circuits" to describe how motherhood and the creation of family is the primary way through which migrant women from Cameroon create a sense of security after relocating to Germany, similarly recognising that the sociality of African motherhood plays out over transnational contexts in ways that express broader experiences of migrant (in)securities. Recognising that the relations between peoples from Africa that persist after migration and across transnational borders also include the ways in which those who remain in Africa transfer goods, conjugal and fostering opportunities, reminders about and re-workings of cultural practices, and social obligations to those who have migrated beyond the continent, Cole and Groes (2016) and Feldman-Savelsberg (2016) characterise these webs of enduring relatedness as "circuits" because these relations are of affective exchange, not unidirectional transfer.

The immediate action taken by refugees in Australia to provide care to relations affected by the 2012 takeover of Goma can appear, at a surface level, to represent one such unidirectional transfer of resources from refugees resettled in Australia to their kin who remain in Africa. Indeed, in the introduction to this chapter, I use the word "response" to describe the actions of resettled refugees to this event, which implies a singular direction of intervention. However, the care that resettled refugees provide to family cannot be singularly understood in the immediate context of a distinct event because these refugees are expending their care in order to protect not only life in the present but life in the future tense.

If the point made by Jane Guyer (1993), that peoples in Africa often view wealth in terms of people, is taken seriously, then the seemingly unidirectional flow of support from Central African refugees in Australia to their kin who remain in Africa can indeed be seen as an exchange rather than a transfer because it is by "feeding" family who live in Africa that lives, futures, and possibilities of reciprocity and regeneration are secured. When wealth is understood in terms of financial and material resources, then the relations between refugees resettled in Australia and their families in Africa appear to be a unidirectional transfer because there is little possibility of their being able to reciprocate through similar means. But when wealth is understood in terms of people, then the support of family that remains in Africa can be seen as an investment in the future by protecting the lives of those peoples, and especially children, who will embody it. As such, refugee women resettled in Australia, like Nyomanda, are often deeply implicated in the ongoing support of family in Africa. As "mothers" whose imperative to create, protect, and preserve the continuity of life and the regenerative potential of the future extends far beyond the care that is provided to immediate offspring, these refugees are creating transnational circuits of care through which futures can be secured.

Toward a mythico-futurity

Children are viewed by the women I conducted fieldwork with as a living futurity. Their rapidly growing bodies signal the passage of time and in doing so signal the opportunity to cultivate particular practices and values: that is, to produce particular kinds of futures.[1] For the Central African refugees I conducted fieldwork with, whose understandings and experiences are oriented through cosmological logics of regeneration, birthing and rearing children are processes that confirm existential continuity. Motherhood is not simply a vector of biological reproduction, it is a process of constructing futures.

But the future is always as yet unknown: projected but never certain. Describing how the lives of Burundian Hutu refugees in asylum in Tanzania were organised according to cosmological and moral patterns of order, Liisa Malkki (1995a) uses the term "mythico-history" to characterise how the immediacy of life in the present is oriented through mythologisations of the past. For the Central African refugees I worked with, however, it was not the past that was mythologised but the future. Many told me that they wanted "new lives," and their everyday existence, in both asylum and resettlement, was organised toward a future in which their lives could be "better." However, as I describe throughout this book, such projected futures are imaginaries and do not necessarily translate into lived realities. These mythologised futures are what I term, in reference to and extending on Malkki (1995a), a "mythico-futurity" through which refugees, in both asylum and resettlement, live towards a renewed future of regenerative potential. For many, however, this mythico-futurity is contested and made precarious by forces outside of their control.

The refugees I conducted fieldwork with evidently take up their experiences of exodus, asylum, and eventual resettlement with an existing set of understandings about the nature and purpose of existence. They are not passive objects who are void of history, as refugees are predominantly projected across political, public, and scholarly representations (Malkki 1996). When participating in seemingly ordinary activities of childrearing, subsistence agriculture, and preparing and cooking food, they are substantiating a forward momentum and affirming the regenerative potential of their worlds. When engaging with and creating transnational networks of care across geographic and politico-legal borders of asylum and resettlement, as I describe when introducing this chapter, they are not only responding to specific instances of need: they are affirming expansive networks of care that speak to the imperative to regenerate life. For these Central African refugees, whose lives are implicitly organised around cosmological logics of regeneration, existential continuity is realised through human reproduction: that is, by having children and protecting the lives of children. And, as I further argue in chapters that follow, through the violences that are imposed on refugees during their experiences of exodus, asylum, and resettlement, it is the lives of children, and the futures they embody, that are at stake.

Note

1 The idea that the reproduction of children is a primary or sole locus of worth and futurity is described by Lee Edelman (2004) as "reproductive futurism" and is recognised as problematic because privileging heterosexual reproduction as the sole basis of future continuity is a way to encode those who are unable or unwilling to reproduce as peoples with "no future" and to consign them to social exclusion. With many groups in Africa valuing high fertility and placing emphasis on reproduction, there is a general tendency to presume a kind of pan-African heterosexuality (Epprecht 2008): an assumption that is not only false but that serves to reify and homogenise African peoples whilst at the same time legitimating the exclusion and stigma of peoples whose sexuality does not align with heteronormativity. My intention here is not to reproduce that imaginary of pan-African heterosexuality. However, since children are considered a social and economic resource to gain status in the present (Guyer 1993) as well as an emblem of the future, when I speak about the emphasis placed on reproduction, I do not mean to reduce that to an associated assumption of compulsory heterosexuality.

References

Amadiume, I. 1987. *Male Daughters, Female Husbands: Gender and Sex in an African Society*. Basingstoke: Palgrave Macmillan.

Butler, J. 1988. Performative Acts and Gender Constitution: An Essay in Phenomenology and Feminist Theory. *Theatre Journal* 40(4): 519–531.

Chodorow, N.J. 1999. *The Reproduction of Mothering: Psychoanalysis and the Sociology of Gender*. Berkeley: University of California Press.

Cole, J. and Groes, C. (Eds.) 2016. *Affective Circuits: African Migrations to Europe and the Pursuit of Social Regeneration*. Chicago, IL: University of Chicago Press.

De Haas, H. 2007. International Migration, Remittances and Development: Myths and Facts. *Third World Quarterly* 26(8): 1269–1284.

Delaney, C. 1991.*The Seed and the Soil: Gender and Cosmology in Turkish Village Society*. Berkeley: University of California Press.

Devisch, R. 1993. *Weaving the Threads of Life: The Khita Gyn-eco-logical Healing Cult among the Yaka*. London: The University of Chicago Press.

Douglas, M. 1966. *Purity and Danger: An Analysis of the Concepts of Pollution and Taboo*. London; New York: Routledge.

Douglas, M. 1973. *Natural Symbols: Explorations in Cosmology*. 2nd Edition. London: Barrie & Jenkins.

Edelman, L. 2004. *No Future: Queer Theory and the Death Drive*. Durham: Duke University Press.

Epprecht, M. 2008. *Heterosexual Africa?: The History of an Idea from the Age of Exploration to the Age of AIDS*. Athens: Ohio University Press.

Feldman-Savelsberg, P. 1999. *Plundered Kitchens, Empty Wombs: Threatened Reproduction and Identity in the Cameroon Grasslands*. Ann Arbor: The University of Michigan Press.

Feldman-Savelsberg, P. 2016. *Mothers on the Move: Reproducing Belonging between Africa and Europe*. Chicago, IL: University of Chicago Press.Guyer, J. 1993. Wealth in People and Self-Realization in Equatorial Africa. *Man* 28(2): 243–265.

Holbraad, M. and Pederson, M.A. 2014. The Politics of Ontology. Available at: https://culanth.org/fieldsights/461-the-politics-of-ontology (Accessed 4 December 2016).

Horst, C. 2006a. *Transnational Nomads: How Somalis Cope with Refugees Life in the Dadaab Camps of Kenya*. New York: Berghahn Books.

Horst, C. 2008. The Transnational Political Engagements of Refugees: Remittance Sending Practice amongst Somalis in Norway. *Conflict, Security & Development* 8(3): 317–339.

Horst, C. and van Hear, N. 2002. Counting the Cost: Refugees, Remittances, and the "War against Terrorism." *Forced Migration Review* 14: 32–34.

Jansen, B.J. 2008. Between Vulnerability and Assertiveness: Negotiating Resettlement in Kakuma Refugee Camp, Kenya. *African Affairs* 107(429): 569–587.

Jones, P. and Smith, D. 2012. Congo Rebels Take Goma with Little Resistance and to Little Cheer. Available at: www.theguardian.com/world/2012/nov/20/congo-rebel-m23-take-goma (Accessed 19 June 2016).

Kaspin, D. 1996. A Chewa Cosmology of the Body. *American Ethnologist* 23(3): 561–578.

Levitt, P. 1998. Social Remittances: Migration Driven Local-Level Forms of Cultural Diffusion. *The International Migration Review* 32(4): 926–948.

Levitt, P. and Lamba-Nieves, D. 2011. Social Remittances Revisited. *Journal of Ethnic and Migration Studies* 37(1): 1–22.

Lewin, E. 1993. *Lesbian Mothers: Accounts of Gender in American Cultures*. London: Cornell University Press.

Lindley, A. 2009. The Early-Morning Phonecall: Remittances from a Refugee Diaspora Perspective. *Ethnic and Migration Studies* 34(2): 1315–1334.

Lindley, A. 2010. *The Early Morning Phonecall: Somali Refugee Remittances*. Oxford: Berghahn Books.

MacCormack, C.P. and Strathern, M. (Eds.). 1980. *Nature, Culture and Gender*. Cambridge: Cambridge University Press.

Malkki, L. 1995a. *Purity and Exile: Violence, Memory, and National Cosmology among Hutu Refugees in Tanzania*. Chicago, IL: University of Chicago Press.

Malkki, L. 1996. Speechless Emissaries: Refugees, Humanitarianism, and Dehistoricization. *Cultural Anthropology* 11(3): 377–404.

Moore, H. 1988. *Feminism and Anthropology*. Minneapolis: University of Minnesota Press.

Ortner, S. 1972. Is Female to Male as Nature Is to Culture? *Feminist Studies* 1(2): 5–31.

Ortner, S. 1990. Gender Hegemonies. *Cultural Critique* 14: 35–80.

Ortner, S. and Whitehead, H. (Eds.). 1981. *Sexual Meanings: The Cultural Construction of Gender and Sexuality*. Cambridge: Cambridge University Press.

Oyewumi, O. 1997. *The Invention of Women: Making an African Sense of Western Gender Discourses*. Minneapolis: University of Minnesota Press.

Oyewumi, O. 2000. Family Bonds/Conceptual Binds: African Notes on Feminist Epistemologies. *Signs* 25(4): 1093–1098.

Oyewumi, O. 2002. Conceptualizing Gender: The Eurocentric Foundations of Feminist Concepts and the Challenges of African Epistemologies. *Jenda: A Journal of Culture and African Women Studies* 2(1): 1–9.

Rich, A. 1977. *Of Women Born: Motherhood as Experience and Institution*. London: Virago.

Richards, A. 1956. *Chisungu: A Girl's Initiation Ceremony among the Bemba of Zambia*. London: Tavistock.

Silva, S. 2009. Mothers of Solitude: Childlessness and Intersubjectivity in the Upper Zambezi. *Anthropology and Humanism* 34(2): 179–202.

Strathern, M. 2012. Eating (and Feeding). *Cambridge Anthropology* 30(2): 1–14.

Tambiah, S. 1985. *Culture, Thought, and Social Action: An Anthropological Perspective*. Chicago, IL: University of Chicago Press.

Taylor, C.C. 1988. The Concept of Flow in Rwandan Popular Medicine. *Social Science and Medicine* 27(12): 1343–1348.

Taylor, C.C. 1990. Condoms and Cosmology: The "Fractal" Person and Sexual Risk in Rwanda. *Social Science and Medicine* 31(9): 1023–1028.

Taylor, C.C. 1992. *Milk, Honey, and Money: Changing Concepts in Rwandan Healing*. Washington, DC: The Smithsonian Institution Press.

Taylor, C.C. 1999a. *Sacrifice as Terror*. Oxford: Berghahn Books.

Taylor, C.C. 1999b. A Gendered Genocide: Tutsi Women and Hutu Extremists in the 1994 Rwanda Genocide. *Political and Legal Anthropology Review* 22(1): 42–54.

Thomson, M.J. 2012. Black Boxes of Bureaucracy: Transparency and Opacity in the Resettlement Process of Congolese Refugees. *PoLAR: Political and Legal Anthropology Review* 35(2): 186–205.

Turner, V. 1967. *The Forest of Symbols: Aspects of Ndembu Ritual*. Ithaca, NY: Cornell University Press.

Williams, R. 1977. *Marxism and Literature*. Oxford: Oxford University Press.

2 Conflict and historicity

The conflicts that have erupted in the Central African region over the past decades have become synonymous with the idea of ethnic conflict. I did not ask refugees I conducted fieldwork with to disclose their ethnicities, if indeed that is how they would even choose to identify themselves. When the topic of ethnicity came up in conversations amongst them during my fieldwork, as it occasionally did, the conversation often lapsed into terse silence. At most, refugees would sometimes tell me about the small villages and tribal groups they belonged to in Africa.

Refugees from Central Africa are a population whose lives have been irrevocably transformed by the violence produced from contested claims to dominance that rest on those very classifications of ethnicity. But after fleeing violence and seeking asylum in neighbouring countries, the problem of ethnicity does not disappear. Despite the best attempts of humanitarian organisations to provide safe and secure lodgings for refugees where they are surrounded by peoples of a similar background, refugees often have to live in camps, settlements, or urban areas amongst people from diverse ethnic groups, including those that may be associated with violence and persecution in the countries they have fled. Those I conducted fieldwork with in Uganda told me that they never felt safe because they were sure that that the persecution they had fled could follow them into their country of asylum. Although refugees would often make private guesses at the backgrounds of other peoples around them, I rarely heard refugees talk openly about their own ethnicities or personal backgrounds in Uganda. Doing so would, according to them, make them vulnerable to violence.

Given that the stakes of disclosing a particular ethnic affiliation can be considered akin to claiming affiliation with a particular version of history and a stance on contemporary politics, it did not surprise me, as an anthropologist who evidently conducts research with refugees who have diverse ethnic backgrounds, that ethnicity was one topic of discussion that did not elicit open responses. But the silence that surrounded the topic of ethnicity did not necessarily indicate that the ethnicity had no salience in the lives of these refugees. Rather, the silence signalled, without words, that the politics of ethnicity that are so deeply implicated in the violences that have erupted in Central Africa endure even when refugees are in situations where they are supposed to be protected from it.

The continuing salience of ethnic identification as a basis of enduring violence and re-traumatisation became clear early into my fieldwork in Australia, when I visited Yolande and her husband after they had been on their first visit to a psychologist. I had already been sceptical about the efficacy of what is an essentially Eurocentric approach to managing issues of trauma, but a magistrate in a court case that Yolande and her husband had become embroiled in had requested that they attend an appointment with a psychologist for a psychological profile. When I walked into the house and saw Yolande hunched over the coffee table in the living room, grasping at her stomach and rocking gently, I knew immediately that something had gone very wrong during the psychology session.

"What happened?" I asked immediately, coming to sit beside Yolande. Seemingly unable to speak, she pushed a pile of paperwork across the coffee table toward me in response. At the top of the pile was the report from the psychologist. With the wave of her hand, Yolande encouraged me to read the report.

One of the first questions that the psychologist had asked Yolande was, "You come from Rwanda, is that correct?" Receiving a response in the affirmative, the psychologist, who was not an expert in working with refugees or survivors of torture and trauma and was, presumably, acting on the basis of popular understandings of the Rwandan genocide, then asked, "Are you Hutu, or Tutsi?"

Gaping at the question, which seemed from my admittedly non-expert perspective to be entirely irrelevant and indeed non-conducive to the purpose of having her psychological state profiled, I asked Yolande how she had responded to the question. "Nothing," she said, "nothing." Indeed, as the report went on to say, she had spent the rest of the one-hour session in complete silence.

That experience emphasised to me that directly asking the refugees I conducted fieldwork with to disclose their specific ethnic backgrounds would be, for many, an unnecessarily traumatic line of inquiry. And yet the silences around ethnic identity and the absence of collective histories that punctuated my fieldwork were not empty. Those silences spoke to the salience of histories and contemporary renderings of marginalisation in producing the kinds of lives these refugees had come to live (Kidron 2009). To ignore the complexity and contestations that surround these issues of conflict and ethnicity would itself be a way to disrespect the silences that refugees themselves place on such subjects, which are not absences of meaning, but reflections of suffering. In this chapter, I trace the backgrounds of conflict and the politics of history that have shaped the lives of the refugees I conducted fieldwork with.

A region in conflict

Millions of people have died in Central Africa over the past 25 years as a direct result of conflict. The following numbers, compiled by Patrick

Kanyangara (2016) for The African Centre for the Constructive Resolution of Disputes, are only estimates, but they speak to the scale of violence and destruction that has characterised conflicts in the Central African region. In the DRC, around 6,000,000 people have been killed and 2,000,000 people have been forced to flee their homes since war was declared in 1996. In Rwanda, the 1994 genocide resulted in around 800,000 deaths, and more than 2,000,000 people became refugees. Following an attempted coup in Burundi in 1993, about 300,000 people were killed, and more than 800,000 people were forced to flee. It is, of course, difficult to ascertain accurate numbers of the peoples affected by these conflicts in terms of either victims or refugees because the violence is wide-reaching and problematic to quantify. Nonetheless, however, the scope and scale that these statistics suggest is numbing, seemingly beyond comprehension.

These statistics emphasise the sheer volume of death and dislocation that has erupted in Central Africa in the past three decades alone. But numbers can have a distancing and desensitising effect. As Allen Feldman (1995: 237) recognises, in reference to statistical representations of Holocaust victims, "quantification, no matter how necessary, contributes to the stratification and hierarchical objectification of victims by number and abbreviates and numbs the material-spiritual cosmos of the event." To have a single number come to represent the extremity of violence that has been imposed on a population that has been exposed to conflict can be a way to sanitise the effects of those processes into a singular experience of violence and reduce the peoples whose lives are counted within the statistic to an indistinct mass. Recognising that the statistics recounted above represent a lived reality of violence for such large numbers of people can seem overwhelming. But, ultimately, it is another form of violence to singularly reduce the lives of those who have fled, and the deaths of friends and family who they mourn, to numbers without attention to the kinds of experiences that such numbers render intelligible. They are people whose futures have been irrevocably altered by exposure to violence. And they are people who I met and became close to while conducting fieldwork.

But just as the refugees I conducted fieldwork with have each been uniquely exposed to violence, so too does the diversity of their personal experiences defy a common labelling of their backgrounds. The kinds of labels that are popularly used to group populations are, for these refugees, the same labels that were in contention during the conflicts that had forced them to flee. The refugees I got to know during fieldwork did not share a common marker of identification based on nationality, ethnic group, or tribe. But what these refugees did share was a common geographic origin. Each had been born and raised in the region that is termed in popular renderings as either "Central Africa" or the "Great Lakes" region, or by the UN as "Middle Africa." Each of these labels refers to the region in the centre of Africa surrounding what are termed the Great Lakes, which includes Burundi, Rwanda, parts of southwestern Uganda, and the eastern region of the DRC.

I use the term Central Africa throughout this book to refer to the backgrounds of the refugees I conducted fieldwork with because this was the geographic region in which they had each been born. Given that I worked with people who had become refugees from this distinct region, it seemed necessary to apply a descriptive label to them when writing about them. I felt that referring to them more generally as refugees would obscure specificities about the violences they have fled and assume that their experiences can be subsumed into a more general "refugee" category.

I realise that this label of "Central African" is itself problematic, as is any label that is applied to classify and categorise what are heterogeneous populations. However, other possible labels, such as "African" refugees or "sub-Saharan African" refugees, seemed more problematic because they were too general or loaded with negative assumptions. Using a more specific national or ethnic label seemed similarly generalising, but also problematic because it was the contention over national and ethnic labels that had been implicated in the experiences through which women I conducted fieldwork with had become refugees in the first place. Although referring to "Central African" refugees is vague, I do not mean to imply that those peoples I categorise within that label are a homogenous group. I only mean to imply that each person I worked with fled the same geographic region.

Nonetheless, the Central Africa label can be more useful beyond indicating a shared geography because it also signals the distinct, but overlapping, series of conflicts that have specifically erupted in that region. In a book documenting the conflicts that have developed in Burundi, Rwanda, and the DRC since independence from colonial rule, Rene Lemarchand (2009: x) intentionally uses the label Central Africa because "viewing their agonies in isolation from each other reveals only a fraction of the regional forces at work." Sharing the perspective of Lemarchand (2009), I similarly consider it impossible to analyse the conflicts that have occurred in Burundi, Rwanda, and the DRC as incidents that are isolated from broader regional and international forces. By referring to the people I conducted fieldwork with as Central African refugees, I mean to indicate the conflicts and persecution from which they fled have a regional, rather than specifically national or ethnic-based, context.

In giving a history of specific dynamics of conflict that are the basis of why the peoples I conducted fieldwork with became refugees, I do not mean to discount the local, and even more broadly continental and international, forces that are implicated within these historical and contemporary conflicts. Since the majority of the refugees I got to know had fled as a result of conflicts that erupted in this region in the 1990s and into the 2000s, it is this time period that I especially focus on. However, it is important to recognise that the events of the past 30 years are deeply rooted in histories of colonial occupations and imperialist violence, shaky transitions to independence and the formation of new regimes of concentrated political power, the everyday inequalities of failed or fragile states and inadequate infrastructure, and various fluctuations of regional and international interventions, which have led to ongoing political instability and continuing outbreaks of violence.

Problematising ethnicity

The 1994 genocide in Rwanda gained more international attention than any other conflict in Central Africa over the past 30 years but this is not the only or defining conflict of the region, which has been a setting for numerous instances of war and violence. Peoples in and from the Central African region more broadly have nonetheless been exposed to a number of instances of violence prior to and following 1994, particularly the multiple outbreaks of genocidal violence in Burundi during the 1970s and the outbreak of two extremely deadly civil wars in the DRC from the mid-1990s to the mid-2000s. Yet the 1994 genocide in Rwanda evoked a global response of attention and condemnation for a number of reasons. The scope and scale of the violence, the failure of international peacekeeping missions to intervene despite clear indicators of the impending genocide, and the media attention given to the genocide in the weeks and months that followed mean that the Rwandan genocide stands, as Peter Uvin (2001: 76) describes it, as a "defining moment" in situating not only the Central African region, but the African continent, within a global context of conflict and intervention. In reports about and analyses that followed the Rwandan genocide, it was ethnicity that was continuously referenced as the focal point of the violence and that was presented as the key explanatory factor of the genocide (Hintjens 2001; Newbury 1998). Indeed, the massacres were predominantly—although not exclusively—directed by peoples identifying with the ethnic Hutu group towards ethnic Tutsi victims. However, although assumptions and experiences of ethnic difference were certainly central to the outbreak of violence, there were numerous historical and contemporaneous international, regional, and national factors at play in the degeneration of ethnic difference into genocide (Reyntjens 1996). Yet the reduction of the Rwandan genocide into a primary dialogue of ethnic conflict can be read as a barometer of how other conflicts in the region have gained, or rather been dismissed, from attention within public spheres internationally.

It is impossible, then, to give an account of the conflicts that have erupted in the Central African region without also discussing ethnicity. International attention that is focused on Central Africa, and continental Africa more broadly, often simplifies the causes of conflicts that erupt in the region to internal factors, with the most ubiquitous claim made about conflicts that arise in Africa being that these are predominantly "ethnic conflicts" (Newbury 1998; Uvin 1999). When considered critically, however, the idea of "ethnic conflict" actually reproduces logics of group division, and it is these divisions that are, supposedly, the focal point of contention through which conflicts based on ethnic difference are produced. It is important, as Rogers

Brubaker (2002) argues, not to accept the seemingly common-sense reduction of specific instances of conflict as being the result of division between ethnic groups—a reduction which dominates everyday talk, policy analysis, and media reporting—because doing so naturalises those very assumptions of difference. The narrative of conflicts in Central Africa being the result of contestations over ethnicity is problematic because it does not reflect the complexity and range of factors that contribute to the outbreaks of violence that have occurred across different African contexts. More perniciously, however, the reduction of conflict in Africa to singular explanations of ethnic divisions reproduces the trope of Africa as a place of tribalism: a "heart of darkness" that is incapable of progress and outside of modernity (Apter 1999; Mbembe 2001).

But what is ethnicity? And why do claims of ethnic-based conflict, particularly in Africa, become represented as routine and thereby made dismissible? Ethnicity became a prominent concept in the social sciences in the 1960s, culminating in the publication of Fredrik Barth's (1969) landmark book *Ethnic Groups and Boundaries*, in which the concept of ethnicity was characterised as an interactional, rather than static, process of boundary formation based on factors conducive to collectivism, such as similar physiological features, shared fundamental values and cultural forms, distinct modes of communication and interaction, and a distinguishable group identity, which is recognised by both those within the group and those external to it. The concept of ethnicity was taken up extensively in social science scholarship, and eventually public vernacular, because it was a term that was able to capture, but nonetheless recognise the flexibility of, key markers of collective affiliation without reifying them to distinct structures of group identity. Prior to ethnicity gaining traction as a social science concept, groups of people had been primarily defined by structural factors, which were assumed to map onto collective formations, such as distinctions based on perceived tribal, racial, cultural, and/or language groupings (Cohen 1978). Ethnicity provides a way to think about the factors that distinguish groups in reflexive, rather than essentialist, ways (Erikson 2002).

For ethnicity to be utilised as a basis of more reflexive understandings of identity is, however, somewhat more optimistic in terms of potential, rather than actual, usage. As John Comaroff (1995) has argued, ethnicity has come to be characterised as a universal potentiality: that is, as a sense of collectivised identity that is available to all but only activated in response to external forces and under certain conditions of diminished power. As a seemingly latent cultural essence, the "primordial infrastructure" of ethnicity, as it is applied in both public and scholarly contexts, means that a "bedrock of essentialism is left intact—along, potentially, with the racist politics of difference which it so often legitimates" (Comaroff 1995: 294). What this means is that ethnicity can be used to signal seemingly essentialist divisions between groups in much the same way that the predecessor concept, race, was applied to characterise seemingly natural differences between peoples.

When used without recognition of the contingency and flexibility of ethnic identity, the term can become another euphemism for supposedly ingrained natural differences, and these assumed divisions between peoples then translate into seemingly natural hierarchies of people. Ethnicity can be used as a euphemistic way to signal inferiorised difference.

The label of "ethnic conflict" also suggests inferiorised difference. After a mass of new ethnonationalist wars and genocides in the early- to mid-1990s, the talk of a "new world order" characterised by peace and cooperation following the end of the Soviet Union came to be replaced by the idea of a "new tribalism" (Freeman 1998), exemplified in the work of Samuel Huntington (1997) and the "clash of civilizations" thesis. The term "tribalism" was rarely defined in such analyses of ethnic conflict: rather, the pejorative connotations of the term, and the implied backgrounding of social Darwinism, was left open and unchallenged. Michael Freeman (1998) argues that this discursive construction of specifically "ethnic conflict" serves to neutralise other ways of explaining outbreaks of violence: especially political. The lack of conceptual clarity between ethnic conflict and tribalism has meant that rather than view outbreaks of violence in Africa, particularly, as stemming from contestation between elite actors seeking to gain political power or as an indicator of the fragility of nation state building processes, these formations of violence are viewed as a reversion to primitivism. Freeman (1998) describes the common-sense discursive construction of ethnic conflict as a way to signal an inversion of the primitive/civilised distinction, a version of history in which:

> [O]nce there was the primitive, the irrational, the violence; then there was progress towards the civilized, the rational, and the orderly; a progress, however, that has been interrupted from time to time by reversions of primitive barbarism.
>
> (Freeman 1998: 17)

The irony pointed out by Freeman (1998) is that it was not early human groups, those so-called primitive tribal groups, who engaged in large-scale wars and massacres of extensive destruction. Rather, the first institutions to practice systematic and large-scale warfare were probably the city–states that have come to form the basis of the nation state structure through which global geopolitics are contemporaneously organised. Nonetheless, the labelling of conflicts as specifically "ethnic" is a way to strip the political origins of these outbreaks of violence and make these conflicts out to be the inevitable outcome of interactions between peoples who are imagined as primitive and whose lives are defined by violent tribalism.

Such racialised political imaginaries of ethnic conflict shape readings of the conflict in Central Africa at the same time that locals themselves take up and mythologise ideas about ethnic identity (Stone 2004: 137; Taylor 1999a, 1999b). Although it would be misleading to wholly characterise ethnicity division as the basis of conflicts in Central Africa, ideas about ethnic difference, as understood by locals within those contexts, were nonetheless at the centre of outbreaks of violence in the region and require critical attention, as I describe below.

The politics of history in Central Africa

The Hutu and Tutsi ethnic groups are those most closely associated in popular understandings with outbreaks of violence across the Central African region. Identifying as—or *being* identified by others as—either a Hutu or a Tutsi has, for many, been a matter of life and death. Conventionally, it has been peoples of the Hutu ethnicity who vastly outnumber those who identify as Tutsi in the region. Despite representing a smaller group of people, political power during the colonial period and following independence was, however, often concentrated into the influence of peoples of a Tutsi ethnicity (Lemarchand 2009; Young 2006). This imbalance of power, and conflicting mythologies around rightful claims to power (Malkki 1995a; Taylor 1999a, 1999b), has significantly shaped how conditions of genocidal violence have been made possible across Central Africa.

The matrix of ethnic groupings across Central Africa is, however, more complex than just these two dominant ethnic groups. The Hutu and Tutsi groupings are overarching ethnic labels that are comprised of numerous other layers of identity based on clan, language group, and kinship affiliations (Lemarchand 2006). These factors may occasionally overlap to produce a distinct sense of ethnic identity but are at other times used as points of distinctions themselves. Ultimately, ethnic identity in Central Africa is highly contingent on factors related to personal identification, external perception, and context. It is, however, the distinction between Hutu and Tutsi ethnic groups that has been the focus of international attention. And, certainly, it was the polarisation of these two dominant ethnic categories in political and popular imaginaries that led to the deaths of hundreds of thousands, if not millions, of peoples across the Central African region.

Controversy surrounds how the distinction between Hutu and Tutsi ethnic groups developed historically. There is a myriad of origin mythologies that are used by peoples across social groups in Burundi, Rwanda, and the DRC to interpret contemporary constellations of power in relation to ethnic identity (Apter 2012; Jackson 2006; Malkki 1995a). However, there is no consensus on how the division and antagonism between peoples of the Hutu and Tutsi ethnicity developed historically. As Peter Uvin (1999), a political scientist who has conducted extensive research on the role of international development and aid in Rwanda in contributing to outbreaks of violence in the region, suggests, "Burundians, Rwandans, and outside specialists of the region disagree almost totally on the nature of precolonial social relations." What can be agreed upon is that there is a politics of history at work in any attempt to classify and historicise the distinction between the Hutu and Tutsi.

There is a basic sense of the pre-colonial trajectory of inter-ethnic relations in the region, even if controversy surrounds other aspects, such as the nature of ethnic distinctions. Peter Uvin (1999) describes this history as follows:

> In all likelihood, the cattle-rearing Tutsi, fleeing famine and drought, arrived in Burundi and Rwanda in successive waves from the north during the fifteenth and sixteenth centuries. The agriculturalist Hutu they met had immigrated into this fertile region some centuries earlier, probably from central Africa... The integration of these different groups was extensive: by the time the colonizer arrived, they spoke the same language, believed in the same god, shared the same culture, and lived side by side.
>
> (Uvin 1999: 255)

But this attempt to generalise the history of the Central African region by Uvin (1999) cannot be taken as authoritative: it represents one dominant perspective. Another, described by Catherine Newbury (1998), a historian of ethnicity in Rwanda, suggests that this idea of ethnic relations between Hutu and Tutsi in the past being harmonious and complementary is false:

> A different version of these relationships asserts that Hutu were conquered in the distant past by clever and wily Tutsi, who imposed an oppressive, exploitative rule on Hutu and made them servants of Tutsi.
>
> (Newbury 1998: 9)

Again, what little can be agreed upon is that differentiations between the Hutu and Tutsi ethnic groups existed prior to the colonial period, with the primary distinction between the two groups being that Hutu have primarily been associated with a lifestyle of subsistence agriculture and the Tutsi were known to be pastoralists. What is widely agreed upon in academic scholarship is that whatever the nature of the pre-colonial distinctions that were drawn between Hutu and Tutsi, these were exacerbated and made especially antagonistic after the imposition of colonial administrations (Lemarchand 2006, 2009; Prunier 1995; Young 2006).

Colonial histories

Burundi, Rwanda, and the DRC share intertwined pre- and post-colonial histories. Prior to colonial occupation, both Burundi and Rwanda were separate kingdoms, each ruled by a monarchy (Chrétien 2003; Newbury 2009). As a larger geographic area comprising of diverse groups of people, the region that is now known as the DRC was not a single kingdom but a set of different kingdoms and governing formations. In the 19th century, colonial powers in Europe began to take an interest in occupying and expanding territorial control into continental Africa. This led to the colonial rule of Burundi, Rwanda, and the DRC. Stemming from these occupations, these three distinct nations have intersecting histories of colonisation that are each marked by violence and terror.

In the late 19th century, King Leopold II of Belgium identified a large portion of the Central African region—what was to become the DRC—as a basis of potential enterprise (Nzongola-Ntalaja 2002: 13–59). After much negotiation with other European powers, Leopold assumed power under the guise of ruling with philanthropic and humanitarian intent to improve the lives of locals. But the rule of Leopold was characterised by brutality (Rose-Hunt 1999, 2008). The operations of large rubber plantations in the region under the rule of Leopold are especially renowned as spaces of terror, in which control was wrought by the systematic murder of people who did not meet work quotas as well as through more arbitrary instances of violence and killings designed to invoke a generalised state of terror. The signature method of governance was bodily mutilation. Eventually, the atrocities committed by Leopold came to light, and the regime came under international pressure to reform, including calls for the rule of the king to be taken over. In 1908, the territory was transferred to the colonial enterprise of Belgium and renamed the Belgian Congo.

Burundi and Rwanda have a different history of colonial occupation but one that nonetheless intersects with that of the DRC (Chrétien 2003; Newbury 1988; Prunier 1995). After contact with German colonists, in 1899 both territories became part of what was known as German East Africa. In 1916, after the outbreak of the First World War, however, German control of the area was dissolved. Belgium became the mandated administrator of both territories, which was subsumed into a single site of governance, Ruanda-Urundi.

In 1925, the territory of Ruanda-Urundi was officially annexed into the governing administration of the Belgian Congo (Chrétien 2003). These three territorial units were, as such, ruled by Belgium as a single colonial entity until the independence of what is now the DRC in 1960. Although the overtly violent regime of King Leopold II collapsed, the colonial rule over what are now the territories of Burundi, Rwanda, and the DRC during the 1900s continued to stoke tensions within the local populations and to create situations of insecurity (Nzongola-Ntalaja 2002: 13–59). In addition, the colonial administrations are implicated in setting up the conditions through which later, post-independence situations of war and conflict broke out. Colonial governments across the Central African region solidified the symbolic power of ethnic groupings by enforcing institutional recognition of ethnic identity and concentrating administrative power within particular ethnic groups (Chrétien 2003; Nzongola-Ntalaja 2002). Specifically in Rwanda, for example, the colonial administration attempted to systematise ethnic identity by requiring people to disclose a specific ethnicity when requested and even, at times, issuing locals with identity cards that demarcated the specific ethnic group they belonged to (Newbury 1998: 11). Despite the Hutu ethnic group being dominant in terms of numbers, colonial rulers frequently sought to concentrate power into the domain of the Tutsi minority, thereby channelling dissent away from the rule of the colonisers and toward and between the locals themselves.

Independence

By the late 1950s, an independence movement was sweeping the African continent. Following years of rebellions and uprisings, the DRC was the first to gain independence in 1960. Although the Belgian colonial administration had attempted to ease the transition to independence by supporting with the set up of governance infrastructure, the post-colonial governing system proved to be unstable (Nzongola-Ntalaja 2002: 94–119). Soon after the DRC gained independence the newly-formed country was plunged into a series of leadership upheavals and coups as different people with competing political agendas attempted to take control over the country. These conflicts were exacerbated by the interests and agendas of international governments, particularly the Soviet Union and the US, who had become interested in the vast wealth of rare mineral resources in the DRC and were attempting to exert influence on who would rise to power the DRC as a result. In 1965, these leadership upheavals ceased when Mobutu Sese Seko, then-commander in chief of the national army, took control of the country declared himself president of a one-party national government. The Mobutu regime was overtly authoritarian, and lasted from 1965 until the outbreak of war in 1997. The decades long rule of Mobutu was characterised by systematic exploitation and corruption, with little investment in the infrastructural changes that would benefit local populations. As such, the generalised insecurity of the colonial period did not dissolve after the DRC became an independent nation.

Prior to withdrawing from Burundi and Rwanda, the Belgian government sought to diffuse what had become intense ethnic divisions by developing a plan to create an independent Ruanda-Urundi with joint Tutsi–Hutu power-sharing (Lemarchand 1994: 51; Newbury 1988). Democratic elections were held in the joint state in 1960. Predictably, the predominantly Hutu population elected primarily Hutu representatives. With violence escalating in response to the election results, a referendum was held to determine whether Rwanda should become a republic. This led to the separation of Burundi and Rwanda into two distinct countries in 1961.

With ethnic hierarchies still simmering, however, the fates of people within each territory remained nonetheless intertwined (Prunier 1995; Uvin 1999). Following independence, Rwanda became a one-party state dominated by a Hutu political party (Newbury 1988; Prunier 1995). Burundi began as a constitutional monarchy, but this was dissolved in 1966 after a series of attempted coups ended with the instituting of a de facto military regime comprised primarily of Tutsi military officials (Lemarchand 1994). Between the independence and separation of Burundi and Rwanda in 1961 until the mid-1990s, numerous instances of guerrilla warfare and outright uprisings broke out within and between both countries. These frequently led to outbreaks of government-led conflict, with violence being directed toward civilians who were identified as not being of the same ethnic group as that associated with the ruling government. The largest of these outbreaks of violence was the genocide of an estimated hundreds of thousands of Hutu civilians in Burundi in 1972 by the Tutsi military regime, following an attempted Hutu uprising (Lemarchand 1994: 76–104).

Following independence, Burundi, Rwanda, and the DRC were embroiled in decades-long regional political antagonism and conflicts. These tensions were fuelled by the concentration of power and resources into the influence of political elites who came to represent hierarchies of ethnic affiliation (Chrétien 2003; Lemarchand 1994; Prunier 1995, 2009). This context of instability and violence forms the context from which the spectacular violences that occurred in Central Africa in the 1990s, and which continue today, were produced.

Conflict in Central Africa: 1990s and beyond

Again, the instances of violence that occurred in Burundi, Rwanda, and the DRC cannot be approached as isolated events (Malkki 1995a: 259–264). In 1993, Burundi held inaugural democratic elections. These resulted in the election of a Hutu president, who was in power for 100 days before being assassinated. The successor of this first elected president in Burundi was also assassinated, along with the then-president of Rwanda in 1994, when the plane that both were flying in was intentionally shot down. In Burundi, the response to the assassination of the first and second presidents led to outbreaks of retaliation violence from civilians, specifically Hutu peoples attacking those understood to be Tutsi. Ostensibly to restore order, the predominantly Tutsi army began to kill those Hutu civilians who were seen as rebellious. As a result of this eruption of violence and generalised insecurity, civil war was declared in Burundi in 1993. The conflict lasted formally until the signing of a peace agreement in 2006. This period of terror in the 1990s and early 2000s was the impetus for many of the refugees I conducted fieldwork with to flee and become refugees (Malkki 1995a: 259–264).

The assassination of the Burundian presidents in 1993 and 1994 is widely considered to have been the impetus for the events that unfurled in Rwanda in 1994 (Prunier 1995). The Hutu-dominated government in Rwanda began to increase anti-Tutsi sentiment in response to the assassination of the first Burundian Hutu president in 1993. By the time the plane carrying both the Rwandan president and the successive Burundian president, both identifying as ethnic Hutu, was shot down in 1994, the conditions of animosity that are necessary to enact a systematic genocide were already in place. After the plane went down on 6 April 1994, military and militia groups began to round up Tutsi civilians, who were then murdered. Media outlets, dominated by pro-government actors, began broadcasting hate speech and advocating for the use of violence against Tutsis. Ordinary citizens began to join in on committing violence. Eventually, the deaths ceased after Tutsi rebels defeated the Hutu regime, but it was years before the millions of peoples who had fled Rwanda to avoid the violence felt that it was safe to return. Some never did return and were exiled from the country permanently, including some of the people I conducted fieldwork with.

The conflict in Rwanda eventually affected the DRC (Lemarchand 2009; Prunier 2009). Over two million people had fled Rwanda during and following the genocide. A great number of these refugees crossed into the DRC. Many of those who fled to the DRC were former soldiers and militants of the ceded Hutu administration in Rwanda, meaning that it is likely that they were directly involved in acts of genocidal violence.

As life in the camps in the DRC became more established, a social and political organisational structure emerged, in which many of these former militants were deeply implicated. An increasingly militarised system of funnelling humanitarian aid to be received specifically by these elites emerged in the camps (Chaulia 2002; Lischer 2006). In response, humanitarian aid organisations withdrew their administrative and resource support from the camps in attempts to distance themselves from what increasingly appeared to be an ethical quagmire referred to as "feeding the killers" of the Rwandan genocide (Chaulia 2002). The militants in the camps used what access to resources they had as a basis from which to expand military activities until eventually this resulted in raids into Rwanda and outright attacks on ethnic groups affiliated with the Tutsi. In 1996, a military intervention into the eastern states of what is now the DRC, headed by Laurent Kabila and backed by both the Rwandan and Ugandan governments, succeeded in entering the country and, in attempting to liberate and take control of camps there, instigated a string of massive outbreaks of violence (Prunier 2009; Reyntjens 2009).

These events were the beginning of what has been popularly termed the First Congo War, which spanned officially from 1996–1997, which then spiralled into the Second Congo War, which spanned from 1998–2004. In an extensively researched book that documents the events of both the First and Second Congo Wars, Gérard Prunier (2009) describes how the first war was initiated in 1996 after Laurent Kabila, who was heavily supported by the governments of Rwanda and Uganda, solidified ethnic Tutsi resistance in the east of the DRC and marched with those forces across the country. Reaching the capital, Kinshasa, in 1997, Kabila overthrew the Mobutu administration and took control of the country, seemingly ending the war: symbolically, at least. In 1998, however, the governments of Rwanda and Uganda attempted to overthrow Kabila, leading to the outbreak of the second war. During the Second Congo War numerous rebel militia groups formed, fighting against not only government forces but also each other: and often inflicting violence on civilians. In addition, the attention focused on the civil war meant that essential services were neglected and made unavailable to civilians. Even those people who were not impacted directly by the physical violence of the conflicts were nonetheless affected by the disintegration of what were already generally weak public health and medical care services, meaning that many people died of preventable illnesses during the period of the second war simply because there was no stable government from which to ensure essential services were being made available to local populations. The Second Congo War formally ended in 2003. Nonetheless, outbreaks of fighting continued to erupt, especially in the eastern states where tensions between ethnic groupings remained especially salient. In the context of this seemingly perpetual cycle of instability, violence, and insecurity, millions of refugees fled the DRC, including many of the women I conducted fieldwork with.

Strategic silences

Described as a series of linear events and with the scale of violence quantified into calculated statistics and estimated death tolls, it is easy to become distanced from the lived reality of these wars and conflicts. But these were the processes that forced the women I conducted fieldwork with to flee their homes and rearrange their ways of living. Despite the violence of being forcibly uprooted from their lives, when I spoke with these women they did not attempt to make sense of the conflicts or to make political claims in regard to them: in fact, they were reticent to the discuss the conflicts, except in relation to personal experiences. This hesitancy to discuss the political contexts of the conflicts in Central Africa is in direct contrast to the ways in which other researchers have documented how refugees respond to and mediate experiences of conflict, especially Liisa Malkki (1995a), who describes how, for Burundian Hutu refugees in an isolated refugee camp, mythologising the past is a way to make sense of violent experiences and to imagine futures in which supposedly rightful claims to nationhood and land are made possible. The mythologisation of the past as a process that both creates and reflects cosmological logics of inclusion and exclusion is what Malkki (1995a) describes as a "mythico-history," which is solidified not only by long-standing origin narratives amongst the Hutu but also by the contemporary context of their being isolated in a refugee camp as a singular ethnic group, limited by the humanitarian order to an everyday life with very little to do and little opportunity to interact with those from outside the camp.

But the refugees I conducted fieldwork with were not living in insular social environments. They were either living in the diverse urban sprawl of Kampala or had been resettled to Australia. They were forced to mediate the precarity of existing as refugees independently of humanitarian aid or through the complex and unfamiliar bureaucratic context of everyday life in Australia. These women were suffering the exhaustion of the present, rather than the boredom and anticipation of it. Their general silence in regard to the political and ethnic dynamics of the conflicts that they had lived through, and which continue to erupt in the region spoke loudly: these women were attempting to move past those hostilities in order to create, rather than destruct, new livelihoods. They were not focused on a mythico-history through which to make sense of their experiences. Rather, they were focused on a mythico-futurity from which to strategise new possible lives.

Fleeing the direct context of conflict and insecurity does not, however, resolve the lingering effects of violence that persist and endure. This is because the kinds of displacement that such experiences of conflict and violence produce cannot be essentialised or reduced to a problem of statelessness or even physical insecurity. The logics that both drove formations of violence in Central Africa are cosmological in scope: not only surfacing at the level of immediate physical harm, but also aimed at or experienced as existential violences that throw whole worlds and ways of living into jeopardy.

References

Apter, A. 1999. Africa, Empire, and Anthropology: A Philological Exploration of Anthropology's Heart of Darkness. *Annual Review of Anthropology* 28: 577–598.

Apter, A. 2012. Matrilineal Motives: Kinship, Witchcraft, and Repatriation among Congolese Refugees. *Journal of the Royal Anthropological Institute* 18(1): 22–44.

Barth, F. 1969. *Ethnic Groups and Boundaries: The Social Organization of Culture Difference*. London: Allen & Unwin.

Brubaker, R. 2002. Ethnicity without Groups. *European Journal of Sociology* 43(2): 163–189.

Chaulia, S. 2002. UNHCR's Relief, Rehabilitation and Repatriation of Rwandan Refugees in Zaire (1994–1997). *The Journal of Humanitarian Assistance*. Available at: http://www.jha.ac/articles/a086.htm (Accessed 27 July 2016).

Chrétien, J. 2003. *The Great Lakes of Africa: Two Thousand Years of History*. New York: Zone Books.

Cohen, R. 1978. Ethnicity: Problem and Focus in Anthropology. *Annual Review of Anthropology* 7(1): 379–403.

Comaroff, J.L. 1995. Ethnicity, Nationalism, and the Politics of Difference in an Age of Revolution. *International studies in Global Change* 7: 243–276.

Erikson, T.H. 2002. *Ethnicity and Nationalism: Anthropological Perspectives*. London; Boulder, CO: Pluto Press.

Feldman, A. 1995. Ethnographic States of Emergency. In *Fieldwork Under Fire: Contemporary Studies of Violence and Survival*. C. Nordstrom and A. Robben (Eds.), pp. 224–250. Berkley: University of California Press.

Freeman, M. 1998. Theories of Ethnicity, Tribalism and Nationalism. In *Ethnic Conflict, Tribal Politics: A Global Perspective*. K. Christie (Ed.), pp. 15–33. Surrey: Curzon Press.

Hintjens, H.M. 2001. When Identity Becomes a Knife: Reflecting on the Genocide in Rwanda. *Ethnicities* 1(1): 25–55.

Huntington, S. 1997. *The Clash of Civilizations and the Remaking of World Order*. Harayana: Penguin Books India.

Jackson, S. 2006. Sons of Which Soil? The Language of Politics of Autochthony in Eastern DR Congo. *African Studies Review* 49(2): 95–123.

Kanyangara, P. 2016. Conflict in the Great Lakes Region: Root Causes, Dynamics and Effects. The African Centre for the Constructive Resolution of Disputes. Available at: www.accord.org.za/conflict-trends/conflict-great-lakes-region/ (Accessed 2 January 2017).

Kidron, C.A. 2009. Toward an Ethnography of Silence: The Lived Presence of the Past in the Everyday Life of Holocaust Trauma Survivors and Their Descendants in Israel. *Current Anthropology* 50(1): 5–27.

Lemarchand, R. 1994. *Burundi: Ethnic Conflict and Genocide.* Cambridge: Woodrow Wilson Center Press and Cambridge University Press.

Lemarchand, R. 2006. The Geopolitics of the Great Lakes Crisis. In *L'Afrique des Grand Lacs–Dix ans de Transitions Conflictuelles: Annuaire, 2005–2006.* F. Reyntjens and S. Marysse (Eds.), pp. 25–46. Paris: L'Harmattan.

Lemarchand, R. 2009. *The Dynamics of Violence in Central Africa.* Philadelphia: University of Pennsylvania Press.

Lischer, S.K. 2006. *Dangerous Sanctuaries: Refugee Camps, Civil War, and the Dilemmas of Humanitarian Aid.* Ithaca, NY: Cornell University Press.

Malkki, L. 1995a. *Purity and Exile: Violence, Memory, and National Cosmology among Hutu Refugees in Tanzania.* Chicago, IL: Chicago University Press.

Mbembe, A. 2001. *On the Postcolony.* Berkeley: University of California Press.

Newbury, C. 1988. *The Cohesion of Oppression: Clientship and Ethnicity in Rwanda, 1860–1960.* New York: Columbia University Press.

Newbury, C. 1998. Ethnicity and the Politics of History in Rwanda. *Africa Today* 45(1): 7–24.

Newbury, D. 2009. *The Land beyond the Mists: Essays on Identity and Authority in Precolonial Congo and Rwanda.* Athens: Ohio University Press.

Nzongola-Ntalaja, G. 2002. *The Congo from Leopold to Kabila: A People's History.* London; New York: Zed Books.

Prunier, G. 1995. *The Rwanda Crisis: History of a Genocide.* New York: Columbia University Press.

Prunier, G. 2009. *Africa's World War: Congo, the Rwandan Genocide, and the Making of a Continental Catastrophe.* Oxford: Oxford University Press.

Reyntjens, F. 1996. Rwanda, Genocide, and Beyond. *Journal of Refugee Studies* 9(3): 240–251.

Reyntjens, F. 2009. *The Great African War: Congo and Regional Geopolitics, 1996–2006.* Cambridge: Cambridge University Press.

Rose-Hunt, N. 1999. *A Colonial Lexicon: Of Birth Ritual, Medicalization, and Mobility in the Congo.* Durham: Duke University Press.

Rose-Hunt, N. 2008. An Acoustic Register, Tenacious Images, and Congolese Scenes of Rape and Repetition. *Cultural Anthropology* 23(2): 220–253.

Stone, D. 2004. The Historiography of Genocide: Beyond "Uniqueness" and Ethnic Competition. *Rethinking History* 8(1): 127–142.

Taylor, C.C. 1999a. *Sacrifice As Terror.* Oxford: Berghahn Books.

Taylor, C.C. 1999b. A Gendered Genocide: Tutsi Women and Hutu Extremists in the 1994 Rwanda Genocide. *Political and Legal Anthropology Review* 22(1): 42–54.

Uvin, P. 1999. Ethnicity and Power in Burundi and Rwanda: Different Paths to Mass Violence. *Comparative Politics* 31(3): 253–271.

Uvin, P. 2001. Reading the Rwandan Genocide. *International Studies Review* 3(3): 75–99.

Young, C. 2006. The Heart of the African Conflict Zone: Democratization, Ethnicity, Civil Conflict, and the Great Lakes Crisis. *Annual Review of Political Science* 9: 301–328.

3 Fear and violence

Fear is a defining characteristic of the refugee condition. By the UNHCR definition, a refugee is a person who has fled their country of origin due to a well-founded fear of persecution (UNHCR 2011c: 3). Fear is embedded in numerous facets of the forced migration process: from the reception of refugees, to providing them with asylum, to eventually attempting to resolve their displacement. Fear informs the ways in which refugees are received within a country of asylum, with host governments often detaining them in detention centres or camps because, as non-citizens, refugees are imagined to represent a threat to the civic population (Devetak 2007). The selection of refugees for resettlement often considers whether they are experiencing ongoing fear and insecurity that prevents them from returning to their country of origin (Jansen 2008). The hostility that so often meets refugees upon becoming settled in a host country of resettlement is also often driven by fear of the other (Casmiro, Hancock, and Northcote 2007; Klocker 2004). The generalised fear of the refugee has been amplified in recent years by the international political and media response to the increased numbers of refugees seeking asylum in Europe (Berry, Garcia-Blanco, and Moore 2016; Greenhill 2016; Kokkonen 2017; Marino and Dawes 2016; Rettberg and Gajjala 2016). A bloc of countries that had previously prided itself on fluidity of travel suddenly returned to putting up borders and obstructions, legal and physical (Holmes and Castañeda 2016; Kallius, Monterescu, and Rajaram 2016). Media reporting of terror attacks and other instances of Islamic extremism in recent years has quickly sought to make links between those events and asylum seekers and refugees in Europe, compounding the fear that is already attached to those populations (Cannizzaro and Gholami 2016; Walsh 2016). It seems, then, that refugees must objectify their own fears by narrating and documenting them in required ways and, at the same time, be themselves objectified as people to fear by the people and systems that respond to them. If refugees were able to be characterised by one affective register, then surely it is fear that defines it.

But how do refugees themselves know fear? The objectification of fear that is required of refugees through processes of humanitarian governance, and the objectification of refugees as peoples to fear, treats fear as an external and identifiable object or experience, referring to either the danger of the situations refugees flee or the danger of refugees themselves. Abstracting fear in this way into a distinct and knowable object, however, ignores the temporal register that is foundational to the way fear is experienced. Fear cannot be singularly understood as an emotion that is constituted in the immediacy of the present, although it is also that. Fear is an emotion that transforms insecurity of the present into anxiety over the future.

"We were afraid," I was told by one woman, Camille, during one of the rare occasions when people I spoke with referred to the situations that had forced them to flee. When I asked what it was she was afraid of, she told me that is was the "soldiers" who had stormed her village. But more than that, she told me, "We were afraid for the children." Her words echoed those of so many other refugees I worked with. Whether talking about the insecurities of fleeing their country of origin, the insecurities of living in a refugee camp or in urban asylum, or the insecurities of adjusting to life in Australia, the refugees I conducted fieldwork with generally articulated a sense of fear that was relational and future-oriented. Fear is primarily experienced, by them, when the futures of their family, and especially the lives of their children, are made precarious.

It is these temporal and relational dynamics of fear that are so often lost in popular accounts and tropes of refugee experiences. Instead, dominant representations of refugee experiences tend to focus on, and often sensationalise, the acts of direct violence that occur in the lives of peoples forced to flee their homes and that generate fear, such as physically violent attacks during conflict or acts of sexual and gender-based violence. Although these direct acts of violence can and do compel people to flee, the fear that these acts generate is not only that of having one's physical life threatened. The fear that such acts generate is also constituted within a social context of projected futures. For the refugees I conducted fieldwork with, the possibility of death or physical harm is understood in relation to the potential to be both socially and physiologically (re)productive: that is, to the potential to recreate life and to protect familial continuity.

Since the only essential dimension of fear, as usefully described by Wendy James (1993: 121), is that it is an "essential situatedness," this chapter is a response to the dominant tropes that are used in popular renderings of conflict in Central Africa to explain the events that compel refugees from there to flee. Focusing on the ways in which experiences of sexual and gender-based violence especially, and the general instability of highly militarised contexts of ordinary life in conflict zones, compelled the refugees I knew to flee, I describe below how the fears they attached to these specific events were not only located in the direct action of acute violence but were more intensively related to a fear of possibility: that is, to the potential effects or outcomes of those acts of direct violence. Specifically, it is the fear that such acts can disrupt the regenerative potential of physical and social reproduction that situated how refugees themselves came to know and experience violence.

Between victims and perpetrators

It is fear of persecution that determines the legal status of refugee, and it is fear that is so often attached to refugees in contexts of asylum and resettlement. In the former scenario, fear is crucial to legitimating the international protection of refugees, and in the latter, fear is crucial to destabilising their rights to protection. However, the fear that is associated with refugees in both scenarios is understood in relation to violence.

There is, however, no single definition of violence. Acts and processes that kill and harm, acutely and slowly, directly and indirectly, are both invisibly embedded into structures of everyday life and directly realised through exceptional events that punctuate the ordinary. Just as there is no objective determinant of violence, fear is a similarly subjective state (Scheper-Hughes and Bourgois 2004). Yet becoming labelled as a refugee requires that private fears and subjective understandings of violences are rendered invisible and replaced by assumptions of violence that can be publically recognisable (Jansen 2008). Refugee status signals, as was recognised by Hannah Arendt (1994: 110) in speaking about her own experiences of becoming a refugee, the "rupture of our private lives."

During refugee status determination processes, peoples who seek to claim asylum are often required to narrate the experiences that have led them to have a "well-founded fear of persecution" that stops them from being able to return in safety to their country of origin (Hathaway and Foster 2014). The legitimacy of a persecution story depends on the credibility of an asylum seeker and their testimony. However, assessments of credibility, according to Michael Kagan (2002), while purporting to be objective, are informed by the subjectivities of decision makers. Physical evidence is one way that an asylum seeker can attempt to verify the truth of their claim to refugee status. The scars, injuries, and diseases that physical violence often produces on the bodies of asylum seekers are often viewed as the most legitimate markers of truth during processes of refugee or asylum status determination (Fassin and D'Halluin 2005). Didier Fassin (2005) describes the emphasis that is placed on the physical bodies of migrants, rather than on their personal narratives, as a way to legitimise rights to protection as a "moral economy," that is, a hierarchy of morals and values through which populations in a given society are both implicitly and explicitly organised in ways that attach differential value to specific kinds of lives and ways of being. Based on an analysis of asylum seeker policy in France, which is applicable more broadly, Fassin (2005) describes how the veracity of the political basis of an asylum seeker's claim to persecution has become increasingly dependent on an appeal to what is taken to be a seemingly universal basis of shared human experience: physical suffering. It is not enough to fear persecution: this persecution must be suffered through, and evidenced by, the physical body. Not only fearing violence, but physically suffering it, has become both a politico-legal and moral indicator of legitimacy when deciding who is, and who is not legally recognised as a refugee.

The fear that is so often attached to refugees or asylum seekers in popular, political, and media renderings of them is, in contrast, that which associates them with the potential to commit acts of violence (Balch 2016; Devetak 2007). The attacks that took place in the US on 11 September 2001 intensified what had already been a prevalent tendency in Western media to represent and associate those peoples classified as a non-white other, or what Ghassan Hage (1998) describes as a "third world-looking migrant," with difference. Overnight, seemingly, these peoples became not only associated with difference, but now with danger: and, specifically, with the potential to commit acts of violent terrorism (Poynting and Mason 2007). Since 2014, which saw a significant increase in peoples from North Africa, the Middle East, and Central Asia trying to travel to and seek asylum in Europe, this association of the non-white migrant with terrorism has been further amplified (Berry et al. 2016; Greenhill 2016; Marino and Dawes 2016). In addition, a new layer of fear has been introduced into this dialogue in recent years, which attaches, specifically, a fear of sexual violence to non-white migrant men. Especially since the 2015 New Year's Eve attacks on women in Cologne, Germany, and subsequent media reporting that sought to identify, or at least suggest, that those who were involved in the attacks on non-migrant women in a public space were from a migrant background, asylum seekers and refugees have increasingly become discursively constructed in Western media as potential perpetrators of sexual violence (Rettberg and Gajjala 2016).

Such constructions of migrants as potential perpetrators of violence are also indicative of a moral economy, in which, again, the legitimacy of the peoples seeking asylum or claiming refugee status is at stake. The association of non-white migrants with potential to commit acts of violence is now filtering from mass media representations into practicalities of organising how those who seek asylum are legally allowed entry to, and publically received in, host nations of asylum (Holmes and Castañeda 2016). The legitimacy of refugees, asylum seekers, or just peoples who are generally coded as non-white migrants to reside in the public spaces of nations dominated by white populations seems to be continually in jeopardy as the tenuous association of migrants with violence becomes amplified and normalised in media representations, political rhetoric, and popular understandings.

Fear and violence have become intrinsic to the ways in which refugees and migrants are represented globally, and crucial to the development of an emergent moral economy of deservingness (Holmes and Castañeda 2016). The veracity of a claim of refugee status is often dependent on being able to evidence physically suffering violence, whilst the legitimacy to be accepted into a particular host nation of asylum is increasingly dependent on legal systems in which processing claims of asylum is often treated as a problem of security clearance rather than a problem of persecution. The same paradox of the refugee was recognised by Hannah Arendt (1994: 112), who describes the refugee figure as both "prospective citizen" and "enemy alien" at the same time. This continuum, in which the deservingness of the refugee to be accepted within a host nation of asylum or not is adjudicated, increasingly depends on how they are understood in relation to violence. What these contemporary moral economies of deservingness have produced is the routine objectification of refugees as either vulnerable victims or potential perpetrators of violence, with little scope to recognise how refugees themselves experience fear or are impacted by the fears that are attached to them.

Fear and possibility

Becoming a refugee is, it seems, a process that renders the personal lives of peoples who have fled their homes dissolvable into easily recognisable tropes. The label of the refugee, as taken up in popular representations, serves to homogenise and generalise what are the diverse experiences of peoples who have been forced to flee their homes and to seek asylum into what used to be a category of universal suffering (Malkki 1996), and which is now increasingly expanded to include another category in which refugees can also be understood as a universal threat (Gale 2004; Huysmans 2006; Kokkonen 2017). The subjectivities through which the violences and fears that create the conditions of refugee lives are known and experienced by refugees themselves are too often reduced to tropes and assumptions, particularly around specific acts or events of physical violence. Doing so overlooks and conceals how fear can also be experienced as a violence of existential possibility.

Fear is both a tangible effect of violence and an invisible violence of possibility. Although neither fear nor violence is entirely reducible to, nor mutually constitutive of, the other, both dynamics of experience and affect are often interwoven. This interweaving of fear and violence is especially evident for peoples who live in situations of persistent and generalisable insecurity (Green 1994). In those contexts, the seemingly omnipresent possibility of violence, whether in terms of direct acts of harm or ongoing conditions of structural precarity, situates violence not simply an abstract concept but as an everyday reality of existential insecurity.

This was certainly the context of existence, both pre- and post-fleeing their country of origin, for the Central African refugees I conducted fieldwork with. The historical legacy of colonial occupation and contemporary context of post-colonial political instability meant that, prior to fleeing, many of these refugees had lived without access to infrastructure to support their everyday lives, especially in terms of medical and health care, education, and transport. When regional conflicts spilled into their own lives, threatening their very physical existence, these were events that punctuated the ordinary, but it was an ordinary life that, for many, was already characterised by uncertainty and the routine possibility of violence (see also Beckett 2017; James 2010). Indeed, the everyday violences experienced by refugees prior to and following their seeking asylum, and the events of direct and acute violence that compelled them to do so, actually stem from the same fear: that of the possibility of having the regenerative potentiality of existence destroyed, especially the fear of losing a child or being unable to bear children.

So often reified into narratives of persecution and violence that are then able to be assessed in processes of refugee status determination, or translated into applications for resettlement, or consumed by public audiences through media renderings of a seemingly typified refugee experience, the violences that compel people to fear, and ultimately to flee their homes and become refugees, are often rendered intelligible by figurations of fear as identifiable events and processes. In the context of Central Africa specifically, particular tropes about the violences that have become attached to conflicts and the experiences of refugees in the region relate specifically to the use of rape as a weapon of war (Kirby 2013), conflict spurred by ethnic division (Dunn 2009), and generalised violence and state failure (Trefon 2004). These tropes dominate how the motivations for refugees to flee the region are understood across public, political, legal, and scholarly imaginaries, and, especially in relation to sexual violence, are often sensationalised.

These tropes are based on actual dynamics of conflicts in the region and have brought to light particularities of the violences inflicted there. However, they also emphasise a generalisability of the violences that characterise conflict in Central Africa, thereby locating the source of violence in the act or event of violence itself, rather than the effects it produces. Relying on such tropes as a way to explain the seemingly self-evident motivations for refugees to flee Central Africa closes off ways to think about the logics that motivate perpetrators to inflict particular forms of violence onto victims and mutes the ways in which those who experience violence attach specific fears to those acts and the effects of them. It is assumed that the very event or act of violence is the source of fear. For the refugees I conducted fieldwork with, however, violence is not singularly located in the tangibility of a direct act. Rather, there is an invisible violence that creates and intensifies fear: it is the violence of possibility, the potential outcomes and effects of the acts of physical violence that drove them to flee. These nuances are lost when the violences that are experienced by refugees are reduced to tropes or singular events of violence.

Beyond the "rape capital of the world"

The "rape capital of the world" is how Senior UN official, Margot Wallstrom, referred to the DRC in 2010 (BBC News 2010). Solidified in the words of Wallstrom but also reproduced in many other media renderings, the conflicts that have occurred since the 1990s in Central Africa, broadly, but in the DRC, especially, have become defined in global imaginaries by the use of rape as a weapon of war (Bell 2016). It is not the millions of people who have died since the outbreak of war in the DRC that grabs international media headlines, nor the continuing political unrest and the foreign interests that are implicated in it. Rather, the dominant narrative to emerge in international dialogues about the DRC, which is typified in the comments by Wallstrom, is that which characterises conflicts in the DRC by the use of rape as a weapon of war and which positions women, to the widespread exclusion of men and children, as victims (Baaz and Stern 2013).

In Uganda, I worked exclusively with women who had fled the DRC, and in Australia, the majority of women I conducted fieldwork with had also originated from the DRC. That the conflicts in the DRC had become popularly synonymous with the mass rape of women was painfully evident to me every time I came to present material from my research at a public event or academic conference. When I would describe my research as being primarily conducted with women from Burundi, Rwanda, and the DRC, I was inevitably asked about the prevalence of rape amongst those I had worked with as if it was assumed that I would have made this a leading focus of my research.

I share with other researchers a sense of relief that the issue of sexual violence during conflict and the suffering of persons who experience it are being rendered visible in academic scholarship as well as popular understandings (Baaz and Stern 2013; Heaton 2013; Mertens 2016). However, like them, I am uneasy about the apparent reductiveness of this narrative, in which the lives of women from regions where sexual violence is experienced at high rates too often become generalised as, and defined by, an identity of victimhood. Women from the DRC, at least in global media narratives and often in academic research, have come to embody a seemingly generalisable identity of "rape victim" (Baaz and Stern 2013; Bell 2016). Through this process of global attention, misrepresentation, and silencing, these women have also been stripped of their personal identities and experiences.

In attempting to draw attention to what are terrible acts of violence, many well-intentioned foreign activists and academics have, it seems, inadvertently invoked what Gayatri Chakravorty Spivak (1994: 93) refers to as the trope of "white men saving brown women from brown men," except that, in the case of the DRC, it is white women, specifically white liberal feminists, who are positioned into the role of saviours. In a more extensive analysis of sexual violence in the Central African region, Baaz and Stern (2013) describe how the construction of a "rape epidemic" in the DRC has created ripe conditions for hierarchical formations of post-colonial feminist intervention. They describe how generally white, Euro-American women have become increasingly attached to the issue of sexual violence in the DRC, which is seen as a "cause" that is largely forgotten by the rest of the world and which, therefore, requires the intervention and aid of daring and willing white feminist women warriors. Consequently, as Baaz and Stern (2013) point out, recognising and representing the atrocities of sexual violence in the DRC to global audiences has become more about documenting the personal growth of white women saviours and selectively re-telling the most sensational stories of violence from the DRC, effectively silencing those who have lived through those experiences.

It is perhaps unfair to dismiss what can be seen as genuinely well-intentioned efforts to provide support to women who have suffered sexual violence within the context of a country that provides little support, medical or otherwise, to them. However, it is still necessary that such efforts, and indeed any instance of international intervention into a continental African context, be approached reflexively, especially in regard to the ways in which such encounters can reinforce and reproduce post-colonial relations of power. The narrative that women in the DRC require "saving," no matter how well intentioned, reinforces a still pervasive neo-colonial narrative in which the African continent continues to be understood through a lens of savagery: as Achille Mbembe (2001: 11) describes, as the antithesis to a supposedly civilised and developed "West."

The entry point to my encounters with women I conducted fieldwork with was not as potential victims of sexual violence. I sought instead to open up a general dialogue from which the peoples I worked with could themselves direct our encounters and identify from their own perspectives the experiences in their lives to which they attached particular significance. As such, I never directly asked women I worked with to recount personal experiences of sexual violence. Nonetheless, some women chose to talk to me about such experiences. But their experiences complicated the sensationalist narrative of rape as a weapon of war that I had become accustomed to from global media representations. As Baaz and Stern (2013) have similarly recognised, those women who have experienced sexual violence in the DRC are not necessarily as distressed over the actual event of violence, as the selective representations of their experiences might lead global audiences to believe. Rather, the ancillary effects of the violence on their lives add a further, and more persistent, layer of fear to their experiences. Baaz and Stern (2013) describe how:

> Another and related aspect of the Raped Woman's story which somehow seems to go unregistered by the visitor/spectator is her accounts of her main worries, which, in most instances, concern her lack of basic means of survival; concerns over lack of land to cultivate, lack of clean water, concerns over her hungry and often malnourished, sickly children. These worries are frequently amplified by the workings of other aspects of violence committed while she was raped, such as pillage and the burning of fields and houses, which left her with nothing.
>
> (Baaz and Stern 2013: 95)

Rather than being caught in the trauma of the specific event of sexual violence, women I spoke with who talked with me about their experiences of assault appeared, as Baaz and Stern (2013) also recognise, to be distraught over the effect of these acts on their lives following the assault. Often, women I got to know in Uganda had fled from the DRC because their husband or a male family member had been killed or had "disappeared" during a raid, meaning that the women were unable to provide protection for their family. Being without a partner and often having their home villages destroyed, women were placed into a situation of impoverishment and generalised insecurity that would force them to flee. In addition, many women became the targets of sexual violence during such raids. Such experiences were not only horrendous during the actual events of violence, but also made the future of reproductive potentiality unclear. Injuries sustained during experiences of sexual violence could prevent further pregnancies. And, it is often the case that after experiencing sexual violence women become ostracised from their male partners and their immediate community. Sexual violence threatened not only biological reproduction of children for these women but also the reproduction of their social lives by changing, and cutting off, particular forms of sociality.

It was the quietness of Janelle that especially struck me as unusual when I first met her. A friend had asked me to visit a church in Kampala that had become foundational in the early reception of experiences of many refugees claiming asylum in the city. Many newly arrived refugees were directed there, and almost as many ended up staying there while they arranged independent accommodation, sleeping in what must have been unbearable heat in the dilapidated, beaten tin and wood structure. A group of thirteen women had gathered there to speak with me, and so I spent most of my day getting to know them and hearing about the experiences that had caused them to flee the DRC. Sometimes, we spoke as a group about the general problem of violence in the DRC and the specific problem of sexual violence, and other times, as tea and food were prepared sporadically throughout the day, I spoke with women individually. At one point, as we sat together in a group, one of the women asked, "Who here has not seen or know about rape during the wars?" The question was met by all with blank silence.

None of the women, however, spoke as little as Janelle. She sat slightly apart from the others and kept her head and gaze turned down. Though it was hard to guess her age, I knew enough to tell that she was an age at which many of her peers were married and having children. Yet it appeared that she was single and childless. I also noticed that she appeared to be especially gaunt: her clothes hung off her thin frame and her cheeks were pinched. I made a point to approach her and start a conversation when the room had quietened down, and tea was being prepared.

I asked her name and where she had come from. Her responses were short, at first, but not terse. I asked about her life in Kampala, and she spoke for a few minutes about how the people who ran the church we were standing in had taken her in and helped her find safety after first arriving in the city. She was very grateful to them. I noticed, however, that unlike the other women I had spoken with, Janelle spoke of no other relatives. She appeared to be close to tears as we spoke.

"But you have a future here, now," I said. I hoped that talking of the future might drive Janelle away from thoughts of the past or present that she might find particularly troubling.

"I am alone," she replied, looking away from me.

"But that could change," I said, "You could meet someone here, and not be alone."

Janelle closed her eyes slowly, then gestured to her seemingly emaciated body. In an unexpectedly forceful stream of conversation, she told me, "With this virus? The virus in my blood? No one will want me. No one will have me. I am nothing. They did this to me. Those men, the soldiers. Now I am nothing."

I did not push Janelle to explain herself further. The source of her visible distress seemed obvious enough from our short conversation, and I would have felt uncomfortable pursuing further details from her. What struck me, however, was that it was not the violence of the specific event or acts that had left Janelle in her current state of ill health that was the source of her distress. Rather, it was the effect that these events were having on her present and future through which Janelle articulated her pain. In a social context in which existential purpose and social recognition is dependent on a capacity to create relationships with people and especially to create sociality through biological reproduction, being "alone," as Janelle describes herself, is itself a kind of death sentence: a social death to preclude, it seemed, an imminent physiological one.

The fear that acts of sexual violence and assault generate is often understood as intrinsically bound to the immediacy of the event of violence. Kirsten Hastrup (2003: 211), for example, describes rape as a "highly localized" act in which "terror hyper-individuates the victim because pain cannot be shared." But what if the sufferer, whose individual body is that which becomes the target of sexual violence, does not understand themselves as a singular individual? Rather, what if the sufferer understands themselves, foremost, as a person whose recognition as an individual is understand exclusively in relation to connections to and with others?

As reflected in the way that Janelle articulates her suffering, the experience of pain in a context in which persons are understood primarily as relational rather than singular beings is never entirely individualised: it is amplified across the relationships through which the person who has suffered violence knows themselves in the present and through which they have imagined themselves in the future. Indeed, it is the individualising aftereffect of the violence, and not the individualisation of the violent act itself, that creates distress for Janelle.

Talking with other women who described to me the experiences that had led them to flee the DRC, I was to find, repeatedly, this future orientation to be crucial to the ways in which the violences they experienced were understood. The severity of violence was articulated by the impact it had on their capacity to bear children or the effect it had on the lives of those children to whom they were already mothers. Indeed, the futurity embodied by children appeared to be not only the epicentre of fear and violence for the women I conducted fieldwork with, but also central to the logics around which the violences imposed on them were organised.

The logics of senseless violence

Violence is rarely senseless. It can be tempting, when confronted with stories of the apparent brutality and extremity of violence inflicted during conflicts in Central Africa, to immediately characterise such acts as senseless barbarism and condemn the attackers as savages. Doing so, however, reproduces the dominant trope of continental Africa as a place of exceptional, and seemingly inhuman, violence (Mbembe 2001). Not only does such a racially charged narrative make it possible to dismiss violences that are committed in Africa as just another example of the assumed brutality of African peoples: it also silences the experiences of those targeted, who are reified to passive victims of barbarism rather than people who are themselves implicated and involved in deeply politicised and complex conflicts.

Just as peoples who fear or have experienced physical attacks and sexual violence during conflict may understand such assaults in more expansive terms than just the immediacy of the violent event and the impact it has on the singular individual who is the target of violence, so too can the violence that is inflicted during conflict signify social and political meanings that transcend the interpersonal dynamic of a violent encounter between two or more people. As Allen Feldman (1991) has theorised, based on research focusing on the Republic and Loyalist conflicts in Northern Ireland, when people become targets of physical violence in times of war and conflict the harm that is inflicted on them is never arbitrary. The physical bodies of targeted individuals or groups, during and following incidents of physical harm or physical control, are being made into symbols of political action. If, as Feldman (1991) suggests, the physically damaged bodies of those who suffer violence during conflict are not simply targets of violence but conduits of political meaning, it is necessary to move beyond the sensational dynamics of extreme violence that has occurred in Central Africa to consider what it means to enforce such specific formations of violence in processes of seeking and attaining social control.

The use of sexual violence in situations of conflict, whether in the DRC or otherwise, is extreme, but not barbaric, senseless, or incomprehensible. Such acts are not, as Thomas Turner (2007) points out, a violent form of sexual activity but rather a sexual form of political action. This is not, however, to suggest that such enactments of sexual violence during outbreaks of conflict are always organised and strategic. As Baaz and Stern (2013) point out, having conducted research with peoples responsible for militia that have directly engaged in such acts, the use of sexual violence can be as much indicative of a breach of control in a military operation as an attempt to gain military control. However, when broaching the possibility of sexual violence and rape as a specific tactic of war, it is necessary, as Paul Kirby (2013) argues, to go beyond this claim of such acts as "weapons." Instead, researchers must be sensitive to the specific meanings, purposes, and ends that such acts may be intended to evoke and achieve.

When considering the complexity of how and why incidents of sexual violence are enacted in times of conflict, sexual violence cannot be dismissed as senseless barbarism. However, although I was consciously wary of getting caught in the seeming incomprehensibility of stories of violence I was told during fieldwork, there were times when I was initially overwhelmed by the affective horror of experiences that refugees recounted to me. Being so overwhelmed, I risked losing the "essential situatedness" of those experiences (James 1993). Recognising that documenting and absorbing such stories of violence can feel overwhelming for researchers, Wendy James (1993) urges for the emotional affect of fear be approached in the context of the "essential situatedness" in which it is constituted, which requires attentiveness to the specific socio-political context in which actions of violence take place. Following this perspective, I was conscious to recover from the shock of such stories, because sensationalising them in the process of documenting them would only serve to abstract the violence of these events that had been lived and experienced by peoples who, at the time of sharing their experiences, I was often sitting next to.

In Kampala, I was visited one afternoon by Emily, a woman who I had gotten to know previously at events at a local church. On that day, she had brought her daughter, Meredith, with her. Meredith was about 11 years old, but she had an intellectual disability that meant she communicated non-verbally with others around her. One of the first things I had noticed about Emily had been the way that Meredith almost always clung to her. Especially shy amongst strangers like myself, Meredith would clutch at her mother's *kitenge* skirt, burying her face into Emily's back and stomach.[1] But I also often caught Meredith giggling, pointing to me as an object of her attention that she apparently found amusing.

I fixed tea for us, and we sat together in a quiet area of the shared courtyard outside of where I was staying. Meredith sat close by her mother, gazing from her to myself. Since we had not had an opportunity to talk in detail previously, Emily and I spoke about her experiences in Kampala, where she had lived for about a year. Eventually, the topic of our conversation came to focus on why Emily had fled the DRC.

It was unclear to Emily why, exactly, that rebel group had chosen to target her village, specifically. She suspected that it was because the land occupied by peoples in her village was fertile and well maintained: "[A] good place for children" was how she described it. But, whatever the reason, one evening, around a year prior to our conversation in 2013, her village had been stormed by members of a militia group. Before the situation had descended into the outright chaos, soldiers had rounded up many of the villagers, including Emily and Meredith, and forced them into one of the shared open spaces between houses in the village. The militia began to discuss their intention of taking control of the village and the surrounding land, but as protest and dissent broke out, they began to demonstrate their handle over the situation by threatening to inflict sexual assault on people. Eventually, this had been what had occurred. But rather than target those who had been most outspoken in their resistance, the militia chose to assault those who seemed to be most vulnerable. Older women and children of either sex and of varying ages were pulled into the open and assaulted. Meredith, who had been whimpering alongside her mother, was one of those who had been chosen by the militia to be a target of assault. Her mother had watched on, powerless to stop the violence, until eventually the panic of her friends and family spilled into outright resistance and the control of the rebel militia was momentarily broken. She had been able to grab her daughter despite the resulting chaos. They had managed to flee.

As her mother relayed this story, Meredith, who sat across from me, appeared to have grown more comfortable. She had let go of her mother and sat quietly, staring at me with wide eyes. For a moment, I was struck by the seemingly senseless brutality of attacking Meredith. Later, after they had left, the image of Meredith staring at me seemed retained, unable to be erased, from my mind as I thought longer about what Emily had told me.

It could appear that the violence inflicted on Meredith and Emily was opportunistic and senselessly barbaric. The assault did not conform to the typical expectation of how rape as a weapon of war is enacted as an act intended to specifically bring sexual gratification to the attacker. Such expectations generally assume that rape during conflict involves a heterosexual encounter of enforced sexual intercourse, involving at least one male perpetrator and at least one female victim. It is often assumed that personal gratification, based on heteronormative sexualisation, is at least a partial motivating factor (Baaz and Stern 2009). This is a limited stereotype, of course. Much good work is being done to draw attention to the experiences of those who have suffered sexual violence in the DRC and in other conflict contexts that do not conform to this trope of heterosexual rape, especially in regard to male sufferers and the experiences of sexual violence for people who identify as LGBTQI (Henry 2015; Lwambo 2013; Solangon and Patel 2012).

During my research I was told about many experiences of violence that reflected the dominant trope of heterosexual rape. However, I also heard about other instances in which violence could not be understood in terms of normative sexuality as primarily based on sexual gratification of a male attacker with a female victim. I was told about instances where militia specifically targeted elderly people. Or situations in which it was young adolescents or children who were the focuses of violence. In still other scenarios, I was told about how militia would force family members to engage in sexual acts with each other.

Engaging in sexual activity with children, assaulting elderly people, and forcing incestuous sexual relations are widely considered to be acts of sexual violence that are especially perverse and that transcend the normative explanation for heterosexual rape as an act that is motivated by sexual gratification (Palmer 1988). Indeed, it is this very perversion of what are considered to be normative dynamics of sexuality in contexts of conflict and war that is crucial to the domination that is symbolised by such acts (Taylor 1999a, 1999b). The intent, it appears, is not to sexualise the targets of violence. Rather, the intention of such acts is to dehumanise.

These specific formations of violence violate cosmological logics of regeneration, in which sexuality is so often understood in relation to the potential to reproduce children. Assaulting those who are not potentially fertile—that is, children and the elderly—and forcing family members to become sexually intimate, inverts the reproductive potentiality that can result from sexual connection. In Central African contexts of conflict, such acts both symbolically and physiologically invert the relations of reproductive connectedness that are the basis of a cosmological belief system in which human purpose is understand in terms of regenerative potentiality (Taylor 1999a, 1999b). In doing so, such formations of violence position those who are targeted as peoples who are not part of this shared basis of humanity. Sexual violence can, in this way, be seen as a distinct method of dehumanisation.

Destroying and obstructing the regenerative potential of those coded as an enemy has been the theme of violences enacted in conflicts across Burundi, Rwanda, and the DRC. Based on her work with Hutu refugees in Tanzania, Liisa Malkki (1995a) recounts the violences they described when referring to outbreaks of conflict in Burundi in the 1970s and 1980, in which:

> There were certain body parts on which mutilation and destruction converged; and these body parts were also the points of thematic convergence in the narrative .... Women's bodies were said to have been destroyed largely through the vagina and the uterus. When the women captured were pregnant, the violence seems invariably to have focused on the womb and specifically on the link between mother and child .... The disemboweling of pregnant Hutu women was interpreted as an effort to destroy the procreative capability, the "new life," of the Hutu people. In several accounts, the unborn child or embryo was referred to, simply, as "the future" .... How one dies is important here, as it is elsewhere in the world. And again, forcing a woman to eat the flesh of her own "flesh and blood," of her child, is imposing, not only cannibalism, but autophagy in the literal sense of devouring oneself. It represents a complete reversal of the "progress of nature" in which the mother's body nurtures, forms, and brings into the world "new life."
>
> (Malkki 1995a: 92–93)

It is regenerative potential, embodied through processes of physiological reproduction, that became the focal point of violence during outbreaks of conflict in Burundi. These were instances of violence that worked to invert the logics of a cosmology of regeneration.

Recounting the dynamics of the 1994 genocide in Rwanda, Christopher Taylor (1999a: 101) similarly points out that the violences enacted during the most intensive days of the conflict seemed to follow what he calls "cultural patternings," in which it was the reproductive and metabolic systems of victims, that is, those through which life-generating fluids and processes of physical regeneration flow, that were the focal point of violence. Taylor (1999a) describes how, during the genocide, men were castrated and breasts of women were cut off as a way to impede fluids like semen and milk, Additionally, Taylor (1999a) describes how the bodies of victims were also impaled from vagina or anus to mouth, symbolising the obstruction of the flow of regenerative potential through the human body.

It is the humanity of the perpetrators that may be in question when analysing such acts of violence from an outsider's perspective. Yet, as the analyses of both Malkki (1995a) and Taylor (1999a) suggest, it is the dehumanisation of the victim that seems to be the intent of such specific formations of violence. Such specific techniques of violence are enacted with a purpose that goes beyond simply destroying or harming the physical existence of the victim. Ultimately, such formations of violence work to exclude the victim from a shared humanity by obstructing their future potentiality to not only be alive but to regenerate life itself.

Sexual violence and other forms of assault that have been committed in Central African conflicts, and which compelled many of the refugees I conducted fieldwork with to flee their homes, are often enacted in ways that can seem senselessly barbaric to an outsider, but which are distinctly logical and attuned to incite terror onto the specific population upon which the violence is inflicted. These are methods of harming and killing that not only result in damage and death: these are methods that, ultimately, both physically and symbolically seek to render the targets of violence as less than human, as peoples whose continuity of social and physiological reproduction needs to be destroyed. The fear that compelled women I came to know during fieldwork to flee their homes and become refugees was never simply a response to an immediate fear of a distinct event or situation of physical violence. Rather, the epicentre of their fears was the potential for such violences to diminish or obliterate their capacity to contribute to what they experience as a fundamental cosmological imperative to regenerate life, especially through bearing and rearing children. Becoming a target of violence during conflict is not only, for them, a personal tragedy. These are incidents that can eject them from the social context of their worlds, meaning that even if their physical death does not result from the violences that are inflicted on them during situations of conflict, the viability of their social existence is not necessarily secure. For these refugees, the fear that compels them to flee situations of conflict in Central Africa is a fear of the violence of existential possibility.

Necrographic maps and social death

Sexual violence and the use of rape as a weapon of war occupies a specific place of horror in the imaginaries of Western outsiders who commentate and report on war atrocities (Gibson 1993). Such acts are seen as a pinnacle of violation. Perhaps, however, this special attention that is granted to acts of sexual violence in Western renderings of conflict and war does not only represent the apparent pervasiveness of such forms of violence but also reflects a distinct fixation that Western audiences have with the individual body as the foundation through which violence is enacted, therefore casting sexual violence as the seemingly most personal and extreme kind of violence that can be inflicted on a person (Gibson 1993). For the women I conducted fieldwork with, it is not, however, the individual body that is at stake during situations of conflict violence: rather, it is the entire matrix of social relations through which their lives are suspended that is at stake. For them, rape and sexual violence are indeed terrible violations. However, the greatest atrocity imaginable to them was not the sexual violation of their individual bodies but the violation of their bodily capacity to reproduce children or the acts that work to sever the relatedness that they already shared with their children. They feared, above all, that militarists would inflict violence on their children. Unfortunately, such occurrences were not uncommon.

When I first met Sifa in Kampala, I did not ask why she, unlike so many other women, was not accompanied by a family or a brood of children. The story came out one afternoon in the apartment I shared in Kampala. Although I did not ask Sifa why she had fled the DRC, it seemed that her current existence in Kampala was so defined by those events that it was impossible to speak of her contemporary life without reference to the reasons that had compelled her to flee. Speaking softly and slowly, she told me that the day she had fled her town had begun like any other. "We," she said, referring to herself and her husband, "did not even know that soldiers, rebels, were near. We did not know..." She shook her head, then continued, "If we did..." The silence that followed was infused with pain. "But, we did not know...."

Sifa told me that the church that she and her husband had begun attending was about an hour's walk from the town where they lived. On a Sunday morning, Sifa and her husband had left to go church and allowed their children, all six of them, to remain at home since the walk was arduous and the children had been sick. "Everything was good," she said, but the strain of the story was making her voice high and sharp. "We were at the church for many hours," she went on, "but when we walked the road to our town we knew something was bad. Smoke over the trees. Bodies on the ground sometimes. Dead people. Dead children. And smoke, so much smoke and fire ahead."

There was a pause before Sifa continued. Her blank expression did not shift. Before she even went on to finish her story, I guessed that she had relived the particular moment she was about to recall many times.

"When we got to the house, where it should have been, it was not there. It was gone. Burnt. They had burnt it...We looked all over for the children... Screaming, screaming for them..." I wrapped my hand around Sifa's as she let out a strangled gulp. "They were inside. They were inside the house when it burned."

The entire future that Sifa and her husband had projected for themselves and their family was, in a matter of mere hours, totally annihilated. Theirs is the kind of experience that the refugees I worked with most acutely fear.

The devastating fate of Sifa's children can be considered here within the framework of what Malkki has termed (1995a) "necrographic maps." Malkki (1995a: 89–90) describes necrographic maps as the charting of techniques for mutilating and killing that are intended to target and obstruct the reproductive potentialities of victims. Whilst the atrocity that Sifa has experienced does not directly target her own body, she is, nonetheless, made an embodied victim through the logics of the violence intending, and succeeding, in destroying her familial lineage by ending the lives of her children. It is necessary, in this context, to take Malkki's (1995a: 89–90) concept of necrographic maps beyond the limits of individual bodies. Within a sense of social necrographic mapping, the targeting of children and biological reproduction within contexts of violence in Central Africa can be examined as a "necrography" of the social body. In this sense, necographic mapping is not simply inscribed on the individual bodies of victims but is imprinted on their social milieu through the destruction of familial lineage. The violence aims to obstruct and decimate the regenerative potential and corporeal presence of victims and in doing so to devastate the lives and futures of those interwoven within their social worlds.

When being attentive to the formations of violence that refugees themselves fear, rather than those that are sensationalised in popular renderings of violence in Central Africa, it is evident that cosmological logics orient how refugees understand and experience violence. The cosmological logics through which these refugees attach purpose and meaning to life are based on an assumption of the regenerative continuity of existence, which is embodied directly through the bearing and rearing of children. To them, children symbolically and physiologically embody the future and the continuity of existential life. Violence that severs their relatedness to children, even if it is not physically inflicted on their individual bodies, is a violence that severs the existential possibility of regenerative continuity and which ultimately creates the conditions of social, if not physical, death.

The concept of social death refers to a condition of being physically alive but not recognised in socially meaningful ways as a person. Being both physically alive and socially dead is a state that occurs, according to Orlando Patterson (1982), who used the concept to describe how mass enslavement is made possible through techniques of social death, when a person is ejected from the structures and norms of their social worlds, leaving them with no set of relations or common methods of communication through which to create a meaningful social existence. Of course, Patterson's (1982) broad historical analysis overlooks the ways in which many enslaved peoples, despite being removed from their existing social worlds and forced into conditions of domination, still created forms of communication and social meaning that eventually transformed into whole cultural systems (Scott 1990). Yet the concept of social death remains a useful heuristic to describe the experience of having a way of existing—that is, a cosmological orientation toward the world—unexpectedly severed.

This was what Sifa experienced when she realised that the entire future she had projected for herself, which had always been in relation to the future of her children, was no longer available for her. This is not to say that she will not re-make her social world in the future. But at the time I met her, Sifa appeared to be in a state of severe detachment from the world: because she was unable to recover from the loss, she and her husband had separated, and she lived a transient existence, floating between family members in Kampala, supporting them with daily tasks like laundry and childcare in exchange for shelter and food. But I noticed the people around Sifa struggled to introduce her or call her by name. This indicated not only the loss of her children but also the destruction of her social status as a mother. According to Patterson (1982), the replacement of a slave's birth name with one determined by the slave owner was one of the crucial ways through which their personal identity was lost and their social death affirmed. For Central African women like Sifa, the use of their birth name is only common until they give birth to their first child, upon which time the woman is referred to as "Mama," followed by the name of her first child. Effectively, the birth name is dropped from common usage: some women I knew, who were friends, even occasionally forgot the birth name of their close friends. It was this naming practice, and this status of "Mama," that Sifa also lost following the death of her children. No longer a mother, the violences that had caused Sifa to flee the DRC were those that had forced her to become a single woman living in what is, for her, an inherently plural social world.

The futures that follow fear

The UNHCR recognises a refugee as a person who has a "well-founded fear of persecution" from which they cannot be protected in their country of origin, and which requires them to seek asylum from another state. This process of being recognised as a refugee requires that peoples who are seeking asylum articulate their fear as a distinct and identifiable object or event. However, part of the intensity of fear is created from those apprehensions that cannot necessarily be defined, objectified, or evidenced. For even when refugees are linking their contemporary and ongoing fear of persecution to distinct events and experiences of the past, they are always projecting this likelihood of violence into a trajectory of future possibility. What the refugees I conducted fieldwork with ultimately fear is this intangibility and volatility of a future that has been made precarious by years and decades of conflict and war. If they stay, will they wake up tomorrow to live with the rhythm of ordinary life: rising with the sun, working through the day, eating at sundown, surrounded by family? Or will they, like Sifa, rise with the sun only to have their whole world irrevocably altered, perhaps even destroyed, by sundown?

The cosmological mythico-futurity that guides how these refugees conceptualise and aim to experience ordinary life is based around an assumption of existence as a cyclic temporal rhythm. It is the continuity of this cyclic rhythm, and the future life that is regenerated through it, that is both targeted for destruction, either symbolically or physically, in the violences inflicted during conflicts in Central Africa and that is the intangible epicentre of fear for those who are targeted. It is not simply an individual in a specific event of violence that is the basis of fear for these refugees: it is the future effects of such acts on the whole social nexus in which their lives are intimately intertwined.

Note

1 *Kitenge* is a material, often waxed, with printed patterns that is worn throughout Central and East Africa.

References

Arendt, H. 1994. We Refugees. In *Altogether Elsewhere: Writers on Exile*. M. Robinson (Ed.), pp. 110–119. Boston, MA; London: Faber and Faber.

Baaz, M.E. and Stern, M. 2009. Why Do Soldiers Rape? Masculinity, Violence, and Sexuality in the Armed Forces in the Congo (DRC). *International Studies Quarterly* 53(2): 495–518.

Baaz, M.E. and Stern, M. 2013. *Sexual Violence as a Weapon of War? Perceptions, Prescriptions, Problems in the Congo and Beyond*. London: Zed Books.

Balch, A. 2016. *Immigration and the State: Fear, Greed, and Hospitality*. London: Palgrave Macmillan.BBC News. 2010. UN Official Calls DR Congo 'Rape Capital of the World.' Available at: http://news.bbc.co.uk/2/hi/africa/8650112.stm (Accessed 17 October 2016).

Beckett, G. 2017. A Dog's Life: Suffering Humanitarianism in Port-au-Price, Haiti. *American Anthropologist* 119(1): 35–45.

Bell, B. 2016. The Wartime Rape Narrative in the Democratic Republic of Congo. Masters Thesis, University of Ottawa, Canada.

Berry, M., Garcia-Blanco, I., and Moore, K. 2016. Press Coverage of the Refugee and Migrant Crisis in the EU: A Content Analysis of Five European Countries, Project Report. Geneva: United Nations High Commissioner for Refugees. Available at: www.unhcr.org/56bb369c9.html (Accessed 27 December 2016).

Cannizzaro, S. and Gholami, R. 2016. The Devil is *Not* in the Detail: Representational Absence and Stereotyping in the 'Trojan Horse' News Story. *Race Ethnicity and Education*. doi:10.1080/13613324.2016.1195350.

Casmiro, S., Hancock, P. and Northcote, J. 2007. Isolation and Insecurity: Resettlement Issues among Muslim Refugee Women in Perth, Western Australia. *Australian Journal of Social Issues* 42(1): 55–69.

Devetak, R. 2007. In Fear of Refugees: The Politics of Border Protection in Australia. *The International Journal of Human Rights* 8(1): 101–109.

Dunn, K.C. 2009. 'Sons of the Soil' and Contemporary State Making: Autochthony, Uncertainty and Political Violence in Africa. *Third World Quarterly* 30(1): 113–127.

Fassin, D. 2005. Compassion and Repression: The Moral Economy of Immigration Policies in France. *Cultural Anthropology* 20(3): 362–387.

Fassin, D. and D'Halluin, E. 2005. The Truth from the Body: Medical Certificates as Ultimate Evidence for Asylum Seekers. *American Anthropologist* 107(4): 597–608.

Feldman, A. 1991. *Formations of Violence: The Narrative of the Body and Political Terror in Northern Ireland*. Chicago, IL: University of Chicago Press.

Gale, P. 2004. The Refugee Crisis and Fear: Populist Politics and Media Discourse. *Journal of Sociology* 40(4): 321–340.

Gibson, S. 1993. On Sex, Horror and Human Rights. *Women: A Cultural Review* 4(3): 250–260.

Green, L. 1994. Fear as a Way of Life. *Cultural Anthropology* 9(2): 227–256.

Greenhill, K. 2016. Open Arms Behind Barred Doors: Fear, Hypocrisy and Policy Schizophrenia in the European Migration Crisis. *European Law Journal* 22(3): 317–332.

Hage, G. 1998. *White Nation: Fantasies of White Supremacy in a Multicultural Society*. Sydney: Pluto Press.

Hastrup, K. 2003. Violence, Suffering and Human Rights: Anthropological Reflections. *Anthropological Theory* 3(3): 309–323.

Hathaway, J. and Foster, M. 2014. *The Law of Refugee Status*. 2nd edition. Cambridge: Cambridge University Press.

Heaton, L. 2013. What Happened in Luvungi? *Foreign Policy* 199(10): 32–36.

Henry, N. 2015. Theorizing Wartime Rape: Deconstructing Gender, Sexuality, and Violence. *Gender & Society* 30(1): 44–56.

Holmes, S.M. and Casteñada, H. 2016. Representing the "European Refugee Crisis" in Germany and Beyond: Deservingness and Difference, Life and Death. *American Ethnologist* 43(1): 12–24.

Huysmans, J. 2006. *The Politics of Insecurity: Fear, Migration and Asylum in the EU*. London; New York: Routledge.James, W. 1993. The Names of Fear: Memory, History, and the Ethnography of Feeling among Uduk Refugees. *Journal of the Royal Anthropological Institute* 3: 115–131.

James, E. 2010. *Democratic Insecurities: Violence, Trauma, and Intervention in Haiti*. Berkeley: University of California Press.

Jansen, B.J. 2008. Between Vulnerability and Assertiveness: Negotiating Resettlement in Kakuma Refugee Camp, Kenya. *African Affairs* 107(429): 569–587.

Kagan, M. 2002. Is Truth in the Eye of the Beholder? Objective Credibility Assessment in Refugee Status Determination. *Georgetown Immigration Law Journal* 17(3): 367–415.

Kallius, A., Monterescu, D., and Rajaram, P. 2016. Immobilizing Mobility: Border Ethnograpy, Illiberal Democracy, and the Politics of the 'Refugee Crisis' in Hungary. *American Ethnologist* 43(1): 25–37.

Kirby, P. 2013. How is Rape a Weapon of War? Feminist International Relations, Modes of Critical Explanation, and the Study of Wartime Sexual Violence. *European Journal of International Relations* 19(4): 797–821.

Klocker, N. 2004. Community Antagonism towards Asylum Seekers in Port Augusta, South Australia. *Geographical Research* 42(1): 1–17.

Kokkonen, O. 2017. A Faceless Threat of Vulnerable Individuals? Representations of Refugees in British Newspapers during the European Refugee Crisis. Bachelors Thesis, University of Jyväskylä, Jyväskylä, Finland.

Lwambo, D. 2013. 'Before the War, I was a Man': Men and Masculinities in the Eastern Democratic Republic of Congo. *Gender & Development* 21(1): 47–66.

Malkki, L 1995a. *Purity and Exile: Violence, Memory, and National Cosmology among Hutu Refugees in Tanzania*. Chicago, IL: University of Chicago Press.

Malkki, L. 1996. Speechless Emissaries: Refugees, Humanitarianism, and Dehistoricization. *Cultural Anthropology* 11(3): 377–404.

Marino, S. and Dawes, S. 2016. Introduction to Fortress Europe: Media, Migration and Borders. *Networking Knowledge: Journal of the MeCCSA Postgraduate Network* 9(4): 1–6.

Mbembe, A. 2001. *On the Postcolony*. Berkeley: University of California Press.

Mertens, C. 2016. Sexual Violence in the Congo Free State: Archival Traces and Present Reconfigurations. *The Australasian Review of African Studies* 37(1): 6–20.

Palmer, C.T. 1988. Twelve Reasons Why Rape is not Sexually Motivated: a Skeptical Examination. *The Journal of Sex Research* 25(4): 512–530.

Patterson, O. 1982. *Slavery and Social Death: A Comparative Study*. Cambridge, MA: Harvard University Press.

Poynting, S. and Mason, V. 2007. The Resistible Rise of Islamophobia: Anti-Muslim Racism in the UK and Australia before 11 September 2001. *Journal of Sociology* 43(1): 61–86.

Rettberg, J.W. and Gajjala, R. 2016. Terrorists or Cowards: Negative Portrayals of Male Syrian Refugees in Social Media. *Feminist Media Studies* 16(1): 178–181.

Scheper-Hughes, N. and Bourgois, P. (Eds.). 2004. *Violence in War and Peace: An Anthology*. Malden, MA: Blackwell Publishers.

Scott, J.C. 1990. *Domination and the Arts of Resistance: Hidden Transcripts*. New Haven, CT; London: Yale University Press.

Solangon, S. and Patel, P. 2012. Sexual Violence against Men in Countries Affected by Armed Conflict. *Conflict, Security & Development* 12(4): 417–442.

Spivak, G.C. 1994. Can the Subaltern Speak? In *Marxism and the Interpretation of Culture*. C. Nelson and L. Grossberg (Eds.), pp. 271–313. Urbana and Chicago: University of Illinois Press.

Taylor, C.C. 1999a. *Sacrifice As Terror*. Oxford: Berghahn Books.

Taylor, C.C. 1999b. A Gendered Genocide: Tutsi Women and Hutu Extremists in the 1994 Rwanda Genocide. *Political and Legal Anthropology Review* 22(1): 42–54.

Trefon, T. (Ed.). 2004. *Reinventing Order in the Congo: How People Respond to State Failure in Kinshasa*. London; New York: Zed Books.

Turner, T. 2007. *The Congo Wars: Conflict, Myth & Reality*. London: Zed Books.

UNHCR. 2011c. The 1951 Convention Relating to the Status of Refugees and it's 1967 Protocol. Available at: www.unhcr.org/en-us/about-us/background/4ec262df9/1951-convention-relating-status-refugees-its-1967-protocol.html (Accessed 5 January 2017).

Walsh, J.P. 2016. Moral Panics by Design: The Case of Terrorism. *Current Sociology*. doi:10.1177/0011392116633257.

Part II

Asylum

4 Liminal asylum and circular time

Living as a refugee in a country of asylum is to live in what can feel like a state of indefinite indeterminacy. This is because the rights and protections that are attached to refugee status and the granting of asylum are generally only intended to be temporary, and yet the periods that refugees spend in contexts of protracted asylum are often not. The rights and protections that are granted to refugees in a country of asylum are not mandated by the UNHCR but are provided at the discretion of the host nation (Hathaway 1991, 2005; Hathaway and Neve 1997). This means that surviving in a country of asylum as a refugee can mean years, sometimes even decades, without necessarily having access to the rights and protections that are generally granted to citizens or permanent residents, such as rights to residency, employment, health care, education, and political participation. Many refugees have little or no way to remove themselves from this impasse: they cannot repatriate to their home country because it is too dangerous, and it is unlikely that they will be selected for resettlement. They may spend years, even decades, living in asylum in conditions that do not necessarily protect them or provide opportunity for social mobility. Simply surviving in asylum does not mean that refugees are able to actively create a future.

Protecting their lives from futures of destruction was, however, precisely the reason that so many of the refugees I conducted fieldwork with had sought to escape situations of war and conflict and seek asylum elsewhere. Becoming refugees meant that they had managed to remove themselves from the immediate danger of imminent physical harm. But being recognised as a refugee, and being granted permission to live in a host nation of asylum, does not necessarily mean that the more intangible and existential problem of being able to live lives of regenerative possibility is solved. In this chapter, I consider whether the international system of refugee protection can provide them with a space in which to regenerate their futures, especially since refugee status and rights to asylum are so often understood to be temporary conditions. How is it possible for refugees regenerate the future when, in asylum, the status of their present life is so often temporary and indeterminate?

Because existing as a refugee in asylum can so often mean that activities of ordinary life become subsumed with concerns about immediate survival, sites of asylum and irregular migration create distinct temporal registers of suspended time and protracted liminality. Based on work with Palestinian refugees living in camps in Lebanon, Adam Ramadan (2013: 72) has described the experience of being a refugee in asylum as "a time of interruption, waiting, stasis." Ruben Andersson (2014: 795) describes how "time became suspended" for irregular migrants who had been detained during their attempts to enter Europe. Working with asylum seekers detained in the UK, Melanie Griffiths (2014: 1997) considers the ways in which their lives unfold within a context of "suspended time" and within a "timeless present." Even the UNHCR (2006: 1) acknowledges that many systems of providing asylum to refugees work on the assumption of providing temporary and immediate humanitarian relief, meaning that when those situations spiral out to many years, as they so often do, asylum comes to be experienced by refugees as a state of perpetual dependency in which "Refugees find themselves in a long-lasting and intractable state of limbo. Their lives may not be at risk, but their basic rights and essential economic, social, and psychological needs remain unfulfilled after years in exile." The asylum that is provided to refugees so often situates them in what is supposed to be a temporary state of emergency assistance, which nonetheless extends indefinitely (Ramadan 2013). Asylum can be seen as much as an existential condition of indefinite liminality as a space of refuge.

The concept of liminality has become crucial to the ways in which the temporalisation of asylum and irregular migration is theorised. Liminality, as initially theorised by Arnold van Gennep (1960), refers to the middle stage of a tripartite passage of social transition. Extending on van Gennep (1960), Victor Turner (1967) further theorised the liminal stage of the rites of passage as that in which a ritual subject has lost their social status but has yet to be recognised with a new one, describing how the subject is effectively betwixt and between categories of classification. It was Liisa Malkki (1995a) who recognised how the concept of liminality can be applied to the experiences of refugees, whose status is, effectively, that of non-categorisation: refugees are peoples who are politically and legally suspended between categories of national identification through which populations across the globe are governed. Other researchers followed suit, tapping into the distinct temporal rhythms of indefinite temporariness that seem to characterise the experiences of asylum seekers, refugees, and other kinds of irregular migrants. Michel Agier (2002: 337) describes, for example, the "liminality of all situations of exodus that gives a frustrated, unfinished character." Building on the work of Agier (2002), Zygmunt Bauman (2002: 438) describes the "permanence of transitoriness" that characterises existing in asylum. Referring to research conducted with asylum seekers awaiting their status to be determined in the UK, Rebecca Rotter (2016: 96) describes how their "waiting was akin to the liminal phase in the rites of passage." The concept of liminality, however, implies linearity.

Liminality implies a distinctly unidirectional transition of a subject through a ritual that progresses cumulatively through linear time. Subsequently, conflating the suspended and indefinite temporal rhythm of asylum as a state of extended liminality attaches linearity to the ways in which refugees and other migrants experience forced migration: as if their sense of temporal discordance is resolved upon ritual incorporation into rhythms of ordinary life as active citizens or residents of their host society. Doing so assumes that their sense of being removed from the temporal rhythms of ordinary life can be resolved in the same way that the ambiguity of their politico-legal status as refugees can be resolved, that is, by restoring to them a distinct national identity and the rights and protections attached to that identity. Recounting how the refugees I conducted fieldwork with experience life in asylum, in this chapter, I consider how their focus on regenerating futures of cyclic continuity means seeking to create temporal registers of circular time that do not necessarily conform to assumptions of time as a linear trajectory.

Reproduction and suspended futures

Nadine came to speak with me with a manila folder tucked tightly under one arm. We exchanged greetings but, almost immediately, Nadine set about fanning the paperwork from the folder on the table in front of us in my apartment. The first was an identity card from the UNHCR, registering her as a refugee. Another document was a letter from the Office of the Prime Minister in Uganda, officiating her refugee status. I do not know exactly what it contained since I did not have time to read it. Upon setting out her world of paperwork, Nadine had quickly directed my attention to a larger stack of medical documents, and the murky darkness of an ultrasound scan.

"Here," she said, stabbing a finger at the scan, specifically. "No babies. I can have no babies here."

I was not able to interpret the scan of her womb and could offer Nadine no comfort or explanation, which was precisely the response that Nadine had been confronted with over and over again since she had begun seeking an explanation for, and support to assist, the problem she was having with conceiving a child in Uganda. In the DRC, she told me, she had fallen pregnant easily. Before the conflicts had begun to escalate in her region in 2011, forcing Nadine and her family to escape and seek asylum in Uganda, she had given birth to four children. Since seeking asylum in Uganda, Nadine had attempted to conceive a child with her husband, but they had no success. She had attended medical appointments at two different facilities in Kampala, attempting to determine a biomedical explanation for her problem with fertility. Neither examination had resulted in identifying a specific medical issue that would cause either temporary or permanently reduced fertility. Nadine had been sent away with general advice to try and eat nutrient rich foods, sleep well, reduce stress, and have regular sex with her husband.

As she relayed this advice to me, Nadine was looking at me with an expression of exasperation. These were not exactly unusual recommendations for anyone, let alone a woman attempting to conceive a child. Nonetheless, as refugee attempting to eke out a self-sustainable livelihood in a context of urban asylum, such seemingly basic advice can be difficult to follow.

Pointing back to the ultrasound, Nadine emphasised, "Nothing wrong! Nothing! It is not me. It is the life here." Such sentiments of frustration were not uncommon amongst the refugees I conducted fieldwork with in Uganda. Nor was Nadine the only woman I spoke with who told me about struggles to conceive and bear children to term since becoming a refugee in Uganda.

Uganda has what the UNHCR (2017b) considers to be one of the most favourable refugee protection environments in the world. It is one of few nations in continental Africa to have in place a policy of asylum that does not require refugees to be warehoused in camps. Rather, the provision of asylum to refugees in Uganda is based on what is termed a "self-reliance strategy," in which refugees are provided with the means to independently meet their own essential needs, including housing and food, rather than rely on humanitarian relief provided by governments or independent organisations (Betts, Bloom, Kaplan, and Omata 2017; Svedberg 2014). The implementation of the self-reliance strategy in Uganda, which was first introduced in 1999 and which has since become the dominant structure of asylum policy in the country, was intended to reduce dependency on humanitarian assistance and to ease the financial burden that such dependency places on Uganda as the host nation of asylum and the involved international organisations (Svedberg 2014). The self-reliance strategy requires that refugees support themselves through subsistence agriculture. The Ugandan government provides newly arrived refugees with a small plot of land in an area that is designated for refugees, although still in close proximity to Ugandan locals who the refugees are encouraged to trade and interact with, as well as the tools necessary to cultivate it. The self-reliance strategy provides a way for refugees to live in asylum in Uganda without being fenced in or otherwise contained. However, the reliance on subsistence agriculture is not sustainable for all. Problems with the long-term fertility of the land and experience with farming complicate the ability of refugees to create subsistence livelihoods from an agricultural enterprise (Ilcan, Oliver, and Connoy 2015; Krause 2016).

The self-reliance strategy, in which refugees' independent survival in Uganda is supported through settlements that help them to engage in subsistence agriculture, is not suited to all refugees. Many choose not to live in the designated settlements and to settle instead in Kampala. Self-settling in urban areas of Uganda is not a new trend. Indeed, the expansive policy of asylum in Uganda, which allows refugees to have freedom of movement and live legally in Kampala, is in part a response to the large numbers of refugees, primarily from the DRC, who were already self-settling in Kampala after war erupted in the mid-1990s (Dryden-Peterson 2006; Hovil 2007). It was not until the introduction and implementation of a new asylum policy, the 2006 Refugee Act, that refugees in Kampala were able to live there legally and seek formal refugee status, however (Dryden-Peterson 2006; Hovil 2007). The 2006 Refugee Act allows refugees to legally live in Kampala and other urban areas that they choose, and gives them the right to work in Uganda. Both of these rights are set out in the UN 1951 Convention and 1967 Protocol Relating to the Status of Refugees. However, these rights are rarely implemented by host nations that receive refugees (Hathaway 2005), making the system of asylum in Uganda on of the most progressive that currently exists worldwide (Betts et al. 2017).

The asylum policy that is in place in Uganda clearly offers refugees some of the most expansive freedoms of any other asylum system in the world. But the rights provided are conditional: they require that refugees create self-reliant livelihoods, either with the support of humanitarian aid if refugees choose to reside in a settlement or completely independently if refugees choose to reside in Kampala or anywhere else other than a settlement. What is framed by the Ugandan government and the UNHCR as a progressive and emancipatory policy of asylum is one in which, in practical terms, refugees, especially those in urban areas, are provided with expansive rights to freedom of movement but with very little infrastructural support to fully realise them.

Eveliina Lyytinen (2015) describes how the ways in which refugees themselves experience urban asylum in Uganda does not necessarily reflect the overly optimistic portrayal that is put forward by the UNHCR and the government. Lyytinen (2015) describes, for example, how many refugees claim that it has been specifically requested that they return to the designated settlements rather than live in the city, relaying a conversation in which an officer overseeing matters relating to the settlement and asylum of refugees expressed, "If you decide that you are going to move to Kampala, there are definitely conditions to meet… If we are to provide the same provisions in the settlement and in Kampala, I do not think we would have settlements." What this means is that what little support that is provided to refugees in Uganda to create independent livelihoods is almost exclusively focused on those refugees who live in settlements at the exclusion of refugees who decide to settle in an urban area. The hardship of settling outside of the settlements acts as an implicit way to discourage refugees to reside in Kampala, even if the official policy gives them the right to do so.

Another problem with attempting to create a self-reliant existence in Kampala is that providing with refugees with the right to work, which they rely on as the primary source of a self-sustaining livelihood since they do not have the support of humanitarian aid, is not the same as empowering them to gain meaningful employment, especially if the role of employers and the labour market in making such processes possible is taken into account. The economic life of refugees in Uganda is the focus of a report produced through the Refugee Studies Centre at the University of Oxford (Betts, Bloom, Kaplan, and Omata 2014), which rightly points to the ways in which the flexibility of asylum policy in Uganda has allowed refugees to become integrated into trade and labour economies with local peoples, subsequently stimulating the Ugandan economy and creating opportunities for refugees to work and create self-sustainable livelihoods. That report indicates that, of the 200,000 refugees in Uganda, only around one per cent are unemployed (Betts et al. 2014: 42). This is a formidable statistic that certainly challenges the commonly held assumption that refugees place an economic burden on the host nation of asylum in which they have sought protection. And yet there is a need to examine the empirical experiences of the refugees who are employed and integrated within those labour markets. That report describes how, in Kampala specifically, refugees have become a crucial component of local trade markets on *kitgenge* material and jewellery. But such markets favour those peoples who have the resources and skills to become entrepreneurs. Not all refugees are able to successfully negotiate what seems to be an often competitive market of self-employment nor do they necessarily have the language skills, educational background, and professional experience to be attractive potential employees outside of self-created businesses. Being legally allowed to work is not the same as having access to meaningful employment that can sustain an independent livelihood.

Many of the refugees I got to know in Kampala were actively seeking employment that could support the needs of their families. But securing such work was often difficult. The refugees I conducted fieldwork with were not the small business operators and entrepreneurs that the Ugandan government and the UNHCR hold up as examples of success that have resulted from the implementation of a flexible policy of asylum that allows freedom of movement. These were refugees who struggled. These were refugees who grasped together enough piecemeal work in the informal sector to make enough money to pay for housing to shelter their family, and sometimes, but not always, to pay for food to fill their bellies. These were refugees who awaited the sporadic remittances from relatives overseas who could ease their economic burden for a week or so. Many worked a series of casual jobs in an informal labour market. Some women I knew had occasional work cleaning the houses or assisting with the laundry of local Ugandan residents or businesses in Kampala. Others sold jewellery on the footpaths of the streets in Kampala City, but their wares were less sought after than those sold in the established market stalls elsewhere in the city. These were jobs to support survival in the immediate sense but not work that would support the futures of regenerative potential so valued by the refugees I conducted fieldwork with. And so, they came to me with stories of economic hardship interwoven with the inability to bear children: two seemingly separate difficulties of their present existences, which were nonetheless intimately bound up in the same existential question about the seeming impossibility of creating a life of regenerative potentiality and purpose.

Poison and stuckedness

So, why do so many refugees live in Kampala when there is, seemingly, so little support to do so? To the officers who oversee and administer the asylum policy to refugees in Uganda, the choice to reside in either a settlement or in the city should, it seems, depend on the economic means a refugee has to support themselves and their family: refugees who have the resources to thrive in the city independently are encouraged to do so, but all others are implicitly expected to live in the designated settlements (Lyytinen 2015). But for refugees themselves, choosing where and how to live is not always about their economic security. Although the designated settlements are policed and segregated into distinct areas of residence that generally correspond to distinct ethnic communities, the settlements are areas in which refugees from different countries, ethnic backgrounds, and with diverse political affiliations, are concentrated. Many of the refugees I spoke with in Kampala admitted that their economic livelihoods in the city were probably worse than if they had attempted to make a living in the settlements, but that they had nonetheless chosen to live in Kampala because they had felt unsafe in the settlements and could be more anonymous in the city. Such claims of danger can be downplayed or treated as farcical by those who oversee refugee protection in Uganda. Kristin Sandvik (2012: 115) describes how, when refugees who are struggling to survive in Kampala continue to refuse to relocate to a settlement, this can be viewed by persons within administrative roles as an indicator that they do not have a "real" need for protection because "if they really had security problems, they would not mind relocating to the settlements." It seems that while refugees in Uganda prioritise being able to feel a sense of security that is existential in scope, the policy of asylum in Uganda, and those administrators who are tasked with operationalising it, prioritises that refugees become self-reliant as soon as possible.

Consolata, a woman I got to know in Kampala, explained to me that the designated settlements are "very bad" places and that she would feel unsafe "everywhere" if she had to live there. When I pointed out to her that there were also many refugees living in Kampala, she shrugged and said, "It is bad everywhere, but it is better here." I wondered what it was, exactly, that these refugees feared about being around refugees: what was the basis of this generalized sense of insecurity? "They will kill us," I was told. When I asked for further clarification on who exactly was meant by this, I was told that the "they" referred to meant, vaguely, "soldiers" who had been sent in to infiltrate the settlements. The refugees I worked with believed that the settlements in Uganda were places where various government army agents and other militarist forces sent people, under the guise of those seeking asylum, to identify and murder political enemies. I asked how it could be that, in the relatively controlled environment of the settlements, where ordinary life is often organised and surveiled by both government institutions and international, non-government organisations, refugees could be murdered by undetected militarists. "Poison," I was told, over and over again, by refugees in Uganda, "They kill using poison." I tried to elicit more detail: where does the poison come from, how is it obtained? The general response to my inquiries about poison reflected what Consolata told me, "How can I know? I do not poison people!"

I have no way to attest to the veracity of these stories. Yet every refugee I got to know had a story about a person they knew who had been a victim of poisoning in a settlement. Some even claimed that they themselves had been poisoned. Consolata had previously lived with her family in a refugee settlement in rural Uganda. She told me that, there, she and her family had become victims of poisoning. "We became sick," she said. "Vomiting every day. When we first came to the camp, we went to a big celebration at a church. There, we ate the food. The next day we were very sick. Even now eating is hard for us." The perpetrator of this specific instance of poisoning was never confirmed, according to Consolata. When I asked why her family had been poisoned, and why poisoning had become a problem in that specific church, she told me, "I don't know why it happened. That is the life there, being a refugee. Things happen to you, and you cannot stop them."

Poisoning did not seem to be understood as a specifically deliberate act, even though refugees claimed that it was militants who were behind such attacks. Rather, refugees like Consolata described poisoning as a generalised risk that goes along with being a refugee in asylum and having to live in the insecure context of a designated settlement or camp. The risk of being poisoned is heightened in situations in which refugees see themselves as having less control over their lives, such as in the settlements, where they have little choice about where to live and who to live near. Even if living in Kampala meant forgoing access to humanitarian aid, at least in Kampala, refugees had more flexibility to relocate when they felt unsafe. Consolata, who worked general service jobs across the city, told me that:

> This work it earns little money, but it is enough to get out of the camp. I have no help here, but it is okay... It is better that I am here, where I can do something to stay alive... In Kampala, there is less poison.

Eating is a fundamental activity of regeneration: consuming food sustains life and ensures survival. For these refugees in Uganda, however, even this most fundamental activity of regeneration, eating, is made precarious. The transmission of poison occurs, according to them, by eating contaminated food. No longer just a source of potential sustenance, food is also considered by them to be a potential source of poison, especially in contexts where they live in close proximity to other refugees. Even in the relative safety of Kampala, the refugees I got to know generally ate in separate family groups, rarely sharing food amongst each other, even when, on some nights, children and families would not have enough food for a meal. For them, eating was an activity that makes them vulnerable to poisoning, and so refugees protected and hid their sources of food from each other and avoided sharing food with people outside of their immediate kinship group. Fears about being poisoned, it seemed, expressed a more generalised experience of uncertainty: a broader fear about existing in unsettled living conditions and amongst people considered strangers.

"Stuck" was how Nela, another woman I conducted fieldwork with, who had also experienced poisoning, characterised the effects of being poisoned. "The poison was in us," she added. She described how the poisoning had occurred, telling me that:

> One day, I was cooking dinner, inside the house, and I fed my children with that food. But that night, my youngest got sick, vomiting, headache… Then the next, then the next… All of us. We could not eat. We could not sleep. The poison was there. It could not be fixed. The poison was stuck in us.

The effect of being poisoned, as described by Nela and other refugees, if it did not directly kill a person, was the disruption and stagnation of the workings of the digestive and metabolic systems, making eating and drinking especially difficult. Poison is a substance of nefarious and uncertain origin that, for these refugees, specifically blocks the regenerative potentiality of eating and feeding, making the cycle of regeneration, which is oriented through preparing, consuming, and digesting food, stagnant and illness-inducing rather than rejuvenating and life-sustaining. With eating and feeding symbolising the regenerative potentiality of life, the effect and very possibility of being poisoned serves to make this fundamental basis of life and future existence seem itself precarious.

"Stuck" is also how displacement is often characterised in anthropological scholarship. Catherine Brun (2015: 19), for example, describes how, in contexts of protracted displacement, "individuals feel stuck in a present that they do not want to inhabit, awaiting a future they cannot reach—a future that is often unpredictable and uncertain." Refugees who live in contexts of protracted asylum across the world often have to endure everyday existence without rights and protections that can, for some, make it seem impossible to create forward momentum and optimistic futures: they may not have the opportunity to participate in education, access adequate health care services, legally work, or have their basic needs for shelter, food, and security supported by the state. Even in Uganda, where refugees are supported by one of the most extensive systems of asylum in the world, refugees continue to lead precarious lives in which the uncertainty of everyday existence means that their attention becomes focused on surviving in the immediacy of the present. They cannot predict or project longitudinal futures with any certainty and so activities that are oriented toward a stable future, such as having children and raising a family, become imagined and experienced as a problem. For the refugees I conducted fieldwork with, poisoning is a metaphor that expresses their experience of feeling stuck and stagnant: removed from the forward momentum of existence.

The problem of displacement is never only a problem of physical survival or of politico-legal ambiguity. The systems in place to provide asylum to refugees and displaced peoples are designed to provide temporary protection to them, but when there is no immediate way to resolve their refugee status, then this supposedly temporary condition of asylum becomes itself a way of life. The seemingly permanent temporariness of existing in asylum means that displacement must be thought of as an existential condition: as an experience of having the cosmological logics through which the future is thought of as predictable made precarious, and in which peoples who are displaced are resigned to living in the present toward an uncertain future.

Cultivating the possibility of new life

How is it possible for refugees in Kampala to create a future, and a sense of regenerative potentiality, when the present is subsumed by concerns over the immediacy of survival? As Catherine Brun (2015) and others suggest (Griffiths 2014; Rotter 2016), refugees and other displaced peoples cannot be totalisatically reduced to being "stuck" in the present. Even if their lives seem dominated by the stuckedness of the present, refugees nonetheless find ways to remain actively invested in the trajectories of their seemingly uncertain futures, seeking out whatever opportunities are available to stabilise their lives. Many of the refugees that I got to know in Kampala had found a way to combine both of these imperatives: that is, to support the immediate survival needs of their families while also creating a sense of futurity and regenerative potential. In the midst of the suburban sprawl of the outer neighbourhoods in Kampala, many of the refugees I knew attempted to maintain subsistence gardens, tucked into the small spaces of laneways or the open areas of empty plots.

Refugees filled their subsistence gardens with plant foods. These plants provided a supplementary, albeit small, source of nutritional value to the meals that refugees served to their families. But perhaps more significantly, tending to these gardens was a seemingly soothing experience for the refugees. Many of them had moved and relocated around the city multiple times, and yet, each time, they seemed to make a deliberate point of creating a garden, even if it was only small and close to where they were living. Doing so seemed to be a way to immerse themselves in the comfort of ecological processes of decomposition and regeneration, which shift with the turning of seasons. By maintaining subsistence gardens, which had little ancillary nutritional value, these refugees were finding a way to make themselves part of circular rhythms of time and to reinforce the regenerative potentiality of their existence.

I was not initially familiar with the types of plants that commonly made up these gardens. When I first arrived in Kampala, I took for granted that the small patches of green that stuck out in what seemed to be odd and random places for plants to grow were weeds. It did not occur to me that these were, in fact, often carefully planned and monitored attempts at agriculture. It was not until I took a walk with Consolata in the residential compound of housing blocks where both she and I lived that I became enlightened about the presence of small plots of plant foods that, until that point, had remained unnoticed to my unfamiliar eyes.

Consolata had taken my arm that quiet afternoon, and we walked the length of the shared courtyard that separated the two major apartment blocks in the compound of residential housing in which we both lived. Consolata lived with her son, his wife, two nieces, and three grandchildren in a three-room apartment. Walking together was a routine that Consolata and I had become used to. We would pace the length of the courtyard together, then go back again, watching her small grandchildren playing nearby. On this particular afternoon, however, Consolata did not turn as we research the spiked gate that marked the threshold between the housing compound and the street beyond. Instead, Consolata guided me through a small passageway between the central apartment block building and the perimeter fence: a pathway that I had not entered before. Leading me into this passageway, Consolata explained to me her motivations for taking me there. "I want to show you my garden," she said.

The restricted space between the building and perimeter wall only allowed about a one-meter-wide gap between the apartments and the retaining wall. The retaining wall itself was tall, reaching about a foot above my own head. On top of the retaining wall was yet another fence, this time made of interlocking wire. The walkway between the apartment building and the retaining wall was constricted, barely allowing more than one person to pass at a time. Since both the apartment and the wall enclosing the housing compound were tall, barely any sunlight reached into the constricted space of the walkway. It seemed impossible to me that a garden could grow in such a space. I assumed that I had misheard Consolata.

And yet Consolata stopped our meander through the back pathway of the building outside of what must have been the back of the apartment she lived in. Pulling a chair beside us, she encouraged me to stand on top of the chair with a flick of her hand. Confused, I did as she indicated. From my stance on top of the chair, I was able to see the top of the retaining wall. There, I was finally able to glimpse the garden Consolata had wanted me to see. In the half a meter of space between the edge of the top of the retaining wall and the wire fence that separated our housing compound from the block next to it, I could see the plants Consolata was referring to: vines and creepers covering the small space, some trailing up into the fence itself, and two somewhat stilted shrubs. Consolata encouraged me to touch the plants, and so I did, gently rubbing the leaves of the shrubs between my fingers. Glancing down, I saw Consolata smiling at me below. After getting down from the chair, Consolata quickly put herself on top of it, where I had been standing, picking a handful of leaves from the creepers and holding them out on her palm to show them to me.

"*Matembela*," she said, indicating to the leaves. "That is what we call this plant." I learned later that *matembela* is the name given to the leaves of the sweet potato plant. The two shrubs, I also learned, were her attempt to grow the *cassava* plant.

The leaves, which were later used to prepare a meal for herself and her family, were still in her hand as we made our way back through the walkway and into the shared courtyard where I asked Consolata why she had chosen to grow plants. I did not say it aloud, but it seemed to me to be a lot of effort to grow plants in such a small and restricted space.

"I have these plants here because if I did not have these leaves, well, myself and my children would die," she responded, a somewhat more direct answer than I had anticipated. She turned one of the leaves over, carefully, in her hand, before she continued. "The soil is bad. And the growing is hard. But I still do it, because there is space to. I could not live here, and not do something. To leave it … no."

I immediately assumed that when Consolata referred to the idea that her family would "die" without the garden, she meant death in an exclusively physical sense. And yet I struggled to comprehend how such a meagre garden could seriously supplement their diet and create a viable source of nutrition for them to fall back on when money for food was scarce. Probing into this question of survival in more depth, I asked Consolata, "If you didn't garden, do you think you would have enough food to survive in Kampala?"

"Maybe," Consolata replied, adding however:

> But wherever I live, I have a garden. Here it has been the hardest. When I first came here, I thought there was no place that I would be able to grow plants. I was thinking that I would have to move away. But then I saw that there was just enough space, at the top there. So, I am here.

I realised, then, that the death Consolata was referring to was not exclusively understood in physical terms. Like myself, she recognised that the supplementary nutrition made available through the plants' being grown was too small to significantly complement the well-being of her family. Instead, she spoke of a sense of being compelled by some seemingly inexplicable force to maintain a garden. It is, I consider, a cosmological imperative to regenerate life that she expresses by maintaining the garden and describing the seemingly obvious need to grow plants. When Consolata refers to the idea that her family might "die," she means not only the possibility of physical death but the cosmological stagnation of life that is bound up in how she understands the destruction of existential purpose and forward momentum.

Circular time

Birth and regrowth, death and decomposition: these are processes that are not viewed by the refugees I conducted fieldwork with as distinct events on a linear timeline of human existence, but are viewed as natural and inexorable catalysts through which the periodicity of human existence is cycled and turned. For them, existence has a distinct momentum, but it is a temporal trajectory of cycles and circularity rather than a linear progression.

There is no universal experience of time. The temporalisation of experience differs across social, cultural, political, and economic contexts, often reflecting the distinctive cosmological assumptions through which people come to understand the nature of the world and of human existence within it (Koselleck 1985; Munn 1992). During fieldwork, I observed how the experience of ordinary life for the refugees I got to know, both in Uganda and Australia, was organised implicitly through cosmological logics of regeneration, emphasising and prioritising activities of both physiological and social reproduction. Regeneration, however, implies a circular conceptualisation of time rather than an idea of time that is linear, progressive, and cumulative. The concept of regeneration conveys a momentum of continuity, according to Jennifer Cole and Christian Groes (2016), who similarly identify regeneration as a foundational cosmological logic through which peoples from Africa negotiate experiences of migration. Regeneration means that connections between people, places, and things are understood in terms of circuits and circularity, according to Cole and Groes (2016: 7), rather than unidirectional flows and linear chains. But this cosmology of regeneration also means that the temporalisation of experience is, similarly, understood to be circular rather than linear.

Circular time is a sense of temporality as a process of ceaseless and cyclical social regenesis. It is a way of experiencing time that is not premised on a singular individual subject but on a way of temporalising experience through sociality. Circular time is reckoned as a lateral plane of temporal co-presence rather than the cumulative progression of an individual trajectory. This is a sense of experiencing time through non-individualist personhood, which Clifford Geertz (1973) also recognises, based on fieldwork in Bali. Geertz (1973: 391) describes how assumptions about personhood in Bali, in which being recognised as a whole person requires that one become a parent and be known as a relation in a wider field of sociality, are reflected in a particular temporalisation of experience, in which "their depersonalizing concept of personhood is a detemporalizing … conception of time." According to Geertz (1973), assumptions about individual personhood produce related assumptions about time as a linear and chronological passage of individual predecessors and successors. Assumptions of personhood as a non-individualistic condition of social relatedness, in contrast, produce assumptions about time that emphasise simultaneity and active co-presence.

Understanding time as a plane of sociality produces an experience of time as a process of continual regenesis. Clifford Geertz (1973) describes how, for people in Bali, this emphasis on social continuity means that time is not experienced as progressive or cumulative but is continuously contemporised, with this temporal rhythm of continuity being fully realised when a person becomes a parent who can then themselves be socially and temporally situated as both a child and an ancestor. Since what matters in that context is becoming a parent, there is no great significance placed on the number of children that are born to a person: rearing one child imbues a person with the same power as another who has five or ten children. Although for the people I worked with, personhood is similarly solidified upon becoming a parent, the amount of social recognition and respect attached to a person is amplified if they are parents to multiple children. For them, as elsewhere is equatorial Africa, wealth is located in people (Guyer 1993), meaning that the reproduction of children is a way to expand social influence. But since Geertz (1973) considers that ideas of personhood directly inform and reflect how time is experienced and conceptualised, how does a view of personhood in which social recognition is amplified by high fertility translate into the temporalisation of experience? The conceptualisation of time and personhood described by Geertz (1973) is one in which the emphasis on parenthood is interwoven with an experience of time as a detemporalised plane of regenesis, that is, a lateral process of ceaseless continuity that is conceived of and lived as a temporal steady state. With personhood being similarly infused with parenthood amongst the refugees I worked with, time is also understood as a plane of continuity, but their emphasis on high fertility produces a distinct sense of time as circular: that is, as a cycle of periods of growth and decline, expansion and decomposition.

What makes the temporalisation of experience distinctly circular amongst the refugees I conducted fieldwork with was their conceptualisation of personhood as realised through parenthood not simply as a static identity, but as a continually reproductive way of being. For them, becoming a parent is a not simply a marker of maturity and social status: it is a cosmological imperative through which a person becomes implicated in the reproduction of social and filial continuity. They become connected to and part of a wider plane of regenesis, in which existence is understood not as a linear trajectory but as a cyclic and continuous oscillation between periods of death and decline and periods of growth and rebirth. This is a sense of circular time that reflects how these refugees experience the world as a plane of regenerative potentiality.

It was as if, for them, the passing of time is inexorably cyclic and, therefore, extrinsic to their own influence as individual people. This circularity of time as cycle of continuity was generally not an explicit topic of conversation, of course: it was expressed and reinforced in the taken-for-granted assumptions embedded in the practice of daily life. Occasionally, however, refugees would nonetheless describe and situate their experiences within a wider sense of temporal circularity. Such overt references to time were most common when refugees would make projections of the future, especially when we would discuss pregnancy and childbearing. Since pregnancy was a topic of much conversation, I had expected that women I got to know might "plan" how many children they would have and their reproductive lives in general. However, it turned out that women viewed their reproductive potentiality in terms of this inescapable circularity of regeneration. "That is not my plan," one woman told me during fieldwork, after I asked her if she planned to have more children. "That is the plan of the universe," she told me, smiling slyly. Although the majority of women I spoke with about pregnancy and childbearing rarely, if ever, fully surrendered control of their reproductive trajectory to some seemingly external force, they still described processes of reproduction as ultimately forming part of a cycle of continuity that is outside of their own influence. Most women who were in relationships practiced methods of controlling reproduction and preventing pregnancy through birth spacing and lengthy periods of breastfeeding. Some, especially in Australia, used hormonal methods of birth control. But even when attempting to control the possibility of pregnancy, they considered reproductive fate to be inescapable. As one woman told me, "When a baby wants to come, it will come. It wants to be born. No pill will stop that."

For refugees living in asylum in Uganda, however, it seems babies do not "want to be born." This perception and experience of reduced fertility is not only troubling to Central African refugees at a personal scale. It is a fundamental inversion of cosmological logics of regeneration, in which the temporal rhythms of ordinary life circulate around activities of reproduction: whether these be tending subsistence gardens, preparing and cooking the meals that provide sustenance to and which ensure the possibility of caring for, and bearing more, children. Becoming a refugee in Uganda is not just a problem of physiological survival. It is an existential crisis, in which the uncertainty of physical survival throws the certainty of future regeneration into question.

Existential displacement

These refugees were experiencing displacement. But this was not a sense of displacement that can be sufficiently captured by conventional approaches to the concept as a disconnection from place or as a politico-legal condition of statelessness. The displacement experienced by these refugees was certainly interwoven with their physical movement from place to place and across national borders, but could not be reduced to an automatic product of those mobilities. Their sense of displacement is an experience of existential uncertainty. The uncertainty of being a refugee in asylum was impacting the activities that these refugees considered to be vital to both physiological survival and existential purpose: that is, preparing, cooking, and eating food as well as bearing and rearing children. Living as refugees in Kampala means prioritising the immediacy of survival in the present, and thereby throws into jeopardy the very possibility of a future. This intertwining of physical and existential insecurity is realised as a sense of discordant temporal rhythms: of living in the present towards an uncertain future.

Displacement, for these Central African refugees, stems from the ways in which the physical, social, and political contexts from which they escaped and into which they migrated coalesce into a sense of being dislocated from time: that is, being removed from, and unable to regain, the temporal rhythms of their ordinary lives. The experience of displacement is, for them, an experience in which the very possibility of a future is itself at stake. Since it is children and processes of reproduction through which this futurity is embodied, it made sense to them that their fertility in Uganda is impacted by the general "problem of the life" there: that is, of having to live as refugees within an uncertain present and, subsequently, in relation to a seemingly uncertain future.

The temporality of displacement has become an emergent focus of anthropological scholarship on refugees and others who are labelled as irregular migrants. Primarily, research has characterised displacement as an experience of being "stuck" in the temporal immediacy of the present (Brun 2015; Horst and Grabska 2015). The geographic stillness of being contained in a refugee camp or detention centre and the politico-legal ambiguity of a non-citizen status can be traced into the ways in which refugees and other migrants come to temporalise their experiences as being stuck in the present with an uncertain future that cannot be aspired to or reached (Ramadan 2013). Characterising displacement as temporal stuckedness is useful but can overlook the ways in which, within those processes of waiting, refugees find ways to actively project their present selves into imagined by futures by participating in activities through which they aim to direct their futures and improve their lives (Brun 2015, 2016; Griffiths 2014). Even if displacement is not simply an experience of temporal stuckedness, however, the idea of displacement as a period of liminality, of waiting for the opportunity for a change in status and social situatedness, is itself problematic.

What is it that refugees and other kinds of irregular migrants are waiting for? What is it that they, and governance institutions through which their lives are organised, imagine will resolve their waiting? Generally, the ambiguity of displacement is imagined as being resolved upon providing refugees with an opportunity to be permanently settled somewhere. Whether this means refugees are repatriated back to their home country, allowed to legally and permanently settled in their host nation of asylum, or are resettled to a third country, the solutions that are predominantly put forward to resolve displacement centre on resolving an experience of liminality: of waiting in temporal stasis. When displacement is characterised as a period of waiting which is resolved through the permanence of settlement, displacement comes to be understood as an experience of liminality.

But characterising displacement as a period of liminality that is solved upon being permanently settled risks inadvertently reducing how refugees constitute and experience what it means to be displaced to the parameters of their politico-legal status. Theorising displacement as a period of liminality that corresponds to the ambiguity of their politico-legal status suggests that displacement is an experience that is activated once a person crosses a national border to become a refugee. What this rendering of displacement as a period or condition of liminality implies, then, is that the experience of being displaced is dissolved once the ambiguity of a refugee's status is resolved and the refugee or migrant is provided with an opportunity to legally and permanently settle. The idea of displacement as a liminal period of waiting is premised on an assumption of linear time and assumes that temporal rhythms of ordinary life are resumed once refugees are no longer forced to survive in the temporal stasis of the immediate present in asylum: as if the certainty of their futures can be restored automatically with the granting of permanent residency. The temporal disjuncture through which displacement is experienced is not an exclusive product of the politico-legal ambiguity of refugee status. Sometimes, as I describe in chapters that follow, the temporal disjuncture of displacement is produced through those very processes that are designed to resolve the temporariness of asylum and to provide refugees with a sense of permanence.

The refugees I conducted fieldwork with did indeed experience their lives in asylum as defined by the immediacy of their physical survival in the present. However, their sense of displacement could not be automatically mapped onto that condition. Rather, their sense of displacement came from being forcibly removed from the temporal rhythms of their ordinary lives. When displacement is theorised as an experience of being removed from what are conceived of as the temporal rhythms of ordinary life rather than as a condition of protracted liminality, then it is possible to approach displacement as an experience that transcends and is constituted outside of the politico-legal ambiguity of refugee status. As I have described in this chapter, it is the perceived absence of a future through which the temporal displacement of refugees is realised in asylum. However, as I consider in the chapters that follow, it is the purposeful control over futures that is a basis of enduring displacement for refugees who are resettled in Australia.

References

Agier, M. 2002. Between War and City: Towards an Urban Anthropology of Refugee Camps. *Ethnography* 3(3): 317–341.

Andersson, R. 2014. Hunter and Prey: Patrolling Clandestine Migration in the Euro-African Borderlands. *Anthropological Quarterly* 87(1): 119–150.

Bauman, Z. 2002. In the Lowly Nowherevilles of Liquid Modernity: Comments on and Around Agier. *Ethnography* 3(3): 343–349.

Betts, A., Bloom, L., Kaplan, J., and Omata, N. 2014. Refugee Economies: Rethinking Popular Assumptions. Humanitarian Innovation Project, University of Oxford: Oxford.

Betts, A., Bloom, L. Kaplan, J., and Omata, N. 2017. *Refugee Economies: Forced Displacement and Development*. Oxford: Oxford University Press. Available at: www.rsc.ox.ac.uk/files/publications/other/refugee-economies-2014.pdf (Accessed 18 January 2017).

Brun, C. 2015. Active Waiting and Changing Hopes: Toward a Time Perspective on Protracted Displacement. *Social Analysis* 59(1): 19–37.Brun, C. 2016. There is No Future in Humanitarianism: Emergency, Temporality, and Protracted Displacement. *History and Anthropology* 27(4): 393–410.

Cole, J. and Groes, C. (Eds.). 2016. *Affective Circuits: African Migrations to Europe and the Pursuit of Social Regeneration*. Chicago, IL: University of Chicago Press.

Dryden-Peterson, S. 2006. 'I Find Myself as Someone Who is in the Forest': Urban Refugees as Agents of Social Change in Kampala, Uganda. *Journal of Refugee Studies* 19(3): 381–395.

Geertz, C. 1973. *The Interpretation of Cultures: Selected Essays*. London: Hutchinson.

Griffiths, M. 2014. Out of Time: The Temporal Uncertainties of Refuges Asylum Seekers and Immigration Detainees. *Journal of Ethnic and Migration Studies* 40(12): 1991–2009.

Guyer, J. 1993. Wealth in People and Self-Realization in Equatorial Africa. *Man* 28(2): 243–265.

Hathaway, J.C. 1991. Reconceiving Refugee Law as Human Rights Protection. *Journal of Refugee Studies* 4(2): 113–131.

Hathaway, J.C. 2005. *The Rights of Refugees under International Law*. Cambridge: Cambridge University Press.

Hathaway, J.C. and Neve, R.A. 1997. Making International Refugee Law Relevant Again: A Proposal for Collectivized and Solution-Oriented Protection. *Harvard Human Rights Journal* 10: 115–211.Horst, C. and Grabska, K. 2015. Flight and Exile—Uncertainty in the Context of Conflict-Induced Displacement. *Social Analysis* 59(1): 1–18.

Hovil, L. 2007. Self-Settled Refugees in Uganda: An Alternative Approach to Displacement? *Journal of Refugee Studies* 20(4): 599–620.

Ilcan, S., Oliver, M., and Connoy, L. 2015. Humanitarian Assistance and the Politics of Self-Reliance: Uganda's Nakivale Refugee Settlement. Available at: http://works.bepress.com/marcia_oliver/6/ (Accessed 12 January 2017).

Koselleck, R. 1985. *Futures Past: On the Semantics of Historical Time*. Cambridge, MA: MIT Press.

Krause, U. 2016. Limitations of Development-Oriented Assistance in Uganda. *Forced Migration Review* 52(3): 51–53.

Lyytinen, E. 2015. Congolese Refugees "Right to the City" and Urban (In)Security in Kampala, Uganda. *Journal of Eastern African Studies* 9(4): 593–611.

Malkki, L 1995a. *Purity and Exile: Violence, Memory, and National Cosmology among Hutu Refugees in Tanzania*. Chicago, IL: University of Chicago Press.

Munn, N. 1992. The Cultural Anthropology of Time: A Critical Essay. *Annual Review of Anthropology* 21: 93–123.

Ramadan, A. 2013. Spatialising the Refugee Camp. *Transactions* 38(1): 65–77.

Rotter, R. 2016. Waiting in the Asylum Determination Process: Just an Empty Interlude? *Time & Society* 25(1): 80–101.

Sandvik, K.B. 2012. Negotiating the Humanitarian Past: History, Memory, and Unstable Cityscapes in Kampala, Uganda. *Refugee Survey Quarterly* 31(1): 108–122.

Svedberg, E. 2014. Refugee Self-Reliance in Nakivale Refugee Settlement, Uganda. Independent Study Project (ISP), Collection Paper 1178. Available at: http://digitalcollections.sit.edu/isp_collection/1778 (Accessed 27 October 2016).

Turner, V. 1967. *The Forest of Symbols: Aspects of Ndembu Ritual*. Ithaca, NY: Cornell University Press.

UNHCR. 2006. Protracted Refugee Situations: The Search for Practical Solutions. In The State of the World's Refugees 2006: Human Displacement in the New Millennium. Available at: www.unhcr.org/4444afcb0.html (Accessed 29 November 2016).

UNHCR. 2017b. Uganda. Available at: www.unhcr.org/afr/uganda (Accessed 7 November 2016).

van Gennep, A. 1960. *The Rites of Passage*. Translated by M.B. Visedom and G.L. Caffee. London; Henley: Routledge and Kegan Paul.

5 Imaginaries and new life

"We need a new life," I was told by Sarah, a refugee in Kampala. This was not an unusual kind of comment: in fact, many of the women I got to know in Uganda expressed similar sentiments. These refugees aspired to futures, to a "new life," that they did not see as a possibility in their contemporary conditions of protracted asylum. Their aspirations for the future centred almost exclusively on the same ultimate desire: resettlement.

Resettlement does not only represent the possibility of resolving refugee status. For these refugees, resettlement offers the possibility of migration outside of Africa and specifically to a nation in the West. There, it is assumed, life will be more prosperous. Refugees are not the only would-be migrants from Africa who imagine that life in a Western nation will provide a better opportunity for a liveable life. Each year, many people attempt to reach the West on the same premise, undertaking precarious and often deadly journeys to do so (Adeyanju and Oriola 2011; Bredeloup 2013; Jackson 2013a; Salazar 2010; Vigh 2009a). The governments of Western nations also organise border protection regimes around the idea that the lifestyles available in their nations create a pull factor for irregular migration. The immigration and border protection regime in Australia, which mandatorily and indefinitely detains people seeking asylum in the country by boat, is premised not only the idea that these peoples represent a threat to the security of the nation but that the Australian lifestyle is a kind of scarce and precious resource that itself requires protecting (Poynting 2004). Even for refugees, transnational migration is never only about securing stability: it is, concurrently, a fundamentally existential endeavour of attempting to secure a liveable life of purpose and fulfilment (Jackson 2013a).

The assumption that resettlement provides an opportunity for refugees to enjoy more prosperous lives also becomes inadvertently replicated in refugee studies. Given that, at current rates, resettlement is only made available to less than one per cent of refugees who are identified as being in need of it each year (UNHCR 2017a), it is perhaps understandable that much research with displaced peoples focuses on the experiences of refugees in situations of protracted asylum, either in camps or as urban refugees. When resettlement is a focus of research, it is often explored in terms of flawed application and selection processes. Since so few placements are made available to refugees for resettlement, the distribution of resettlement slots is often highly contested. Competition for resettlement has created a situation in which its possibility has become a way to informally govern refugees, leading, in some instances, to exploitative exchanges between refugees seeking resettlement and officers who oversee application processes (Jansen 2008; Sandvik 2011). To qualify and apply for resettlement, refugees must convince aid representatives of an ongoing fear of targeted persecution. The processes of interviewing, gathering documentation to advance such claims, and subsequently having applications assessed are long and complex, and the uncertainty that refugees experience during these processes is further compounded by the suspicion they are confronted with along the way because it is commonly assumed by aid representatives that refugees seek to fabricate persecution claims in order to advance resettlement applications (Thomson 2012). Refugees are rarely given information about the status of their applications during the long periods it takes for them to be assessed, and even when an application is successful, the pragmatics of organising the migration are often haphazard and exclude refugees from knowing the details of their own futures (El-Shaarawi 2015). What is supposed to be a process of obtaining a durable solution to resettlement is, itself, a source of uncertainty.

Whether or not resettlement actually resolves these insecurities of displacement is, however, rarely problematised, except in a few cases (Besteman 2016; Jackson 2013b; Lems 2016; McMichael and Manderson 2004). The idea that asylum and resettlement are exclusive domains of experience is implicitly reinforced by this analytical disconnect. In this chapter, I consider how this pervasive assumption about the prosperity of refugee resettlement, as reproduced in scholarly work, government policy, international humanitarian programmes, and even by refugees themselves, can be thought of as a "resettlement imaginary," that is, a "constructed landscape of collective aspirations" (Appadurai 1996: 31). The resettlement imaginary is not neutral in its effects, however. Imagining resettlement as an automatic solution to displacement is a way to conceal how seeking resettlement and being resettled are processes that can themselves exacerbate experiences of displacement.

Existential imperatives to migrate

More than just a movement between places, migration is a process through which the possibility of new ways of living are realised (Pajo 2007). The kinds of imaginaries that compel people across continental Africa to aspire to migrate outside of the continent and participate in often dangerous journeys to do so has become a focus of recent work in anthropology. Migration to the West is often imagined in such contexts as a way to achieve economic and social capital, which can enhance social mobility in ways that are no longer possible in local settings (Adeyanju and Oriola 2011; Jackson 2013a;

Salazar 2010; Vigh 2009a, 2009b). This is not to reproduce the functionalist logics of a push-pull argument about migration, in which the desire to move from Africa to the West is essentialised to the push of deprivation and the pull of assumed prosperity. Many would-be migrants consider that migration to the West will result in an improved economic situation, but these financial motivations cannot be considered in isolation from imaginaries of social possibility, in which monetary gain is just one potential outcome (Vigh 2009a). Migration and mobility are, according to Michael Jackson (2013a: 202), part of a broader existential process of negotiating "external constraints and personal imperatives," meaning that physical movements across and between different countries are a form of existential mobility: an attempt to recompense needs that are fundamentally related to social and personal fulfilment and not singularly reducible to material impoverishment or economic need.

The desire to be physically mobile and to participate in transnational migration can also be understood as a process that is bound up in an existential tension regarding stability and stuckedness. The pervasive appeal of imaginaries of migration has intensified in recent decades, according to Arjun Appadurai (1996: 33), due to the increased media exposure to new and different ways of living. Becoming familiarised with different possible ways of living through the media has destabilised what may have once been more static and stable communities and networks of family, friends, work, and leisure. Now, people are increasingly imagining themselves in relation to and with others across the globe, meaning that entire worlds and ways of being are being imagined and recreated without being rooted to a particular place. Global connectedness has made people aware of the inequalities that shape their daily lives, and many now imagine futures of globalised possibilities (Horst 2006b).

The existential stakes and dimensions of migration, and the ways in which these have been shaped in response to increasingly globalised imaginaries of what it means to live a good life, have become a focus of anthropological scholarship in recent years, particularly in its documenting of the experiences of migrants from Africa (Bredeloup 2013; Englund 2002; Jackson 2008, 2013a; Lems 2016; Lucht 2012; Vigh 2009a, 2009b). The idea of possibility is central to these dialogues. Based on decades of fieldwork conducted with people from Sierra Leone, both those in the country and transnational migrants, Michael Jackson (2008) describes how:

> In a single generation, I had seen Kuranko youth turn away from the ancestral order of things and from the dutiful perpetuation of custom, setting their sights on an uncertain future in some far-flung place and invoke, as migrants do everywhere, the logic of sacrifice. For by giving up the life to which one was born, one stood to gain, through a kind of rebirth, a greater or more abundant life elsewhere at some future time, if not for oneself, then for one's children.
>
> (Jackson 2008: 60)

As the passage from Jackson (2008) suggests, migration and transnational mobility represent, for many people planning or engaged in migration from Africa, the tangible possibility of what they conceive of as a life that is prosperous.

The idea, and very possibility, of "the good life" has become a recent focus in anthropology. This renewed focus on the possibility of achieving "the good life" has developed as a response response to what Sherry Ortner (2016) describes as a turn to "dark anthropology" and what Joel Robbins (2013) terms as a turn to documenting the "suffering slot," in which anthropological research has, over the past decades, become increasingly focused on documenting suffering and violence without considering how people attempt to, and do, experience happiness.

As part of this turn away from documenting suffering and moving towards recognising more optimistic dimensions of human experience, Edward Fischer (2014) characterises "the good life" not as a stable state of existence that is able to be achieved or obtained, but as a dynamic. Fisher (2014) locates "the good life" as a product of continual fluctuations between aspirations and abilities: that is, aspirations toward ways of living that a person perceives as better than those in which they live currently, and the ability to strive towards such seemingly better ways of living within conditions that do not harm or constrain those aspirational processes. The very possibility of "the good life," according to Fischer (2014), then, is itself the basis of experiencing it: existential fulfilment derives from having purpose and being able to pursue it. It is precisely for this reason that when conditions of everyday life for refugees in Africa are so constrained that the very possibility of pursuing a better life seems impossible, that refugees can feel stuck: not only limited in terms of physical containment and legal constraints but also in existential terms. Their sense of displacement arises when they come to be living in the immediacy of the present towards an uncertain or seemingly impossible future.

More broadly, however, there are many reasons why the possibility of "the good life" seems, over recent years, to have become impossible for many people in Africa, not just refugees. Based on fieldwork with African fisherman-cum-migrants attempting to enter and settle in Europe through Italy, Hans Lucht (2012) describes how customary ideals of reciprocity that organise life in African fishing villages have come, seemingly paradoxically, to be crucial drivers in the desire to migrate away from Africa. Migrating to the West is seen as a way to get repositioned within the circulation of symbolic and material goods, which are essential to maintaining influential social status and experiencing existential purpose in local contacts back "home" in Africa. So, paradoxically, migration away from Africa is often viewed as a necessary means through which to achieve fulfilment in terms that are important in local African contexts. A similar situation is described by Henrik Vigh (2009a) based on research conducted with men seeking to, or who have engaged in, migration from Bissau. There, high unemployment and a lack of life chances have left many young men with little possibility to earn the social status and financial security needed to support a household. As such, they are also unable to marry and attain the social status of adulthood. Migrating outside of Africa is imagined by these young men as a way to break the stagnation of living in the stasis of suspended youth. Giving a different but nonetheless related perspective, Sylvie Bredeloup (2013) considers that migrations from Africa are not wholly determined by the misery of social, political, and economic conditions that push peoples to migrate, but that personal motivations and ambitions to explore and invent new ways of life are also crucial to these departures becoming realities. Ultimately, however, it is, as Michael Jackson (2011: 38) points out, a broader, and seemingly universal, existential "yearning to be more than we presently are and to have more than we presently possess" that drives people to migrate. In that way, migration is not an exceptional experience but one that reflects a common drive toward the betterment of life, in which all people can be considered as being in a process of migration towards existential fulfilment, whether engaged in the mobility of transnational travel or not.

But the ability to actualise increasingly globalised possibilities of "the good life" is stratified. The external constraints in some people's lives mean that they are more stuck than others in contexts of everyday life that seem diminished of possibility. Refugees often live stagnated lives of existential and physical uncertainty, dominated by concerns for survival in the present and, in some cases, unable to actively work towards futures of certainty or regenerative potential in asylum (Ramadan 2013). Indeed, for some, the main way to actively seek new futures is to continue to endure the suffering of merely surviving the present and, at times, to even exacerbate or exaggerate the insecurity of everyday life in order to increase the chances of being resettled (Jansen 2008). Resettlement, for many, is not only an imaginary of a better life: it is often conceived of as the only way to escape the existential stagnation of seemingly indefinite asylum.

The resettlement imaginary

Many refugees I got to know in Uganda dreamed of being resettled and actively worked towards that goal. Resettlement was one of the first topics of conversation that came up in my conversations with them, because, as a *muzungu* who evidently originated from one of the nations that hosts resettled refugees, I represented a direct connection to resettlement.[1] Of course, I spent a lot of time explaining to refugees that I had no direct influence on the resettlement of refugees in Australia. However, it was not until they realised that I was committed to living amongst them in the crowded urban sprawl of Kampala that my claim to having "no power" was taken seriously by them. Still, my presence was itself a visible reminder of the possibility of resettlement, and so discussions about the lives of resettled refugees, and my own life in Australia, were never far from our conversations. Yet no matter how intently or how often I tried to explain to refugees in Uganda that the expectations of resettlement that they had come to idealise did not necessarily reflect how refugees I knew in Australia, at least, experienced resettlement, they ignored and downplayed my perspectives, continuing to imagine resettlement as a process that inherently and automatically improves quality of life for refugees.

Nela, for example, told me, "In Australia, we will have a good life. We can get money and the children can go to school. It will be good." I attempted to explain that, even though it is true that education is free and the welfare state in Australia provides financial support to people even when they are not able to find employment, there are other factors that complicate these processes. My comments were occasionally met with fleeting concern or outright denial, but refugees in Uganda would always return to the idea of resettlement as a process through which social and economic prosperity is assured. Rarely did my conversations with refugees about the lives they anticipated upon being resettled reflect the intended aim of resettlement, that is, to protect refugees who are unlikely to ever be able to return home due to ongoing security concerns. Rather, the resettlement imaginary they described was one in which they imagined not only improved safety but also a more generally enhanced quality of life, with more expansive possibilities for social regeneration.

The core mission of the resettlement programme, as administered by the UNHCR and participating host nations of resettlement, is to provide protection to refugees in protracted situations of asylum whose safety and security needs are not being met (UNHCR 2011a). Resettlement is a globally recognised stream of migration in which refugees apply to be permanently relocated to another country, with participating host nations of resettlement then selecting refugees to migrate and providing them with permanent residency and civic rights. The bureaucracy of resettlement does not stipulate that refugees are necessarily migrated to what is considered to be a Western country. Yet because it is primarily the US, Canada, Australia, and nations in Europe that are associated with the resettlement programme, in popular representations and in the viewpoints of the refugees I conducted fieldwork with, resettlement has become synonymous with migration to the West. Resettlement is not, then, simply a method of refugee protection. Bound up in broader dialogues about migration from continental Africa to the West, resettlement has also come to represent more generally an opportunity to lead a better life.

The resettlement of refugees is not reducible to the singular "push" factor of war and conflict, even though this is often how the UNHCR and host nations of resettlement might portray it. The idea that any kind of migration can be reduced to push-pull factors is itself problematic. Initially developed by E.S. Lee (1966), but taken up extensively in migration research, the push-pull theory is based on the idea that migration is driven primarily by the "push" of poverty and deprivation, and compelled by the "pull" of perceived security and provision. But this theory is simplistic and functionalist. It assumes that money and financial security are the central reasons behind migration decisions, reducing complex social motivations to a singularly economic rationale. When applying for resettlement, the refugees I conducted fieldwork with were not only driven by a desire to meet the protection needs of themselves and their families but also believed that resettlement would offer them different and more extensive "social possibility" (Vigh 2009a: 93) than if they remained, living as refugees, in continental Africa. To go beyond the dominant but essentialist rendering of resettlement as an automatic solution to displacement, in which the primary problems associated with resettlement are not related to the experience of being resettled itself but that placements are limited and application processes are unfair, requires recognition of resettlement as both an empirical process and an imaginary: as an idea of social possibility constructed through a pastiche of interlocking push and pull factors.

The idea of the imaginary has become a somewhat ubiquitous term in anthropology over the past two decades. In the late 1980s and 1990s, the idea of culture became a point of disciplinary contention. The concept of the imaginary was a way to try and capture the nuances of shared systems of belief without, potentially, reproducing the same connotations of homogeneity and fixity implied by culture (Strauss 2006). But, just like culture, the concept of the imaginary is also conflicted and requires critical situating when being used by anthropologists to characterise how people experience and understand their worlds. The term imaginary and other renderings of imagination have been used to describe the effects of ideology (Althusser 1971), fantasy, illusion, and escapism (Lacan 1977) and shared and implicit cognitive schema (Anderson 1983; Taylor 2002, 2004).

When referring to the resettlement imaginary, I use the concept of imaginary in the sense described by Arjun Appadurai (1996: 31), based on the work of Benedict Anderson (1983): that is, I refer to the imaginary as a "constructed landscape of global aspirations ... mediated through the complex prism of modern media." Anderson (1983) used the concept of imagination to describe how, especially since the extensive distribution of print media, peoples across the globe have been able to understand themselves as being part of a larger community of others with whom they presumably share a language and concerns. Appadurai (1996) considers that the construction of "imagined communities" described by Anderson (1983) were only a precursor to what he describes as the "imagined worlds" that have erupted since the technological explosion of the 20th century. People are no longer simply creating imagined communities, according to Appadurai (1996), but are situated in whole worlds that are constituted and created through historically positioned imaginations that have spread across the globe. In the sense described by Appadurai (1996), the imaginary is a social practice through which implicit assumptions about the world are collectively constituted in relation to globalised media streams. It is through such imaginaries that peoples come to envision "possible lives" outside of their own immediate situations (Appadurai 1996: 52). These imaginaries are not simply fantasy, however. They can also be the basis of social action as people attempt to create lives in which these imagined social possibilities can be achieved.

The resettlement imaginary does not just emerge out of fantasy. As Arjun Appaduari (1996) describes, imaginaries in contemporary contexts of intensively globalised media networks have expanded to consider ways of living that cross and transcend geographic and national boundaries. For the refugees I conducted fieldwork with, the resettlement imaginary is constituted over time by exposure to representation of the West in global media, by maintaining contact with friends and family who have been resettled and by becoming familiar with what are often selective and overtly positive accounts of resettlement experiences, and by the often very visible markers of resettlement application procedures and departures in the immediate contexts of their everyday lives.

Resettlement placements may be extremely limited, but refugees in contexts of protracted asylum are nonetheless exposed to the possibility of resettlement on a regular basis (Horst 2006b; Jansen 2008). Many have family and friends who have been resettled overseas, with whom they remain in regular contact. Often, refugees also rely on remittances from relations who have been resettled as a way to supplement their own livelihood strategies. Sometimes, refugees who have been resettled will even return to camps and places in which they have lived previously in asylum for the purpose of visiting kin or selecting a spouse, an experience that I became intimately familiar with during fieldwork because, during my research in Uganda, I was accompanied by a refugee who had been resettled in Australia and who was temporarily returning to visit family there. In camps and designated refugee settlements, resettlement is also highly visible because the proximity of refugees in those contexts makes the resettlement departures particularly obvious. Houses that had previously been occupied by refugees suddenly become vacant, families that were previously a part of everyday life become absent. Church groups and NGOs who visit the camps and settlements, who often make direct and indirect promises and attempts to sponsor refugees for resettlement, further reinforce the viability of resettlement selection and migration. Subsequently, what is understood by the UNHCR and the agencies to be an option available to a limited few nonetheless becomes highly visible in the lives of many refugees (Jansen 2008). In this way, the imagined possibility of resettlement does not correspond to the empirical reality of the limited resettlement placements that are made available to refugees each year. Through this exposure to ideas about resettlement, refugees come to popularly and collectively imagine resettlement to be a viable possibility to resolve the hardships of everyday life in asylum (Horst 2006b).

But these resettlement imaginaries are based on selective representations of migration to, and everyday life in, Western countries. The refugees I got to know who had been resettled in Australia admitted to me that, when they made contact with their relations who remained in continental Africa, they would purposely only relay stories that emphasised the positive aspects of their lives in resettlement: they would exclude the hardships, and at times exaggerate or lie about the prosperity that being resettled brings. When preparing for temporary return journeys back to Africa, these resettled refugees would pack and ready themselves in ways that would emphasise their supposed prosperity: buying many new items to take back to family members and even going as far as to put on weight to signify their new lives of excess. They told me, however, that these outward portrayals were mostly falsifications and fabrications based on expectations of resettlement: representations of a life of ease and prosperity that most did not, in fact, occupy in reality. Since their relations in Africa expected, however, that resettlement brings prosperity, these refugees felt pressured to provide remittances and economic support to family, even when their own situations in resettlement were financially precarious and socially strained.

One afternoon, I visited Rachael, a woman in Australia, who told me that she was "taking a break" from her family in Africa. Her husband had just become unemployed, and her shifts as an aged care worker at a local nursing home had been reduced. There was very little money to spare, and the financial tension was causing her social relations to fray. "I have turned my phone off," she said. "It is too much, talking to them. They will be asking for money. They think always that we are doing well."

On another day, as my friend Nyomanda and I prepared for her return journey to visit family in Uganda, the problem of resettlement expectations loomed. Travelling back to Africa was itself a display of the prosperity. Yet Nyomanda and her family had spent two years saving money for the trip, and they were far from financially secure in Australia. They struggled with insecure employment and poverty like most of the other resettled refugees I knew. Still, Nyomanda schooled me in the process of managing resettlement expectations. Her family would expect that she would bring them money and other kinds of material support, but it was important not to make it too obvious to others outside the family that she was a visitor: a returning refugee who had been resettled. If many other refugees in Uganda found out about her status, their assumptions about resettlement prosperity meant that it would be assumed she was rich, and she would become a target for sorcery or other kinds of attacks. "If we told them the truth," Nyomanda told me, as we prepared together for her visit to Uganda, "they would not believe us anyway." Later, after I had been through my own experiences of trying to explain the complexities of resettlement to refugees in Uganda and having my explanations ignored or downplayed, I realised that Nyomanda was right. The resettlement imaginary was difficult to puncture.

Resettlement as cruel optimism

It is through imaginaries that people anticipate and navigate the future. According to Henrik Vigh (2009a: 100), it is the "social imaginary that allows us to anticipate, position and act in relation to a world that is constantly approaching and engaging us rather than merely being subject to our command or solidified surface of enactment."

The resettlement imaginary can generate behaviours that are both constructive and destructive. To these refugees, resettlement is not simply a fantasy: it is an active social practice that mobilises people into action (Appadurai 1996). However, the "cruel optimism" (Berlant 2011) of resettlement can lead some people into action that itself causes damage and hardship.

Resettlement is supposed to be a method of protecting refugees from protracted insecurity. However, since the limited number of resettlement placements made available for refugees each year makes the opportunity to be resettled so restricted, the pursuit of resettlement can itself become a source of anxiety. Based on research conducted with Somali refugees in the Kenyan refugee camps near Dadaab, Cindy Horst (2006b) describes how traditional Somali *buufis*, meaning dreams, hopes and longings, have come to be reinscribed for Somali refugees living in situations of protracted asylum. No longer just a general sense of longing for new futures, *buufis* amongst the Somali refugees in Dadaab are now almost exclusively understood in relation to the desire to be resettled. These "resettlement dreams," as they are described by Horst (2006b), are intensified by the transnational flows of remittances and personal accounts of resettlement that reach Somali refugees in camps, which mean they are able to compare their lives of hardship in the camps to the supposedly prosperous lives of others elsewhere. These resettlement dreams are both a source of hope and a source of despair: they provide comfort that a different kind of life is possible for refugees outside of the camps, but this hope often descends into obsession and depression once the improbability of being resettled is realised.

The pursuit of resettlement can be considered "destabilizing by design" (El-Shaarawi 2015: 52). The bureaucratic procedures to apply for resettlement often exacerbate the anxiety experienced by refugees in asylum: their stories of persecution are assessed by UNHCR workers for credibility, and the paperwork required to lodge an application for resettlement—let alone have that application be deemed successful—can take months or years, leaving refugees in a state of existential uncertainty (Thomson 2012). Even after receiving confirmation that a resettlement application has been approved and preparations for resettlement begin, the process of arranging travel can also take months and even years: sometimes, information is not made available to refugees or information given to them, such as travel dates, is unexpectedly changed (El-Shaarawi 2015). After conducting research with refugees from Iraq living in Egypt, Nadia El-Shaarawi (2015: 51) describes how refugees awaiting resettlement embody the temporal and spatial uncertainty of their statuses, writing, "On more than one occasion I visited a family to find them sleeping on the floor or living out of suitcases that had been packed earlier" because they might begin preparations for their resettlement, such as selling their furniture, with no indication of when and how that journey will take place.

But even before putting in an application for resettlement, refugees generate strategies to boost the chance that their application is accepted and successful and limit the uncertainty that is generated through the process of applying for and receiving resettlement (Jansen 2008). Refugees are acutely aware that resettlement placements are limited and know that there are particular trends in the kinds of refugees who are more likely to be resettled each year. The extensive fraud that occurred during the resettlement of Somali Bantu refugees in the late 1990s and early 2000s is a standout case of how desperation and knowledge of how to strategise the resettlement application system can lead to deception (Besteman 2016: 92–96). After the US decided to resettle Somali Bantu refugees from Dadaab camps in Kenya as a group, many refugees from diverse ethnic backgrounds strategised their applications for refugee status around claiming to be Somali Bantu, some even buying ration cards from Somali Bantu families to authenticate their claims. Such instances of widespread corruption have become embedded in the processes of assessing resettlement applications more broadly. Marnie Thomson (2012: 198) describes how the humanitarian system of resettlement is one that "consistently seeks to discredit" refugees.

Unlike in the case of the Somali Bantu refugee resettlement that occurred in the late 1990s and early 2000s, most of the refugees I conducted fieldwork with were attempting to be resettled as an individual or a family case. As Thomson (2012) points out, however, there seems to be a process of stratifying the kinds of experiences and persecution that lead particular cases for resettlement to be prioritised: those cases that can be documented and verified are especially prioritised. What this means is that it is often those refugees who are able to document an ongoing experience of persecution within the camp setting who are prioritised for resettlement, since those experiences are generally recorded by the camp administration. Those whose marginalisation is a product of political persecution without some kind of physical markers of violence or institutional documentation are especially disadvantaged in the system of applying for resettlement because they are not able to produce a documented ongoing fear of persecution that prevents them from returning home (Thomson 2012). Aware of these dynamics, some of the refugees I knew had attempted to exacerbate their vulnerability while living in camps or settlements during the application process for resettlement in an attempt to increase their likelihood of being selected.

Amal, a woman I got to know in Australia, told me that her resettlement to Australia had probably been made possible because of the strategising of her husband. Amal was from a Muslim background and had lived in one of the Dadaab camps in Kenya since she was around eleven years old. A few years later, she became unexpectedly pregnant and was socially ostracised from her family. She raised her child, and eventually children, alone, until she met her future husband. He had a Christian background and originated from a different country and ethnic background than Amal. Like her, he also had children from a previous relationship. Amal told me that her husband had "chosen" her to be his wife because together, they would constitute a mixed-religion, mixed-ethnicity, and mixed-nationality relationship and surely attract attention and vitriol from others in the camp. After getting married, they did indeed begin to experience further ostracising. At one point, Amal's husband was even beaten up. Amal feared for the safety of their children. Significantly, however, Amal did not like her husband: he was a cruel man who was often violent towards her and the children. Still, Amal told me that she chose to stay with him because the marriage represented the best chance for her and her children to be resettled out of Dadaab. There were many other vulnerable single women with children seeking resettlement, and she would not likely stick out amongst them. Eventually, this attempt to make themselves vulnerable to violence in the camps resulted in the desired outcome: Amal and her family were resettled to Australia.

Not all refugees were assured that their attempts to prioritise their applications for resettlement would be as "successful" as Amal's. Many refugees I spoke to in Kampala told me that they were considering relocating to one of the designated settlements because they could apply for resettlement there. They told me that relocating to the settlements was a risky move, though, because they feared becoming targets of violence by relocating. But this fear was justified, indeed welcomed, in their perspectives because, if they were targeted, it would ultimately increase their chances of being selected for resettlement. Becoming vulnerable to violence was a way, paradoxically, to make the possibility of a better life in resettlement go from being just an imaginary to an empirical reality.

Describing how the resettlement dreams that are experienced by Somali refugees in Kenya generate both hope and despair, Cindy Horst (2006b) considers that the ways in which refugees fixate on resettlement can produce a kind of madness: a state of seemingly perpetual and insolvable suffering. It did indeed seem to be a paradoxical kind of madness that, in seeking the enhanced protection of resettlement, the refugees I came to know during fieldwork would, in situations of protracted asylum, put themselves in further danger in order to increase their vulnerability and improve what remains a very limited chance of having their resettlement application approved.

The destructive potential of pursuing resettlement can be considered from Lauren Berlant's (2011) theoretical framework of "cruel optimism." According to Berlant (2006: 21, 2011), "'cruel optimism' names a relation of attachment to compromised conditions of possibility.... Cruel optimism is the condition of maintaining an attachment to a problematic object *in advance* of its loss." Resettlement, I consider, represents one such "problematic object." Being so limited in availability, yet so coveted by the refugees I conducted fieldwork with, the pursuit of resettlement, despite the probable outcome of failure, makes the imaginary of being resettled a way for refugees to remain attached to, and even focused on creating, "compromised conditions of possibility" (Berlant 2011: 24). Although it is not frequently written about in academic scholarship, it is not uncommon when working with refugees to hear stories and rumours about people who have seemingly "chosen" to seek the status of refugee and enter refugee camps specifically because doing so is seen as an opportunity to be resettled and to migrate to a Western country (Jansen 2008). The resettlement imaginary that drives people to endure in living situations of suffering due to the slim possibility that doing so may result in their being selected for resettlement can be considered an effect of the illusion of the "good life," a concept that Berlant (2011) uses to describe the kinds of prosperous lives and livelihoods that people have come to imagine and seek but which are, in reality, non-existent and impossible to attain. In pursuing what they imagine as the "good life" of resettlement, refugees can purposely sabotage their lives in the present by actively working towards a life that is not only limited in its availability but which is itself an imaginary.

(Re)Productive futures

Experiences of reduced fertility amongst the refugees I conducted fieldwork with signalled the uncertainty of everyday life in protracted asylum: being unable to conceive and bear a child to term was interpreted by them as an indicator of not only the physical strain of life as a refugee in Uganda but also the existential anxiety of living in the present towards an uncertain future. But, as other researchers emphasise, the feeling of being "stuck" in asylum, and existing "between past and possible future lives" (El-Shaarawi 2015: 49), does not necessarily mean that refugees are dominated by this temporal stagnation: many imagine and actively work towards new futures as much as is possible within the constraints of their daily lives as refugees. For refugees in Uganda, this often meant dreaming of and applying for resettlement.

But just as they understood the temporal stagnation of asylum in relation to reduced fertility, the social possibilities of resettlement were articulated in relation to the fertility and children. Although there is certainly a global resettlement imaginary in which policy actors, academic researchers, host nation governments, and refugees themselves across the world continue to implicitly reproduce the idea of refugee resettlement as an automatic solution to displacement, the production of this imaginary in localised situations also reflects particularities of cosmological beliefs about how futures of existential purpose are secured. For the refugees I got to know in Uganda and Australia, the resettlement imaginary, and the futures of social possibility that these refugees assumed resettlement would secure, was understood and articulated in relation to the lives of children and reproductive potentiality.

I became very close to Sarah, a refugee who lived in the same housing compound as me, while conducting fieldwork in Uganda. Practically every morning, we would sit together and do chores, talking intently as we went about washing and hanging out clothes, fetching water, sweeping out the shared courtyard. Unlike so many other refugees I got to know in Uganda, Sarah was pregnant. We did not, however, discuss the pregnancy, even as it became more and more physically obvious: no one in our circle of immediate contacts did. There was no outward excitement surrounding the impending birth or obvious preparations for it. It was as if Sarah was not pregnant at all. And, socially speaking, she was not. Across equatorial Africa, it is common to avoid publically displaying pregnancy because doing so is seen as a way to make pregnant women and unborn children vulnerable to invisible harm from sorcery (Chapman 2006). And yet, for refugees in Uganda, the uncertainty of the future seemingly compounds the insecurity of pregnancy. Although Sarah and I never discussed the impending birth directly, her anxiety about the new baby seemed, to me, to be expressed in her increasing concern over the future, which we discussed often during our almost daily conversations. As her belly expanded with the growth of the baby, so too did her worry about the kind of existence into which it would be born: about the futurity that this baby would embody. One day, she outright told me, "We need a new life in Australia. The life here is killing us. There, in Australia, my children can be free."

The morning of the birth proceeded as every other day had. Life in the compound unfolded in the way it normally did: people went out with empty jerry cans to fetch water, preparations began for those going to work, children played happily in the shared courtyard. Noticeably absent, however, was Sarah. And although no one mentioned that Sarah was not present as we passed each other in the courtyard, I think we all knew what her absence signalled. Finally, in the middle of the afternoon, Sarah's husband trudged into the housing complex and told us the news: the baby, a little girl, had been born. I was invited to go and visit her in the hospital, and so I did. Sitting on the edge of the bed in which, hours before, she had given birth, I asked Sarah what she had named the little girl. "Asha," she told me: a variant of a Swahili word for "life." Affirming the futurity embodied by the birth of their child in what was a difficult situation of protracted asylum, Sarah and her husband had named the baby for the future of possibility that she represented.

For other refugees in Uganda, however, difficulties in conceiving and bearing children to term affirmed, to them, not only the physical insecurity of life in asylum but also what they saw as a lack of a viable future. Seemingly stuck in a stagnated present, unable to situate themselves in a temporal cycle of regenerative continuity, these refugees in asylum developed a resettlement imaginary in which they saw being resettled not only as a way to achieve a better quality of life but as a kind of existential mobility in which their problems of social regeneration and physiological reproduction would also be solved. As Nadine, who had struggled to fall pregnant since coming to Uganda to seek asylum, told me, "I will have a baby overseas. I will." The resettlement imaginary that oriented their experiences in the present and their dreams of the future was one in which they specifically sought to escape the social death of childlessness.

Between possible futures and lived realities

The imaginary of resettlement is a way in which refugees in Uganda are able to locate and work towards futures beyond their immediate situations of asylum, in which they are removed from active temporal rhythms of circular time. They assume that their displacement can be resolved upon their being resettled. This is not only because they expect that countries that provide resettlement to refugees will offer them enhanced physical and material security, although this is often the case. But migration is never only about survival. Rather, refugees see in resettlement the potential for increased social possibility. Specifically, they see the potential to regenerate life. It is only in resettlement, I was told, that it is possible to bear and rear children in ways in which they can be "free." As similarly recognised by Nadia El-Shaarawi (2015: 50), the refugees I got to know in Uganda had developed a specific imaginary of resettlement in which "[r]esettlement, with its promise of permanent residency in a 'secure' country (James 2009) and the ability to exercise rights, presented a promising solution to an uncertain future."

It is not just refugees who dream and produce such resettlement imaginaries. Resettlement is widely imagined throughout institutions of humanitarian governance to be a solution to the displacement that refugees experience in protracted situations of asylum. The idea that resettlement equates to refuge is an implicit assumption that is embedded and reproduced across international systems of humanitarian governance, refugee policy that operates at global and national scales, the work of scholars and researchers who study the experiences of refugees, and the perspectives of refugees themselves. Yet little research connects the experiences of refugees across contexts of protracted asylum and in resettlement in a way that can explore whether the assumptions embedded in resettlement imaginaries are actualised. In the chapters that follow, I explore the lives of refugees resettled in Australia and the ways that their experiences complicate the seemingly obvious assumption that resettlement is an automatic solution to displacement.

Note

1 Colloquial Swahili term for "white person."

References

Adeyanju, C. and Oriola, T. 2011. Colonialism and Contemporary African Migration: A Phenomenological Approach. *Journal of Black Studies* 42(6): 943–967.

Althusser, L. 1971. Ideology and Ideological State Apparatuses (Notes toward an Investigation). In *Lenin and Philosophy and Other Essays by Louis Althusser*. L. Althusser (Ed.), pp. 127–186. Translated by B. Brewster. New York: Monthly Review Press.

Anderson, B. 1983. *Imagined Communities: Reflections on the Origin and Spread of Nationalism*. London: Verso.

Appadurai, A. 1996. *Modernity at Large: Cultural Dimensions of Globalization*. Minneapolis: University of Minnesota Press.

Berlant, L. 2006. Cruel Optimism. *Differences* 17(3): 20–36.
Berlant, L. 2011. *Cruel Optimism*. Durham, NC: Duke University Press.
Besteman, C. 2016. *Making Refuge: Somali Bantu Refugees and Lewiston, Maine*. Durham, NC: Duke University Press.
Bredeloup, S. 2013. The Figure of the Adventurer as an African Migrant. *Journal of African Cultural Studies* 25(2): 170–182.
Chapman, R.R. 2006. *Chikotsa*—Secrets, Silence, and Hiding: Social risk and Reproductive Vulnerability in Central Mozambique. *Medical Anthropology Quarterly* 20(4): 487–515.
El-Shaarawi, N. 2015. Living in an Uncertain Future: Temporality, Uncertainty, and Well-Being among Iraqi Refugees in Egypt. *Social Analysis* 59(1): 38–56.
Englund, H. 2002. Ethnography after Globalism: Migration and Emplacement in Malawi. *American Ethnologist* 29(2): 261–286.
Fischer, E. 2014. *The Good Life: Aspiration, Dignity and the Anthropology of Wellbeing*. Stanford, CA: Stanford University Press.
Horst, C. 2006b. *Buufis* amongst Somalis in Dadaab: The Transnational and Historical Logics behind Resettlement Dreams. *Journal of Refugee Studies* 19(2): 143–157.
Jackson, M. 2008. The Shock of the New: On Migrant Imaginaries and Critical Transitions. *Ethnos* 73(1): 57–72.
Jackson, M. 2011. *Life within Limits: Well-being in a World of Want*. Durham, NC: Duke University Press.
Jackson, M. 2013a. *The Wherewithal of Life: Ethics, Migration, and the Question of Well-being*. Berkeley: University of California Press.
Jackson, M. 2013b. *The Politics of Storytelling: Variations on a Theme by Hannah Arendt*. 2nd Edition. Copenhagen: Museum Tusculanum Press.
Jansen, B. 2008. Between Vulnerability and Assertiveness: Negotiating Resettlement in Kakuma Refugee Camp, Kenya. *African Affairs* 107(429): 569–587.
Lacan, J. 1977. The Function and Field of Speech and Language in Psychoanalysis. In *Ecrtis: A Selection* J. Lacan (Ed.), pp. 30–113. Translated by A. Sheridan. New York: W. Norton.
Lee, E.S. 1966. A Theory of Migration. *Demography* 3(1): 47–57.
Lems, A. 2016. Placing Displacement: Place-Making in a World of Movement. *Ethnos* 81(2): 315–337.
Lucht, H. 2012. *Darkness before Daybreak: African Migrants Living on the Margins in Southern Italy Today*. Berkeley: University of California Press.
McMichael, C. and Manderson, L. 2004. Somali Women and Well-Being: Social Networks and Social Capital among Immigrant Women in Australia. *Human Organization* 63(1): 88–99.
Ortner, S. 2016. Dark Anthropology and Its Others: Theory since the Eighties. *HAU: Journal of Ethnographic Theory* 6(1): 47–73.
Pajo, E. 2007. *International Migration, Social Demotion, and Imagined Advancement: An Ethnography of Socioglobal Mobility*. New York: Springer.
Poynting, S. 2004. Advanced Australia Fear: A Review Essay. *Current Issues in Criminal Justice* 16(2): 241–252.
Ramadan, A. 2013. Spatialising the Refugee Camp. *Transactions* 38(1): 65–77.
Robbins, J. 2013. Beyond the Suffering Subject: Toward an Anthropology of the Good. *Journal of the Royal Anthropological Institute* 19: 447–462.

Salazar, N. 2010. Tanzanian Migration Imaginaries. *Working Paper*, International Migration Institute, University of Oxford, Oxford, pp. 2–29.

Sandvik, K. 2011. Blurring Boundaries: Refugee Resettlement in Kampala—Between the Formal, the Informal, and the Illegal. *Political and Legal Anthropology Review* 34(1): 11–32.

Strauss, C. 2006. The Imaginary. *Anthropological Theory* 6(3): 322–344.

Taylor, C. 2002. Modern Social Imaginaries. *Public Culture* 14: 91–124.

Taylor, C. 2004. *Modern Social Imaginaries*. Durham, NC: Duke University Press.

Thomson, M. 2012. Black Boxes of Bureaucracy: Transparency and Opacity in the Resettlement Process of Congolese Refugees. *Political and Legal Anthropology Review* 35(2): 186–205.

UNHCR. 2011a. UNHCR Resettlement Handbook. Available at: www.unhcr.org/46f7c0ee2.html (Accessed 12 November 2016).

UNHCR. 2017a. Resettlement. Available at: www.unhcr.org/en-au/resettlement.html (Accessed 12 January 2017).

Vigh, H. 2009a. Wayward Migration: On Imagined Futures and Technological Voids. *Ethnos: Journal of Anthropology* 74(1): 91–109.

Vigh, H. 2009b. Motion Squared: A Second Look at the Concept of Social Navigation. *Anthropological Theory* 9(4): 419–438.

Part III

Resettlement

6 Resettlement and contested citizenship

Nyomanda had filled the walls of her living room in her rented home in suburban Australia with photographs. Most had been carefully placed in frames and hung from the picture rails or stood on the fireplace mantle; others were unframed and stuck haphazardly on the walls with tape or wedged in front of other photos already in frames. Some were photographs of family who were still in camps, which had been taken on one of the trips when Nyomanda or her husband had returned to Africa, depicting large groups of people and many children lined up in front of the camera, beaming. Others were photos of Nyomanda and her husband, affectionately standing close to each other and gazing toward the camera. School photos of their children, taken when they were in full school uniform and sitting in front of a professional background, had been framed and hung on the walls. Taken throughout the seven years since Nyomanda and her family had migrated to Australia, the photographs documented the stark progression of growth and changes that had occurred since they had been resettled.

But it was a series of photographs hanging directly across from the main entryway that especially caught my attention whenever I visited Nyomanda at her home. These were photographs that depicted Nyomanda and her family posing together and dressed in formal attire: Nyomanda and her husband in traditional *kitenge* material outfits and the children in formal dresses or suits. One of the photos from that series depicted Nyomanda's husband shaking hands with a person who was dressed in heavy robes with red, yellow, and black stripes: the outfit adorned by the Mayor of the city during ceremonial events. Another photo from that day showed the family posing and smiling with friends who worked at the local migrant resource centre that had supported them with their settlement when they had first arrived. These were photographs from the citizenship ceremony in which Nyomanda, her husband, and their children had become naturalised Australian citizens. Nyomanda told me that becoming a citizen had been one of the happiest days of her life.

But the realisation of permanent residency, and the culmination of this national identity through the celebration of citizenship that takes place during a naturalisation ceremony, does not necessarily translate into benefits that are felt during the experience of everyday life for refugees resettled in Australia. For the refugees I conducted fieldwork with in Australia, the claim to being a recognised and legitimate citizen, or future citizen, is contested.

These refugees are not resettled into a neutral sociocultural context. Upon resettlement in Australia, their lives become embedded in assumptions and expectations that inform how they are perceived and approached within their local communities and how their everyday lives in Australia are organised more broadly. As I describe in this chapter, I observed during my fieldwork that non-white refugees from Africa who are resettled in Australia are often encoded with immediate assumptions of difference and inferiority. The presence of refugees from Africa is more often only tolerated rather than welcomed. Their claims to civic belonging and eventual citizenship are always mediated through these contingencies, making the aspiration to create a "new life" in Australia a process of simultaneously negotiating marginalisation with opportunity and possibility.

Settlement potential

The resettlement of refugees in Australia is not an exclusively humanitarian process of providing those refugees most in need with protection. From the selection of refugees to be resettled to the implementation of programmes and services to support their migration transition, the resettlement of refugees in Australia works to simultaneously resolve their displacement and shape them into particular kinds of citizens. The resettlement of refugees serves as a way to reinforce the exclusive basis of existing formations of civic belonging as much it serves to foster new and inclusive articulations of citizenship.

The selection of refugees for resettlement is not necessarily organised to benefit those who are most vulnerable and supposedly in need. Although ongoing insecurity and vulnerability is a factor that informs the criteria for refugee resettlement in Australia, this is not the only basis of selection. Popular imaginaries of refugees and asylum seekers in Australia depict the resettlement of refugees as an "orderly" process, in which those who are most vulnerable are selected for migration ahead of others (McKay, Thomas, and Kneebone 2012). This means that those refugees who attempt to seek asylum in Australia directly—that is, without being selected for resettlement offshore by Australian officials—are labelled in public discourse as "queue jumpers" (Gelber 2003 Pickering 2001). But the idea that there is an orderly queue of refugees awaiting resettlement who are ranked according to vulnerability, and that asylum seekers are taking the resettlement placements that could be made available to those more needy refugees, is false. There is no queue.

The process of refugee resettlement, as set out in the UNHCR "Resettlement Handbook" (UNHCR 2011a), is not replicated the same everywhere but generally begins with refugees applying to be resettled as individual cases, usually from camps or in other situations of protracted asylum. The UNHCR and other local operating partners assess resettlement applications, determining those that should be accepted as genuine cases for resettlement and those who should not. "Genuine" cases are determined depending on whether a refugee has a demonstrated risk of insecurity in a context of asylum and is unlikely to be able to safely access another durable solution, such as repatriation to their origin country or local integration in their host nation of asylum. Then, cases are selected for resettlement and referred to government representatives from a host nation of asylum, who assess each applicant to determine whether they are suitable candidates for resettlement to that country. Each nation works with a set number of resettlement placements, which can change from year to year, and criteria through which applicants for resettlement are selected and prioritised.

In Australia, cases for resettlement are assessed on the basis of a few factors, including the degree of persecution or discrimination that an applicant is subject to in their country of origin, the extent of their existing connection to Australia, and whether there is another country that could be more suited to providing settlement and protection to an applicant (UNHCR 2016: 4). Since the pool of applicants seeking to be resettled in Australia is far greater than the number of available placements, government officials have to exclude many applicants for resettlement. Some attributes make a refugee less likely to be selected, such as a medical condition that could incur what a government official might consider an "undue" or significant cost (UNHCR 2016: 8). But there is speculation that refugees are also selected on the basis of their having particular social, cultural, and religious attributes that would seemingly make it easier for them to assimilate into Australian society (Colic-Peisker 2005).

There is no publically available information on whether social or cultural parameters are considered when government officials select refugees for resettlement. However, there is a tendency for refugees who are selected for resettlement to embody what is termed by Val Colic-Peisker (2005) as "settlement potential." Unlike the medical and security clearances that applicants seeking to be resettled to Australia are subjected to as part of the application process, considering the "settlement potential" of refugees requires assessing their predicted potential to assimilate into the Australian population. According to Colic-Peisker (2005: 618–620), assessing whether refugees have "settlement potential" means considering how their social, cultural, educational, professional, and racial background will fit into a population that is dominated by highly educated white people with a predominantly Judeo-Christian and European heritage. The family composition of refugees who are resettled to Australia is one factor that suggests that the selection of refugees through the resettlement programme is organised according to assumptions about the kind of peoples who are mostly likely to fit into Australian society.

The resettlement programme in Australia privileges those refugees who fit the conventional model of a nuclear family, or who are at least comprised of a parental member and offspring who are related to them by direct genetic descent. This stems from broader UNHCR policies of resettlement that, according to Brooke Wilmsen (2011: 63), "configure the family in ways that are not meaningful themselves." The UNHCR is not entirely the basis of this exclusionary basis of settlement potential, however. The structuring of resettlement policy and processes in ways that privilege those refugees whose family compositions fit the ideal of a nuclear family model is due to the fact that "resettlement countries largely adopt definitions of the family based on a nuclear family configuration and do not recognize other family formations and relationships as legitimate" (Wilmsen 2011: 63). As such, the composition of family is one factor that influences how the settlement potential of refugees to be resettled to Australia is assessed.

Dominant models of kinship in Central Africa do not, however, correspond to the nuclear model that privileges a hierarchy of direct genetic descent (Oyewumi 2000). Although the full realisation of personhood for men and women across many Central African contexts is predicated on their producing biological offspring (Devisch 1993; Feldman-Savelsberg 1999; Silva 2009), this does not mean that these unidirectional relations of genetic descent define how kinship is understood and practiced. Indeed, many of the refugees I conducted fieldwork with were part of family groups in which lateral relations, such as the brother's sister, had as much power as, or more power than, the mothers themselves, or that included offspring who were not related through direct genetic descent. In addition, conflict situations can impact and change kinship structures (Bruck and Schindler 2009; Sánchez-Céspedes 2016). The premature deaths of family members can also mean that orphaned children become incorporated into the care of kin relations who are not necessarily directly related to them. Although refugees may therefore originate from social contexts that do not privilege direct genetic relatedness or may have experienced situations of conflict that disrupt and change structures of kin relatedness, ultimately, it is host nations that determine the composition of family groups to be resettled (Wilmsen 2011). The application processes through which refugees are selected for resettlement to nations like Australia consistently privilege genetic relatedness and nuclear family models, a process that has intensified in recent years through the use of genetic testing to establish relatedness during resettlement application processes (Cox 2016; Dove 2013; Heinemann, Helén, Lemke, and Naue 2016). This method of selecting refugees who conform to particular formations of family relatedness reflects how the resettlement process works as much to select refugees whose settlement potential fits with particular assumptions about integration and civic life in Australia as it does to provide refugees with protection.

But the settlement potential of refugees does not only consider the social and cultural attributes of applicants. According to Colic-Peisker (2005), the designation of resettlement placements to particular groups of refugees is fundamentally informed by assumptions of integration potential that are based on the racialisation of refugees, especially those who are non-white. Political concerns about societal cohesion, which often depict forces of social instability along lines of racial division, are reflected in the populations of refugees who are designated as resettlement priorities and who are eventually selected for resettlement. Those refugees who are more visibly different to the dominant white population have assumptions of difference attached to them, which reflects in the ways that their settlement potential comes to be perceived in processes of selection for resettlement and subsequent evaluations of resettlement success (Colic-Peisker 2005). Even though the racialisation of refugee populations is not explicitly worked into the selection criteria of individual cases for resettlement, the overall designation of resettlement placements to refugees from particular national backgrounds in recent years, more broadly, reflects a process of implicit racialisation.

In 2007, then-Minister for Immigration, Kevin Andrews, abruptly cut the quota of refugees from continental Africa from approximately 70 per cent of the total resettlement intake to around 30 per cent (ABC 2007). Refugees from Africa were no longer to be considered a priority group for resettlement to Australia. The initial justification for the reduction given by Andrews was that many conflict situations in Africa were no longer considered urgent (Farouque, Petrie, and Miletic 2007), meaning other populations of refugees could be supported through the resettlement programme. That claim itself was spurious. Although the wars in the DRC and what was then Sudan had formally ceased, there were still frequent outbreaks of violence in both countries and elsewhere in Africa, which would prevent refugees from being safely returned to their homes (ABC 2007). It seemed as if there could be another reason for the abrupt reduction in the number of resettlement placements made available to refugees from Africa: one not related to the situations of conflict that produce refugees but related instead to the openness of Australia as a host nation to receive and settle them.

In the months after the Department of Immigration announced the sudden reduction, Kevin Andrews did indeed voice another reason why refugees from Africa were no longer making up the bulk of the resettlement programme in Australia. In October 2007, Andrews claimed that, "Some groups don't seem to be settling and adjusting into the Australian way of life" (Farouque et al. 2007). Andrews, a Minister appointed to one of the highest political offices in Australian politics, was invoking a kind of casual racism that not only stereotypes people from Africa as problems but which, in doing so, also infers that refugees from Africa can be approached as a homogenous group. The comments by Andrews suggest that refugees from across continental Africa all share the same problematic characteristics that would make integration difficult in Australia. In reality, refugees from Africa are incredibly culturally and socially diverse and not able to be homogenised. What they often do share, however, is the experience of being visibly non-white migrants whose presence in a predominantly white population becomes racialised. The dominant fantasy of an "Australian way of life," as it was put by Kevin Andrews and as it is propagated by the Australian government and naturalised in the worldviews of the predominantly white Australian public, is steeped in the seemingly natural authority of whiteness and the necessity of controlling what is perceived as cultural difference.

Citizenship and the "Australian way of life"

The racialisation of non-white people as inferior, which is at the centre of attitudes toward and policies about immigration to Australia, continues, according to James Jupp (2002), to be masked by a denial of difference. Being a citizen in Australia is predominately imagined as a meritocracy in which experiences of exclusion or marginalisation must result from personal failures rather than systematic assumptions of inferiority that are popularly attached to those who are seen to embody cultural difference (Perera 2009: 155). In recent years, the link between citizenship and an idealised imaginary of a specifically, and seemingly homogenous, "Australian way of life" has been solidified in the policy of the Australian government. On 11 December 2006, the then-Prime Minister John Howard announced amendments to the Citizenship Act. The amendments included the introduction of a citizenship test that would require applicants to demonstrate, according to Howard (2006, cited in Perera 2009: 153), "a basic level of English language skills, as well as knowledge of the Australian way of life and our shared values." These are the cultural conditions into which refugees from Africa are resettled in Australia.

Citizenship is a status of political recognition that imbues a person with a particular national identity. Being legally identified as a member of a national group allows people to access particular rights and privileges that are attached to that nationality but also subjects them to particular expectations of citizenship that are inscribed into their lives as laws and societal responsibilities (Heater 2013). Yet citizenship is not simply a category in which the legal parameters around inclusion within and exclusion from a nation state are defined. Citizenship is also a cultural and moral category of recognition (Werbner 1998), making some claims to civic belonging seem more valid in the social context of public life than those made by others.

Citizenship in Australia, other Western democratic states, and increasingly across the globe, is often implicitly stratified according to neoliberal moral economies in which the value of life is implicitly measured in accordance with the market value (Muehlebach 2012; Ong 2003, 2006; Povinelli 2011). Neoliberalism is a term that has become a somewhat "chaotic concept" in anthropological writings (Jessop 2013: 65), that is, regularly used but rarely defined. Indeed, the usefulness of neoliberalism as a heuristic in anthropological research is a topic of debate. According to Tejsawini Ganti

(2014), neoliberalism, as it is popularly used in anthropology, is used to refer to a few different processes, predominantly: neoliberalism as a structural force through which peoples' lives and life chances are organised and stratified; neoliberalism as an ideology of governance through which peoples' lives are subjected and by which peoples themselves come to reproduce as a process of subjectification; and neoliberalism as a basis of practical action through which behaviours are oriented. Whether structure, ideology, or practice, neoliberalism can be broadly traced to a move from collective and state-centred models of societal organisation towards private and competitive free market models: a move that has translated into a moral economy of "good" citizenship across Western democracies, and increasingly globally, in which valued societal participation is dependent on demonstrating markers of individualisation, economic self-reliance, and demonstrations of efficiency and productivity (Ong 2003, 2006). At the core of neoliberalism as a theory of political and economic practices is the idea that human well-being can be best advanced by "liberating individual entrepreneurial freedoms and skills within an institutional framework characterized by strong private property rights, free markets, and free trade," in which "the role of the state is to create and preserve an institutional framework appropriate to such practices" (Harvey 2005: 2). As such, state interests can be taken as those that generally align with neoliberal agendas. Determinations of, and expectations placed on, citizenship are made by states in relation to maximising the effectiveness of neoliberal systems of governance (Ong 2006).

But, as Daniel Goldstein (2012: 304) points out, even when the empirical and practical effects of what are considered to be neoliberal forces of individualisation and economic rationalism are evident in the lived daily reality of global subjects, the analytic of neoliberalism itself should not be used an overarching "explanatory catholicon" in anthropological research. Goldstein (2012: 308) points out that the political and economic landscapes of everyday life across diverse global contexts are "characterised by shifting and overlapping fragments of various theories, discourses, ideologies and practices, which people must navigate as they try to make a living and achieve some kind of security in their lives." As such, the construction of citizenship ideals and the organisation of everyday life, in Australia and elsewhere, cannot be essentialised to moral economies of neoliberal value alone.

The refinement of neoliberalism as a basis of societal organisation has, historically and contemporaneously, been a vector through which ideas about racial superiority and inferiority are constituted and reproduced. To understand this link between citizenship and racialisation, Aiwha Ong (2003) considers that it is necessary to identify how contemporary workings of citizenship derive from historical contexts of slavery and the racial exclusion of non-white immigrants and local indigenous peoples. The enslavement of black people is, according to Ong (2003: 10–14), the basis of a bipolar racial continuum between whiteness and blackness, upon which the worthiness of citizens or potential citizens becomes concurrently mapped across both economic position and racial categorisation. Although dissolved as a formal model of population segregation, racialisation and associated assumptions of economic contribution continue to organise how citizenship is lived and experienced, and the worthiness of citizens is stratified, across the US (Ong 1996, 2003) and elsewhere (Mercer 2010; Ong 2006).

This template of measuring citizenship persists today in the ways that images and imaginaries of self-sufficient, entrepreneurial, and productive citizens are often represented as white people, and lazy, recalcitrant, and ill-disciplined citizens are often represented or assumed to be non-white people. Aiwha Ong (1996) describes how, in the US specifically, but more broadly in other Euro-American societal contexts in which political and social power is concentrated into the domains of those who are identifiable as white, the validity of claims to citizenship is moderated by factors associated with racialisation, cultural background, and socioeconomic class: a combination of attributes that Ong (ibid) considers necessary to constitute a societal context of hegemonic whiteness. Ong (1996: 739) describes how "[a]ttaining success through self-reliant struggle, while not inherently limited to any cultural group, is a process of self-development that in Western democracies becomes inseparable form the process of 'whitening.'" What this means is that the validity of contemporary claims to citizenship in places like the US and Australia have come to be mediated through historicised moral, cultural, and racial assumptions about citizenship through which the idea of a "good" citizen comes to be automatically premised on the citizens embodying whiteness.

Race is not a valid biological categorisation. Although groups of peoples can share certain physiological attributes and genetic markers, these cannot be exclusively mapped onto peoples on the basis of their skin colour or other physical characteristics (Erikson 2002). And yet, categorisations of race continue to remain salient in public discourse across the globe, making perceptions and understandings of race significant to the ways in which peoples' lives are organised and experienced globally (Harrison 1995; Visweswaran 1998). Conventionally, however, analyses in the social sciences of racial categorisations and the effects of these classificatory processes have focused on the demarcation of peoples who are non-white because it is those populations who have been most subjected to the negative effects of racialisation. However, as Richard Dyer (1997) emphasises, the continuing focus on non-white peoples as racialised subjects masks an assumption that those who are white are non-raced. Dyer (1997) considers that because the racialisation of people as white has conventionally been absent in social science research and public imagery more generally, the condition of whiteness has come to represent a kind of fundamental humanity. Dyer (1997: 2) suggests that:

> The point of seeing the racing of whites is to dislodge them/us from the position of power, with all the inequities, oppression, privileges, and

sufferings in its train, dislodging them/us by undercutting the authority with which they/we speak and act in and on the world.

Whiteness is, therefore, a category of racialisation in which the identification of people as white is embedded within a set of corresponding moral and cultural assumptions of their being superior, making whiteness, as Aihwa Ong (1996, 2003) suggests, a fundamental basis of "good" citizenship in Western democracies such as Australia and making those who are labelled as non-white automatically representative of inferiority.

The idea of legitimate citizenship as a cultural and moral category in Australia has historically been grounded in an assumption of whiteness (Mercer 2010; Schech and Haggis 2001), which is especially evident when analysing historical and contemporary controls and restrictions on immigration. Australia became a nation in 1901. Soon after the federation of the Australian nation, one of the first bills to be passed in the new Australian government was the Immigration Restriction Act of 1901, which remained in place until 1958. The policy worked to prioritise migrants from the United Kingdom, and specifically to maintain British hegemony and the domination of the whiteness (Jupp 2002: 6).

The Immigration Restriction Act of 1901 was explicitly racist in its effects, even if those were masked in the policy by the euphemism of immigration "restriction." In an extensive overview of historical and contemporary immigration practices in Australia, James Jupp (2002) describes how the Immigration Restriction Act of 1901 allowed officers to administer a dictation test to would-be immigrants at the point of their arrival in Australia. Although it was never explicitly stated in the policy, it was understood that the test could be given to a potential migrant in any language originating from Europe, even if it was not a language that was known to them. In addition, immigration officers were authorised to judge the degree of "white" blood in the veins of an applicant for settlement. Although it was never explicitly stated that peoples from other "races" were culturally inferior, that implication was nonetheless salient. The actual justifications given by governments for restricting immigration to Australia throughout the early 20th century was that allowing people to settle in Australia who could not visibly fit into the homogenous white society would create unrest and disrupt social harmony. Jupp (2002) argues that this denial of explicit racism, but nonetheless pervasive racialisation of migrants as culturally inferior, is at the centre of Australian immigration policy: not only during the early 20th century but also into the 2000s. The centrality of racism to the implementation of immigration policy, as well as attitudes towards non-white migrants, continues to be reproduced in the contemporary experiences of refugees from continental Africa who are resettled in Australia.

So what is an "Australian way of life," and how does this imaginary of a common lifestyle and shared values impact the experiences of refugees resettled in Australia in recent times? At the centre of this imaginary of core Australian values is egalitarianism: a value that manages to reconcile the deeply individualist neoliberal ideology of productive work ethic with a social expectation of masculinised collectivity and friendship, referred to in Australia as "mateship." The "Aussie battler" is the central figure of this imaginary that both major political parties draw on to justify and legitimise their policy directions: working for the "battler" rather than the "elite" is political rhetoric that speaks to the core of an idealised vision of what it means to be Australian (Dryenfurth 2005).

The concept of egalitarianism means equality for all and the dissolution of hierarchy: a value that would, seemingly, refute racist attitudes that work to segregate and rank people on the basis of false biology. But what elevates the specifically Australian version of egalitarianism to a core national value is that it developed, historically, as a response to and the antithesis of the upper-class British aristocrat, who was seen as the lazy elite benefiting off the hard work of working-class people (Hage 1998: 198–200). The version of egalitarianism that is at the core of the so-called "Australian way of life" is one that is premised on a masculinised vision of White Australian solidarity in opposition to the social elitism of British "high culture." It is a value that excludes as it simultaneously includes and demands that those who are brought into the scope of recognition prove their worthiness, if not through their affiliation to the core white racial identity of Australia, then by demonstrating their commitment to the core value of hard work and sacrifice. Refugees from Africa, whose understandings of the world have been shaped by different cosmological logics of regenerative potentiality and circular time, do not readily fit this mould of moral and cultural citizenship in Australia. As such, the resettlement of refugees from Africa in Australia has emerged in recent years as a perceived threat to the "Australian way of life."

Governing difference

> National security is therefore about a proper response to terrorism. It's also about having a far sighted strong well thought out defence policy. It is also about having an uncompromising view about the fundamental right of this country to protect its borders, it's about this nation saying to the world we are a generous open hearted people taking more refugees on a per capita basis than any nation except Canada, we have a proud record of welcoming people from 140 different nations. But we will decide who comes to this country and the circumstances in which they come.
>
> (John Howard, Launch of the Liberal Party Election Campaign, October 28, 2001, cited in Dryenfurth 2005: 195)

The speech given by then-Prime Minister John Howard to launch his election campaign in 2001, which he went on to win, exemplifies the ways in which the egalitarian values at the core of the supposedly "Australian way of life" serve to exclude as much as include. In the speech, Howard first emphasised the generosity of the Australian nation, then used positive self-representation of Australia as a basis to justify policies of mandatorily detaining refugees, including women and children, as a fundamental right (Dryenfurth 2005). The use of the inclusive "we" that Howard refers to, in the context of this stance of controlled immigration, is one that excludes at the same time as it includes, positioning people like him—that is, the dominant white Australian population—as the people who have a right to govern those whose claim to the nation is perceived as less valid (Dryenfurth 2005).

The assumed authority of whiteness is at the core of mainstream attitudes towards immigration and multiculturalism in Australia. The ways in which white politicians and a predominantly white public "weigh in" to determine whether to exclude, tolerate, or embrace cultural diversity is indicative, according to Ghassan Hage (1998: 17), of an enduring "governor" mentality in which white Australians, whether advocating for or against diversity, nonetheless do so while occupying a seemingly natural authority to speak on behalf of the ethnic other: effectively and simultaneously silencing those who are labelled as such and positioning them as a problem to be debated. Hage (1998) incisively points out that while the Australian public is often divided on the benefits and disadvantages of multiculturalism, it is united on a far more fundamental point: that the Australian public, imagined as a predominantly white population with a homogenous sociocultural background, has the authority to decide how, or by whom, the Australian population is made up. Whether advocating for multiculturalism or condemning it, those who imagine themselves as part of the dominant white population in Australia share a "belief in their centrality as enactors of the Law in Australia, or, to put it differently, as 'governors' of the nation" who also share a "conception of ethnics as people one can make decisions *about*: objects to be governed" (Hage 1998: 17).

I was standing beside Regina on the footpath outside of a grocery store when I first witnessed what Hage (1998: 17) describes as the "governor" mentality toward non-white people in Australia. Regina had turned her attention to the fruit and vegetables that were prominently displayed on the outdoor stalls of a local grocery store: picking up individual oranges in her hands and turning them over, trying to determine which would be the best to purchase for her family to eat. As we stood together, my attention was suddenly caught by a car on the road beside us that had slowed as it came to pass by Regina and me. "Go back to Sudan!" someone screamed from the passenger window. The driver then noisily accelerated past us for maximum attention. Caught by surprise by the verbal abuse, I struggled to restrain myself from responding to the diatribe with a rude gesture. I turned to Regina to express my anger, but my immediate fury diminished as I observed her own reaction: she still seemed very much absorbed in the task of selecting oranges from the display in front of us and checking them for quality. When she finally noticed my own attention and my expression of shock, Regina simply shook her head and told me, "Don't worry. For us, that is normal."

The attempt made by Regina to console my anger at this display of overt racism towards her had the opposite effect. Her reassurance that such incidents are "normal" only reassured me that racist "governor" mentalities continue to maintain salience in the worldviews of the Australian public. "Does it make you upset?" I asked her. "Of course," she responded:

> Before I came to this country, I had never even met someone from Sudan. Not one. And here, people—white people—just think we are all the same. But I can't get sad because of this. If I did, I would be sad all the time.

Regina's casual acceptance of verbal harassment toward her expresses the ordinariness of everyday racisms in Australia. As I have described elsewhere (Ramsay 2017b), this public harassment expresses more than just an individual attitude towards the visible presence of a non-white person, however. Specifically instructing Regina to "go back to Sudan" expresses specific dynamics of the kinds of racisms that circulate more broadly in Australia, which are specifically directed at non-white refugees from Africa. The conflation of her blackness with a "Sudanese" ethnicity, which in itself reveals a problematic misconception about the salience of that label as a national identity, suggests that overwhelmingly negative media attention toward refugee settlers born in what is now South Sudan has filtered into public consciousness (Baak 2011; Due 2008; Nolan, Farquharson, Politoff, and Marjoribanks 2011; Nunn 2010; Windle 2008). The specifically "Sudanese" refugee has become condensed, in the public imaginary in Australia, into the central symbolic figure of refugee migration from Africa. This means that the particularities of national, ethnic, cultural, and personal backgrounds that refugees who originate from continental Africa embody are ignored in popular understandings in Australia.

When Regina refers to the ways in which the Australians she meets treat non-white refugees from Africa as "all the same," she is articulating annoyance at being categorised by an ethnic assumption made purely on the basis of her blackness. This assumption of homogeneity on the basis of skin colour—reproduced not only in the day-to-day experiences of the refugees I conducted fieldwork with but also normalised in the rhetoric of politicians at the highest level of political representation in Australia, as was done by Kevin Andrews in 2007 when reducing the intake of refugees to be resettled in Australia from Africa—is a direct form of racialisation.

Colonial racism

When combined with the reduction of Regina to a particular national identity based entirely on the colour of her skin, the statement "Go back to Sudan" works to racialise her in a way that reflects an assumption of white authority, in which those who are non-white are opened up to being regulated and policed by those who claim authority over Australian nationhood simply because they exist in public space (Hage 1998; Noble 2005; Noble and Poynting 2008). Whether those persons who called out the verbal abuse to Regina can themselves be considered white is peripheral: the authority of whiteness is implied in the statement. Although Regina reacted to her public vilification with casual acceptance, her seemingly calm response to marginalisation has been built up over years of exposure to racism.

Refugees do not begin their settlement in Australia with the expectation that they will become targets of racism. For the refugees I conducted fieldwork with, this realisation of their otherness was generally triggered by particular encounters in which the assumptions of difference that are attached to them are exposed, often in spectacular ways. They experience what Ghassan Hage (2010) refers to as mis-interpellation. This is a kind of racism that involves two intertwined processes. Firstly, the racialised people are interpellated, that is, made to believe that they belong to a collectivity, such as a nation. By providing refugees with permanent residency and the eventual opportunity for citizenship, the resettlement programme implies an equivalent status between resettled refugees and Australian citizens. However, this civic recognition does not automatically equate to social belonging in the ways that refugees empirically experience their resettlement in Australia (Dhanji 2009; Fozdar and Hartley 2013). Refugees nonetheless begin their resettlement immediately as permanent residents, that is, as potential citizens who are structurally interpellated into Australian society. Over time, however, the visible difference that refugees embody to the dominant white population can mean that they become confronted with incidents of racism that seemingly contradict the interpellation implied by the resettlement programme. Upon becoming aware of the difference that is encoded into their blackness through racist encounters, the "symbolic order brutally reminds [refugees] that they are not part of everyone" (Hage 2010: 211): that their resettlement in Australia and interpellation into the structural order of citizenship does not guarantee their social inclusion. This is what Hage (2010) considers to be a process of mis-interpellation.

These moments, in which the mis-interpellation of non-white African refugees is realised and reinforced, came up periodically in my fieldwork. Visiting Christina one afternoon, I asked her how she was experiencing her recent relocation from a metropolitan area to a rural town some ten hours away. I had driven out to visit her and her family, interested to find out how the experience of everyday life in Australia differed for resettled refugees between urban and regional contexts.

"Do you like it here?" I asked her. Shaking her head, Christina replied, "No, it was better before." She told me that her primary motivation to relocate had be the lure of employment opportunities on local farms. Since moving, however, she had found that the farming work was erratic, involved long hours, and was physically draining. But there were additional problems:

compared to her previous metropolitan location, in the rural area, there was less opportunity to take up educational courses and less support services for migrants and obtaining familiar African foods and goods entailed a four-hour drive to the nearest major city. Compounding these practical difficulties, Christina also told me, "Here, people are more racist."

To explain what she meant, Christina told me that when she first arrived in her new rural city, she had begun to visit surrounding neighbours to introduce herself and her family. The neighbours were generally very welcoming. Soon, she even found herself considering these new neighbours her friends. But her relationship with them soured after they gave Christina a nickname in reference to the colour of her skin, which she found offensive: "Chocolate." "That never happened to me before," she told me. "Here, I am called Chocolate."

Even if the neighbours had meant for the nickname "Chocolate" to be playful, the experience shocked Christina. The nickname made her immediately aware that others were attaching an assumption of difference to her on the basis of her skin colour. In Australia, nicknames can often be an indicator of mateship and belonging: attributes that speak to that core value of egalitarianism that is supposedly at the centre of the "Australian way of life" (Johnson 2007). But nicknames and joking in Australia often serve to create connectedness by bringing people into a shared community of ridicule, in which the egalitarianism of mateship is always ambiguous because the supposedly casual and lighthearted racialisations through which connectedness are forged also demarcate assumptions of innate difference (Hage 2014: 234–235): it is only shifts in tone that signal whether the intention of the label is to marginalise or cement mateship. Through such ambiguity, racist nicknames come to do both. Racialised nicknames are one example of the ways in which non-white migrants and refugees can become mis-interpellated in Australia (Ramsay 2017b), reflecting how experiences of social inclusion and exclusion into Australian society, broadly, are inextricably intertwined for these refugees.

Other encounters recounted to me by women I conducted fieldwork with presented more extreme examples of the kinds of innate difference and incommensurability that are attached to them. For example, another woman I got to know, Louise, described to me the time when she had been referred to as a "monkey." She told me that she had been walking in a shopping centre when a woman and a child had walked up beside her. Upon noticing her, the little boy had stopped and pointed at her, saying, "Look mummy, a monkey!"

"He didn't even know I was a person," Louise said:

> I am a human, too, just like him. He thought I was some kind of ancestor, walking the earth, not on the same level. The mother tried to shush him, but I do not know, I felt like the mother might have felt the same as her did: why did he choose to call me a monkey? The mum spoke to

> me. She said, 'Hello, how are you?' so I said, 'Hello, how are you' back. I looked at the little boy and I said, 'You are beautiful.' He pointed back at me and said, 'Look, mummy, the monkey speaks!'

Even though the comments were directed at her by a child, Louise had never before thought of herself as so incommensurably different from others that she could be considered non-human. This experience of mis-interpellation, of the realisation of exclusion, reflects the powerful "Look, a Negro" passage in the work *Black Skins, White Masks* by Franz Fanon (1968). In that passage, Fanon (1968) recalls the moment when his humanity became fundamentally called into question after migrating to France:

> "Look, a Negro!" The circle was drawing a bit tighter. I made no secret of my amusement.
>
> "Mama, see the Negro! I'm frightened!" Frightened! Frightened! Now they were beginning to be afraid of me. I made up my mind to laugh myself to tears, but the laughter became impossible...
>
> I existed triply: I occupied space... I was responsible at the same time for my body, for my race, for my ancestors. I subjected myself to objective examination, I discovered my blackness, my ethnic characteristics; and I was battered down by tom-toms, cannibalism, intellectual deficiency, fetishism, racial defects, slave-ships...
>
> (Fanon 1968: 112)

The passage by Fanon (1968) reflects what Hage (2010) characterises as an experience of mis-interpellation, in which the hierarchies of racial superiority and inferiority that are implicit structures of everyday life in Western nations come to be realised in encounters in which those who are oppressed are explicitly dehumanised. Experiences of racism dehumanise in ways that can lead those targeted to call into question what had formerly been assumptions of their own humanity. It is not necessarily the shock of being called a "monkey," as experienced by Louise, or a "negro," as experienced by Fanon (1968), that ruptures their assumption of shared humanity. Rather, it is the tacit acceptance of these derogatory labels that shocks. The causal acceptance by others peripherally involved in such processes of dehumanisation solidifies the normality of hierarchies of racial difference, in which blackness implicitly encodes a person with assumptions of deficiency.

Such mentalities of racial stratification reflect a colonial mindset, and have shaped both historical and contemporaneous dynamics of racism in Australia. Racism was not only central to the founding of Australia as a colony of the British empire on land occupied by Indigenous peoples but continues to inform public and political attitudes and actions that stem from it. Of course, racism is never a static or uniform attitude of hierarchisation on the basis of physical attributes (Hage 2014). Australian racism towards the non-white other, and specifically towards migrants, has both shifted and maintained continuities since the federation of the country in 1901, generally in response to new waves of migrant populations entering and settling in the country (Jupp 2002). In a review of historical and contemporary formations of racism in Australia, Ghassan Hage (2014) characterises two forms of dominant racist attitudes. The first, numerological racism, is a racism of numbers in the sense that the attitude may be expressed with tolerance or sympathy towards the targeted group but will finish with the sentiment that "too many" people from a specific group will overrun the country and damage the dominant culture and "Australian way of life." The second, existential racism, is more direct and stems from an attitude of extreme dehumanisation: the target of the racialisation is perceived as so incommensurably different that the reaction to them is disgust and an absolute inability to relate to them as a fellow human being. Hage (2014) considers that although most dominant expressions of racism in Australia since the influx of post-Second World War migration have reflected numerological racism, the other more existential and dehumanising kind of racism, which can be characterised as a "racism of disgust," has become prominent in recent years, specifically in response to new populations of non-white migrants from Africa who have been settled in the country over the past two decades.

This upsurge of existential racism in Australia derives, according to Hage (2014: 233), from the persistence of a colonial imaginary in Australia. Hage (2014) describes how the targeting of new African migrants in Australia with these kinds of existential racisms "probably has to do with the complex ways in which the racist English colonial imaginary of Africa and India has seeped into White Australian culture as part of its cultural inheritance." The pervasive racialisation of women I conducted fieldwork with in Australia as incommensurably different and deficient reflects, I consider, this colonial imaginary: it is a "colonial racism" based on internalised and seemingly naturalised attitudes of racial superiority.

Resettlement as a civilising process

These colonial racisms are not isolated from other dynamics of stratification, including gender. Racist discourses of colonial power were historically, and continue to be contemporaneously, realised through segregations, subjugations, and inferiorisations that solidify and reproduce economies of gendered and racialised difference (Bhabha 1996; Stoler 2002). Describing how, historically, white European settlers in Dutch colonies interacted with populations in Indonesia, Ann Laura Stoler (2002) describes how local women were exploited as domestic servants. In those roles, women were expected to provide care for a household. At the same time, however, the difference and inferiority attached to local women meant that they were also imagined to be a danger to the children of colonisers in terms of both physical health and moral development. According to Stoler (1989, 2002), the dangerous non-white mother is a trope that manifests across broad colonial contexts. That figure also continues to hold salience in Australia and significantly organises and controls the lives of the refugees I conducted fieldwork with. Even though African-born peoples have assumptions of inferiority and deficiency attached to them broadly in Australia, women in particular evoke particular reactions of distrust: especially around motherhood.

Many women I got to know during fieldwork had social workers become involved in their lives, particularly around issues related to child and family welfare. It was during encounters between women I conducted fieldwork with and social welfare workers that I witnessed a specific modality of governance being imposed on these women: one in which they were made into subjects of domestication. One afternoon, I was present when a worker who provided settlement support to a participant, Solange, visited her at home. Solange's children had just returned home from school. As she was talking with the worker, Solange began to prepare a meal to feed her children. Doing so, she opened a large tin of tuna and placed it on the ground. The children sat around the tin, and began to use their hands to scoop out the fish and eat.

An intervention ensued. The worker immediately went to the children, picked up the tin, and placed the food on a nearby table. Without directly addressing Solange, who stood nearby, the worker told the children to wash their hands after they had finished their shared meal of tuna from a can as if, somehow, the imagined savagery of the act could be eliminated by hand-washing. When we spoke afterwards, Solange told me that watching the worker preside over her children had made her feel "like I was not a parent." When I was alone with the worker after this visit, I asked why they had moved the meal from the ground to a table. "They were eating like animals," I was told.

It was impossible for me to know the individual motivations that the worker, who may not have personally intended to patronise Solange, ascribed to this encounter. Nonetheless, comparing people to "animals" is a way to dehumanise. The comparison also evokes racial connotations in terms of the colonial trope of black African peoples' being associated with savagery, primitivism, and animalistic behaviours (Apter 1999; Bonsu 2009). Whatever the intent, the experience produced a specifically racialised and gendered effect on Solange, who felt that her authority as a mother had been dismissed on the basis of a reaction to racialised difference. When analysed as an encounter of institutionalised logics of whiteness and reactions to practices of cultural difference, the interaction between the social worker and Solange expresses "racism of disgust" (Hage 2014), that is, an existential racism in which it is the very humanity of the racialised subject that is in question.

During another encounter with a worker from a social welfare agency, I observed similar processes of dehumanisation that, regardless of whether they were intended by workers themselves to be racialised, nonetheless reproduced a colonial imaginary of African savagery that played into a colonial racism of disgust. In a meeting with a worker from a social welfare agency, Camille expressed concern over the way the skin of her children had become dry and brittle, which she attributed both to the climate of Australia and their new living situation, in which she had been separated from them and unable to care for them. After this conversation, Camille turned away to attend to the children. The worker and I stood together, alone.

"It is interesting, you know," the worker then said, turning to me. "I would not have thought she would be so concerned about their skin. I figured that, in Africa, they probably didn't have soap." The worker quickly qualified this statement by saying, "You know, because they were so poor in the camps and everything."

Having only met Camille that day, the worker knew nothing about the past experiences Camille had lived through except that she was a resettled in Australia as a refugee. That limited knowledge had been enough for the worker to consider that Camille and her family were ignorant of norms about hygiene and cleanliness. Catching what must have been my incredulous expression, the worker quickly tried to qualify the original statement by making a vague statement about what they assumed to be the general impoverishment of everyday life in a refugee camp. Nonetheless, the initial comment had evoked a common trope of colonial racism in which the racialised African subject is imagined as unclean, unhygienic, and savage (Bonsu 2009): as, ultimately, less civilised than the colonial ruler (Stoler 1997, 2002).

From these and other encounters, I came to observe that the resettlement of refugees in Australia can be understood as a "civilising process." Describing how notions of cleanliness, manners, and orderly conduct became crucial to post-enlightenment formations of governmentality, Norbert Elias (1978) considered that intersecting ideals of hygiene and personal order during this period became societal aspirations through a "civilising process." These ideals of hygiene and personal order became normalised and internalised as techniques of self-regulation through which marginalised populations, in particular, could be governed and subjugated: marked as different from those with more capacity to maintain those ideals. The effect was to diffuse and decentralise the control of populations through direct intervention by reproducing the normalcy of class hierarchy through markers of personal control, orderliness, and domesticity.

Attaching such assumptions of deficiency to African women reflects, then, specifically "colonial" attitudes in which racism and gender intersect into a general distrust and dehumanisation of non-white women. These dynamics of seemingly automatic racialisation and routine intervention made women I conducted fieldwork with feel surveilled and vulnerable: as if they were already marked as problems. As one woman told me, while discussing how social welfare institutions seemed to her to especially target refugee settlers like herself, "They look at us like we are bad parents."

Becoming problems

> I'm recognising the problem. Many people have recognised the problem. I'm not proposing to apologise for saying what people are concerned about.
>
> (Kevin Andrews, cited in AAP 2007)

These comments, spoken by Kevin Andrews in response to inquiries about the drastic reduction of resettlement placements being made available to refugees from Africa, speak to the core issue that the refugees I conducted fieldwork with were confronted with upon being resettled in Australia. These refugees were immediately made into "problematic" citizens by virtue of assumptions of deficiency that are attached to non-white people in Australia. The resettlement of refugees from Africa begins with this basis of problematisation, meaning that when refugees attempt to recreate the regenerative potential of their lives in resettlement, they are constantly negotiating societal structures that already encode them as burdens in need of intervention.

The core purpose of the resettlement programme that is operationalised through the UNHCR is to provide refugees with an opportunity for permanent residency (UNHCR 2011a)—that is, a stable basis of national identification and legal protection—thereby resolving the politico-legal ambiguity of the "refugee" as a stateless person whose protection and rights fall under international conventions rather than national frameworks. But providing refugees with a national identity following resettlement does not automatically equate to resolving what is an existential sense of displacement that cannot be essentialised to politico-legal ambiguity. In Australia, where resettled refugees are provided with permanent residency and, eventually, the opportunity for full citizenship, this process comes with the expectation that refugees will not only follow legal parameters of residency in Australia but that they will conform to what are implicit cultural and social norms that correspond with an imaginary "Australian way of life." Because these norms are grounded in a heritage of colonial attitudes that reinforce ideas of racial superiority and inferiority, non-white refugees from Africa enter into this context of cultural citizenship (Ong 1996) in Australia with a disadvantage: their skin colour already encodes them with assumptions of deficiency from which they are automatically rendered in public and political attitudes and imaginaries as "problems."

How does this seemingly automatic problematisation of non-white refugees from Africa, whose cultural citizenship in Australia is ambiguous, effect the lives of women from Central Africa whose primary imperative in life is cosmological regeneration? As I describe in the chapter that follows, the programme of resettlement in Australia resolves the politico-legal ambiguity of refugees but does not automatically translate into social conditions in which the refugees can feel free to create the kinds of futures they imagined for themselves prior to their being resettled. When considered as an existential sense of security, rather than a purely politico-legal status of protection, the refuge that is assumed to be provided to refugees who are resettled in Australia is not automatically crystallised at the point of their new residency status. Attempting instead to negotiate the implicit expectations of cultural citizenship that are attached to the settlement and acceptance of migrants and refugees in Australia, the refuge that is provided through resettlement must be seen as conditional.

References

AAP. 2007. Andrews Takes a Swipe at Migrants After Bashing. Sydney Morning Herald 12 October 2007. Available at: www.smh.com.au/news/national/andrews-takes-swipe-at-migrants-after-bashing/2007/10/11/1191696079744.html (Accessed 30 November 2015).

ABC. 2007. Australia Closes Door to African Refugees. The World Today Radio Broadcast. Available at: www.abc.net.au/worldtoday/content/2007/s2049830.htm (Accessed 27 January 2017).

Apter, A. 1999. Africa, Empire, and Anthropology: A Philological Exploration of Anthropology's Heart of Darkness. *Annual Review of Anthropology* 28: 577–598.

Baak, M. 2011. Murder, Community Talk, and Belonging: An Exploration of Sudanese Community Responses to Murder in Australia. *African Identities* 9(4): 417–434.

Bhabha, H. 1996. The Other Question: Difference, Discrimination, and the Discourse of Colonialism. *Black British Cultural Studies: A Reader*. H.A. Baker, M. Diawara, and R.H. Lindeborg (Eds.), pp. 87–105. Chicago, IL; London: The University of Chicago Press.

Bonsu, S.K. 2009. Colonial Images in Global Times: Consumer Interpretations of Africa and Africans in Advertising. *Consumption Markets & Cultures* 12(1): 1–25.

Bruck, T. and Schindler, K. 2009. The Impact of Violent Conflicts on Households: What Do We Know and What Should We Know about War Widows? *Oxford Development Studies* 37(3): 289–309.

Colic-Peisker, V. 2005. 'At Least You're the Right Colour': Identity and Social Inclusion of Bosnian Refugees in Australia. *Journal of Ethnic and Migration Studies* 31(4): 615–638.

Cox, E. 2016. Concealment, Revelation, and Masquerade in Europe's Asylum Apparatus: Intimate Life at the Border. *Lateral: Journal of the Cultural Studies Association* 5(2). Available at: http://csalateral.org/issue/5-2/concealment-revelation-masquerade-europe-asylum-cox/ (Accessed 23 December 2016).

Devisch, R. 1993. *Weaving the Threads of Life: The Khita gyn-eco-logical Healing Cult among the Yaka*. London: The University of Chicago Press.

Dhanji, S., 2010. Social or Unsocial? The Linkage between Accommodation, Health and Well-Being among Former Horn of Africa and Sudanese Refugees Living in Australia. *Australian Review of African Studies* 31(1): 106–136.

Dove, E.S. 2013. Back to Blood: The Sociopolitics and Law of Compulsory DNA Testing of Refugees. *University of Massachusetts Law Review* 8(2): 466–530.

Dryenfurth, N. 2005. Battlers, Refugees, and the Republic: John Howard's Language of Citizenship. *Journal of Australian Studies* 28(84): 183–196.

Due, C. 2008. 'Who are Strangers?': Absorbing Sudanese Refugees into a White Australia. *ACRWSA* 4(1): 1–13.

Dyer, R. 2007. *White*. London: Routledge.

Elias, N. 1978. *The Civilizing Process*. Oxford: Blackwell.

Erikson, T.H. 2002. *Ethnicity and Nationalism: Anthropological Perspectives*. London; Boulder, CO: Pluto Press.

Fanon, F., 1968. *Black Skin, White Masks*. Translated by C.L. Markmann. London: MacGibbon & Kee.

Farouque, F., Petrie, A., and Miletic, D. 2007. Minister Cuts African Intake. *The Age*, 2 October 2007. Available at: www.theage.com.au/articles/2007/10/01/1191091031242.html (Accessed 16 January 2017).

Feldman-Savelsberg, P. 1999. *Plundered Kitchens, Empty Wombs: Threatened Reproduction and Identity in the Cameroon Grasslands.* Ann Arbor: The University of Michigan Press.

Fozdar, F. and Hartley, L., 2013. Civic and Ethno Belonging among Recent Refugees to Australia. *Journal of Refugee Studies,* 27(1): 126–144.

Ganti, T. 2014. Neoliberalism. *Annual Review of Anthropology* 43: 89–104.

Gelber, K. 2003. A Fair Queue? Australian Public Discourse on Refugees and Immigration. *Journal of Australian Studies* 27(77): 23–30.

Goldstein, D. 2012. Decolonialising 'Actually Existing Neoliberalism.' *Social Anthropology* 20(3): 304–309.

Hage, G. 1998. *White Nation: Fantasies of White Supremacy in a Multicultural Society.* Sydney: Pluto Press.

Hage, G., 2010. The Affective Politics of Racial Mis-Interpellation. *Theory, Culture & Society* 27(7–8): 112–129.

Hage, G., 2014. Continuity and Change in Australian Racism. *Journal of Intercultural Studies* 35(3): 232–237.

Harrison, F. 1995. The Persistent Power of "Race" in the Cultural and Political Economy of Racism. *Annual Review of Anthropology* 24: 47–74.

Harvey, D. 2005. *A Brief History of Neoliberalism.* Oxford: Oxford University Press.

Heater, D. 2013. *What is Citizenship?* Hoboken, NJ: John Wiley & Sons.

Heinemann, T., Helén, I., Lemke, T., and Naue, U., 2016. *Suspect Families: DNA Analysis, Family Reunification and Immigration Policies.* London: Routledge.

Jessop, B. 2013. Putting Neoliberalism in its Time and Place: A Response to the Debate. *Social Anthropology* 21(1): 65–74.

Johnson, C. 2007. John Howard's 'Values' and Australian Identity. *Australian Journal of Political Science* 42(2): 195–209.

Jupp, J. 2002. *From White Australia to Woomera: The Story of Australian Immigration.* New York; Port Melbourne, VIC: Cambridge University Press.

McKay, F., Thomas, S., and Kneebone, S. 2012. 'It Would Be Okay if they Came Through the Proper Channels': Community Perceptions and Attitudes Towards Asylum Seekers in Australia. *Journal of Refugee Studies* 25(1): 113–133.

Mercer, D. 2010. 'Citizen Minus'?: Indigenous Australians and the Citizenship Question. *Citizenship Studies* 7(4): 421–445.

Muehlebach, A. 2012. *The Moral Neoliberal: Welfare and Citizenship in Italy.* Chicago, IL: The University of Chicago Press.

Noble, G. 2005. The Discomfort of Strangers: Racism, Incivility and Ontological Security in a Relaxed and Comfortable Nation. *Journal of Intercultural Studies* 26(1–2): 107–120.

Noble, G. and Poynting, S. 2008. Neither Relaxed nor Comfortable: The Affective Regulation of Migrant Belonging in Australia. *Critical Geopolitics and Everyday Life.* R. Pain and S.J. Smith Fear (Eds.), pp. 129–138. Hampshire: Ashgate.

Nolan, D., Farquharson, K., Politoff, V., and Marjoribanks, T. 2011. Mediated Multiculturalism: Newspaper Representations of Sudanese Migrants in Australia. *Journal of Intercultural Studies* 32(6): 655–671.

Nunn, C., 2010. Spaces to Speak: Challenging Representations of Sudanese-Australians. *Journal of Intercultural Studies* 31(2): 183–198.

Ong, A. 1996. Cultural Citizenship as Subject-Making: Immigrants Negotiate Racial and Cultural Boundaries in the United States. *Current Anthropology* 37(5): 737–762.

Ong, A. 2003. *Buddha is Hiding: Refugees, Citizenship, the New America*. Berkeley: University of California Press.

Ong, A. 2006. *Neoliberalism as Exception: Mutations in Citizenship and Sovereignty*. Durham, NC; London: Duke University Press.

Oyewumi, O. 2000. Family Bonds/Conceptual Binds: African Notes on Feminist Epistemologies. *Signs* 25(4): 1093–1098.

Perera, S. 2009. *Australia and the Insular Imagination: Beaches, Borders, Boats, and Bodies*. New York: Palgrave Macmillan.

Pickering, S. 2001. Common Sense and Original Deviancy: News Discourses and Asylum Seekers in Australia. *Journal of Refugee Studies* 14(2): 169–186.

Povinelli, E. 2011. *Economies of Abandonment: Social Belonging and Endurance in Late Liberalism*. Durham, NC; London: Duke University Press.

Ramsay, G. 2017b. A Civilising Process: Colonial Legacies of Racism Toward Central African Refugee Women Resettled in Australia. *Journal of Intercultural Studies* 38(2): 170–188.

Sánchez-Céspedes, L. 2016. The Consequences of Armed Conflict on Household Composition. *Oxford Development Studies*, 1–27. doi:10.1080/13600818.2016.1213798.

Schech, S. and Haggis, J. 2001. Migrancy, Multiculturalism and Whiteness: Re-charting Core Identities in Australia. *Communal/Plural* 9(2): 143–159.

Silva, S. 2009. Mothers of Solitude: Childlessness and Intersubjectivity in the Upper Zambezi. *Anthropology and Humanism* 34(2): 179–202.

Stoler, A. 1989. Rethinking Colonial Categories: European Communities and the Boundaries of Rule. *Comparative Studies in Society and History* 31(1): 134–161.

Stoler, A. 1997. Making Empire Respectable: The Politics of Race and Sexual Morality in Twentieth-Century Colonial Cultures. *Cultural Politics* 11: 344–373.

Stoler, A. 2002. *Carnal Knowledge and Imperial Power: Race and the Intimate in Colonial Rule*. Berkeley: University of California Press.

UNHCR. 2011a. UNHCR Resettlement Handbook. Available at: www.unhcr.org/46f7c0ee2.html (Accessed 12 November 2016).

UNHCR. 2016. Australia: Country Chapter—UNHCR Resettlement Handbook. Available at: www.unhcr.org/en-au/protection/resettlement/3c5e542d4/unhcr-resettlement-handbook-country-chapter-australia.html (Accessed 2 February 2017).

Visweswaran, K. 1998. Race and the Culture of Anthropology. *American Anthropologist* 100(1): 70–83.

Werbner, P. 1998. Exoticising Citizenship: Anthropology and the New Citizenship Debate. *Canberra Anthropology* 21(2): 1–27.

Wilmsen, B. 2011. Family Separation: The Policies, Procedures, and Consequences for Refugee Background Families. *Refugee Survey Quarterly* 30(1): 44–64.

Windle, J. 2008. The Racialisation of African Youth in Australia. *Social Identities: Journal for the Study of Race, Nation and Culture* 14(5): 553–566.

7 Friction and temporal discordance

"I thought, when we came here, that this would be a new life," Maria told me as we sat together on the veranda at the front her house in a suburban Australian neighbourhood, drinking tea. "But the life is different," she went on, "it is not easy."

"In what ways?" I asked her, taking another sip of tea. I had been conducting fieldwork with resettled refugees for a few months by that point of my research. Having observed, by then, numerous instances of hardship as refugees struggled to cope with unexpected problems that surfaced upon their being settled in Australia, I found myself unsurprised that Maria was being so critical about her experience of resettlement.

"Pressure, pressure, always pressure," she responded. "Sometimes I think it would be easier to stay in Africa. The life here is not good."

How is it possible for refugees to move from an imaginary of resettlement in which the possibility of migrating to Australia is viewed as an opportunity for a "new life" to being so critical of resettlement that they would even consider that remaining in Africa could have been a better option? The experience of resettlement is not, it seems, as singularly positive as so many refugees imagine it to be prior to being resettled. Refugees in Australia continue to endure a sense of existential displacement long after their migration. As I observed it, this sense of displacement endures because the organisation of everyday life in Australia, through neoliberal logics of individualisation, does not correspond to their own cosmological logics of regeneration and sociality. This means that, when trying to create the new lives of possibility in Australia that they imagined prior to being resettled, their attempts to do so are constrained.

The Australian government provides one of the most extensive programmes of settlement support to resettled refugees in the world. Resettled refugees receive intensive case management upon arriving in Australia, whereby they are supported for at least the first six months following their migration by government-funded settlement service providers, who develop a package of services that are tailored to meet the specific needs of each refugee (DSS 2017). These services include the following: access to both immediate and longer-term accommodation; provision of basic household goods and an initial outlay of food; assistance with registering with the national health care system and other health services, setting up bank accounts, and enrolling children in local schools and adults in a free English language programme; and support with registering and receiving public benefit payments from Centrelink.[1] After this period of intensive casework support, resettled refugees are then transitioned into more general, but still refugee-specific, support programmes and services that are available to assist refugees for up to five years after being settled in Australia. Resettled refugees also have access to broader public support systems that are available to all permanent residents in Australia, such as Centrelink, the public health care and education system, public welfare benefits, and social support services. With refugees receiving this suite of settlement-specific services and being able to access the services of more general public welfare institutions, it is clear that the system of support that is made available to refugees who are resettled in Australia is extensive.

The effect of this intensive and highly interventionist system of refugee support, however, is that refugees come to be hitherto treated as problems. Directing resettled refugees into these public services immediately upon their arrival can serve to set up a hierarchical dynamic of power and control between refugees and the institutional actors within the organisations that provide support: a relationship dynamic that persists and continues to define how refugees are treated long after the period of intensive support that is provided to them after their initial arrival in Australia ceases.

The programme of settlement support that is made available to refugees who are resettled in Australia is designed, according to the programme's description in the UNHCR Resettlement Handbook, to assist refugees to become "self-reliant and to participate equitably in society" (UNHCR 2016: 13). This statement reveals a key assumption that is embedded in what it means to be an "equitable" member of Australian society. Namely, that the worth and value of societal membership is measured according to a member's ability to be "self-reliant," that is, to demonstrate economic productivity. The services that are provided to assist refugees upon their arrival in Australia exist not only to support the welfare of resettled refugees, then. These services also introduce them to this sociocultural context of neoliberalism, in which the worth of people is individualised and measured by their market value.

Refugees enter Australia as marked subjects: defined by assumptions of deficiency, racialised by colonial logics of inferiority, and situated as problems in need of intervention. The suite of services that are provided to refugees upon their settlement in Australia support their welfare and well-being but also work as disciplining structures through which refugees are supposed to learn and internalise dominant logics of economic productivity that guide how societal membership is valued in Australia. But this emphasis on individual productivity, as measured in economic terms, does not correspond to the cosmological logics of regeneration that guide how the refugees I got to know during fieldwork approach and organise their everyday lives following resettlement. Being resettled in Australia does not, then, necessarily create conditions in which refugees can create and regenerate new life. Rather, resettlement can produce instances of cosmological friction through which the ontological security of refugees is gradually undermined and made precarious, creating new potentialities and lived realities of existential displacement.

Barriers to equity

"That is the life here," one woman, Martha, told me. "Appointment, appointment, appointment." Because the services that provide support to refugees are numerous but highly bureaucratised, the everyday life of resettled refugees often becomes, as Martha suggests, dominated by what can feel like an endless series of meetings, appointments, and other obligations. Without meeting the seemingly endless requirements of these institutions, refugees risk having crucial mechanisms of support, including access to public welfare payments, suspended or withdrawn. Rather than supporting refugees to meet these bureaucratic obligations in an equitable way, however, I observed during fieldwork that many of the organisations that provide services to refugees approach their particular needs with rigidity and an unwillingness to compromise, seeming to purposely ignore the specific barriers that refugees face when attempting to equitably access services and support in Australia. Paradoxically, by ignoring the specific barriers that refugees face when attempting to live independently, those services set them up to fail at achieving that independence. What I came to understand to be the rationale for this seemingly counter-intuitive approach to supporting refugees is that, by being purposely inflexible to the specific needs of refugee clients, these institutions impose a self-reliance model of civic life onto resettled refugees through a "sink or swim" approach. This observation reflects what Lena Dominelli (2014: 80–81) considers to be a general trend in Western welfare states to dismantle universal support services by making self-sufficiency a requirement of access, even when those who are marginalised and often most in need of services are those who are also most likely to be excluded from the labour market and in need of extra support to be self-sufficient.

The mandate of the public institutions through which resettled refugees in Australia receive support, and many of the individual workers within them, are well intentioned and aim to provide care for refugees. To care, however, is not a neutral act with a singularly humanitarian objective. As Elizabeth Povinelli (2011: 160) describes, "to care for others is to make a claim," that is, "to care is to embody an argument what a good life is and how such a good life comes into being." The kind of "good life" that is promoted by the institutions that provide care to refugees is that in which the value of people is measured by demonstrations of self-reliance and displays of economic productivity. Subsequently, the ideal kind of existence that is promoted through public institutions in Australia is that in which, paradoxically, the removal of care can itself be construed as an act of caring. In order for refugees to become familiar with expectations of self-reliance, support must be withdrawn so that they can learn how to survive independently. Strategically withdrawing intensive support can be especially harmful to refugees, however, because they often experience a number of barriers to accessing services and support in Australia in an equitable way. Difficulties related to language proficiency, literacy, transport, unfamiliarity with bureaucracies, and a lack of extensive social support networks all make access to public services especially complicated for refugees.

Language proficiency and a lack of literacy was a major barrier to feeling settled for the refugees I got to know in Australia. Upon first arriving in Australia, few refugees, especially women, are familiar enough with the English language to communicate confidently. Following resettlement to Australia, refugees, and indeed most migrants, are automatically eligible to receive 510 hours of adult English language tuition. Every refugee I came to know during fieldwork had participated in this tuition, and I observed that most refugees were proficient in spoken English and comprehension after a couple of years of being settled in Australia, especially if they had taken most of the free tuition. Still, I was astounded by the capacity of so many women I worked with, illiterate in their own language as well as in English, to maintain a complex schedule of appointments and meetings, bus timetables and public transport routes through only memorising them.

Transport was another barrier to equitably accessing services. In the two Australian states in which I conducted the majority of my fieldwork, obtaining a driver's licence requires learner drivers to accrue 120 hours of driving practice that has been supervised by an experienced driver who has held a licence for many years. To obtain a licence, then, resettled refugees must find an experienced driver to supervise them, which is often difficult in their own networks of newly settling refugees, or pay upwards of $40 AUD an hour to receive supervision from a professional driving instructor. Factoring in the expense of a car itself and the associated upkeep, it is clear that accessing independent transport is often prohibitive for refugees resettled in Australia, especially for those who are newly arrived.

Those refugees who did manage to obtain a licence and a car would often become immediate sources of support to many other resettled refugees who did not have the same scope of mobility. However, such expectations to provide transport assistance and help to others put a lot of pressure on the relations of what were often newly forming community networks and friendships. At the time I conducted fieldwork, many of the women I got to know had husbands or partners who had obtained a licence and a car, but they themselves were still in the process of attaining a means of independent transport. Often attending to their own schedule first, husbands and partners were not always available to take members of their family and others to appointments and meetings. So, women generally still relied on the slow and often unreliable networks of public transport in their local regions. One morning, as I observed one of the women I conducted fieldwork with at 7 a.m. pushing a two-seater pram onto a bus while holding the hand of another older child in order to attend a 9 a.m. appointment across town, I felt that it was wonder that these newly settling refugees managed to make it anywhere at all.

Governmentality and directed futures

The highly bureaucratised nature of public institutions in Australia was another significant barrier to the equitable access of services for women from a refugee background. With social welfare and employment agencies, public services, schools, and medical services all set up in ways that prioritise top-down decision making and pre-organised inflexible structures of interaction, the refugees I conducted fieldwork with struggled to make sense of what seemed, to them, to be highly inefficient and problematic systems of public engagement. For many, the only prior experience they had with a similar system of bureaucracy was the UNHCR, and the partner organisations associated with it, through which they had applied for resettlement and received humanitarian relief. With bureaucracy being associated with the UNHCR, many refugees felt a general sense of unease when engaging with public institutions upon being resettled in Australia. The memories of applying for resettlement and, for many, being treated as a probable "cheat" by having the veracity of their story of persecution and ongoing insecurity undermined many times (Thomson 2012), made this association of Australian bureaucracies with the UNHCR another barrier to participating in public life in Australia and the institutions through which public services are channelled. Most of the women I worked with seemed simultaneously exhausted and perplexed by the expectations placed on them through the public institutions within which their lives had become intertwined. Reporting, paperwork, and appointments dominated their everyday existences, and yet they had little opportunity to speak back to those institutions and take control of their own lives.

Indeed, as Catherine Besteman (2016: 217–219) describes in relation to research conducted with Somali Bantu refugees in the US, the theme of "control" often characterises interactions between resettled refugees and the workers from agencies that are supposed to provide them with services and support. In these hierarchical systems of refugee settlement in nations like the US and Australia, the supposed "bureaucratic incompetence" of refugees is not seen as an indicator of cultural difference but as a marker of deficiency, meaning that refugees are often approached a priori as problematic objects of policy rather than potentially meaningful agents engaged in the construction and success of public policy. The highly bureaucratised nature of everyday life in nations like Australia and the US and the contexts of social and cultural marginalisation within which these institutions are embedded can mean that resettled refugees often become objects of "bureaucratic containment and silencing" (Besteman 2016: 215).

Witnessing one of the women I got to know during fieldwork, Sima, interact with the Centrelink organisation, I got to observe directly one such incident of bureaucratic silencing. Sima needed to go to the Centrelink office to discuss her fortnightly welfare benefit, which was about to be cut off because the week before she had failed to declare her income. Because she did not have a computer at home, Sima was required to go directly to the Centrelink office each fortnight to use a computer there to declare her income. But the week before our visit to the office together she had been unable to declare her income in the usual way. Her daughter had fallen ill, and Sima had spent most of the week indoors caring for her. However, not declaring her income meant that her next payment was in jeopardy. If the payment was cut off, even for a week or so, Sima would be unable to pay her rent. This would not only mean that her current tenancy might be affected, but that the resulting bad tenancy ledger might prevent her from being considered for other rental properties in the future. Somewhat nervous, it seemed, Sima had asked me to accompany her to the office for personal support.

Sima and I had been waiting in the waiting area of the Centrelink office for about 20 minutes before the number she had been provided with upon entering the building was called up. After having her number called, Sima was directed to a cubicle desk. Together, we took seats facing the Centrelink worker who had been assigned to deal with her case. Beside the worker, who appeared to be a white, middle-aged woman, was a computer screen, which had Sima's information pulled up on it. Throughout the encounter, the worker barely drew her eyes away from the screen to make contact with either Sima or myself.

We began the appointment with Sima explaining the current situation, in which she had been unable to declare her fortnightly income due to being prevented from leaving the house in order to care for a sick child. The worker heard the story and nodded, then explained that the problem could be fixed. However, the worker added that the processing period for the necessarily information to go through the "system" could take up to 14 days. This meant that Sima would have to go without income for about a fortnight before a double payment would go through. Sima, visibly distressed, told the worker that she required the payment earlier: otherwise, she said, she would be unable to pay her rent. The worker repeated that the there was no way to negotiate the payment lapse in the immediate days.

Trying to reign in what appeared to be her increasing panic, Sima asked the worker, "You are a mother, yes?"

"That is not a concern," the worker replied.

"Are you a mother?" Sima repeated.

"Well," the worker finally conceded to the question, "well yes, I am." Sima's gaze immediately intensified.

"So," she said firmly, "you cannot do this. You are a mother. I am a mother too. I have children. I have to give them food. I have to keep the house. You are a mother."

Sima spoke these words as if expressing some kind of implicit expectation of mutual care that is automatically embodied through what she imagined to be a collective experience of motherhood. It seemed that Sima expected the worker to relate to her on the mutual basis of motherhood and, in doing so, to find a way to negotiate the bureaucratic problem of the lapsed payment. In response to this appeal, the worker appeared to be genuinely apologetic, saying, "I am very sorry. There is nothing I can do from here."

"But you are a *mother*," Sima interrupted, emphasising the last word.

"If you go back to the front counter you could use the phones to try and arrange an emergency payment in the meantime," the worker went on, all business once again. "I cannot do that from here. You will need to make the call. But it is late in the afternoon and the branch will be closing in the next hour, and it may take longer than that. You would benefit from coming back tomorrow to organise the payment."

We left the Centrelink office unable to solve the problem of the suspended payment. Sima was extremely distressed at the impending financial crisis. However, that was not the direct focus of her shock as we left the office together. Walking out the door, Sima turned to me to say, "These Australians are bad people. They pretend to be mothers, but they are not."

The encounter between Sima and the Centrelink office stood out during my fieldwork as a particularly salient example of the disciplining effects of public institutions in Australia, which guide resettled refugees into becoming particular kinds of citizens. Grounded in routine, inflexible to context, and marked by emotional distance, the encounter between Sima and the Centrelink worker can be viewed as a product of what Michael Hertzfeld (1992) has characterised as the "social production of indifference." This characterisation is used by Hertzfeld (1992) to describe how the rationality of public bureaucratic institutions masks what is a heavily symbolic and socially emotive form of moral policing. These institutions are, according to Hertzfeld (1992), driven towards implicitly reinforcing ideals of individualism and entrepreneurialism. However, this means that when citizens who are engaged within such institutions do not meet the expectations of neoliberal self-sufficiency that are embedded within those encounters, their failure to do so is marked as a personal moral failure rather than an outcome of systematised institutional disregard: resulting in a kind of humiliation and disciplining that then works to produce a specifically neoliberal ordering of society that values maximisation of personal self-reliance. Interactions between refugees and such public institutions are, then, not only guided by the seemingly detached and rational bureaucratic procedures through which their lives become reducible to numbers and records (Graham 2002), but are also informed by the specificities of personal encounters within those bureaucracies that render their struggles to understand and meet the demands of valued societal membership in Australia and elsewhere as personal moral failures.

Such public institutions can be viewed, then, as disciplining forces through which unruly subjects who do not conform to neoliberal ideals defined by economic productivity and self-sufficiency become punished and sanctioned in ways that force people to internalise and reproduce those values. Initially developed by Michel Foucault (1991, 2008), the concept of governmentality refers to mechanisms and techniques through which populations come to govern themselves without the direct intervention of sovereign power. Governmentality depends on populations' internalising the interests of overseeing bodies so that particular ways of being come to be reproduced as seemingly normal and natural. Through this process of normalisation, populations come to "naturally" regulate themselves and, in doing so, reproduce state interests and the power structures that are embedded through them. In this way, the programme of refugee settlement in Australia, and the suite of both specialised and public services that are embedded into the bureaucratic organising of the lives of refugees following their resettlement, can be viewed as system through which modes of governmentality are reproduced within the lives of these new residents.

Neoliberal time

What is missing from Foucault's (1991, 2008) theorisation of governmentality is recognition of the temporal orientation that is implied by the normalisation of particular ways of living. The effect of governmentality is not simply the creation of population control in the present. Rather, governmentality works to also project those controls onto the formation of society in future. This is a theme taken up in the work of Elizabeth Povinelli (2011), who describes how the contemporary context of late-liberal capitalism, which structures population governance in Australia, is based on a very specific articulation of neoliberalism: not simply as some general orientation towards economic rationalism and individualisation but as a system of political organisation in which lives that do not produce market value are lives with no value. These are lives that, under those logics, eventually become excluded from systems of support and care that promote and sustain life in Australia.

The temporal effect of governmentality in Australia, in which those members of society who are valued are those who discipline themselves to be self-reliant citizens, is the production of a future societal horizon in which the economic productivity of the population is maximised and the burden of population-level issues like health care and education is minimised. The support that is provided through public institutions in Australia therefore requires that recipients demonstrate self-reliance. Povinelli (2011) recognises that contemporary social welfare institutions operate as a system of control in which it is the production of a normative future horizon, based on the maximisation of economic productivity, that is at stake.

Clearly, neoliberalism remains a salient organising logic through which populations are governed in Australia. Although researchers like Daniel Goldstein (2012) bring up important critiques of whether neoliberalism remains a sound analytic in anthropological work, especially when local conceptions of power and control are not taken into account, it appears that neoliberalism does continue to hold analytical weight. As Bob Jessop (2013) points out in relation to Goldstein (2012) and others who debate the contemporary salience of neoliberalism as a social science analytic (Hilgers 2012; Peck and Theodore 2012; Wacquant 2012), even if neoliberalism is a potentially problematic concept, global systems of governance that rely on principles of economic liberalisation are increasingly unstable and prone to failure. Since the effects of such processes of decline are felt at the level of local populations, it is necessary to continue focusing analytical attention onto them.

When describing how the Australian government continues to invest particular attention into the seemingly neoliberal project of maximising the market value of citizens rather than investing in the social welfare of the population, I am recognising one set of logics through which the lives of Australian residents become organised and oriented toward generating a future that requires their compliance in the present. Since the success of neoliberalisation requires dominance and governmentality in the present, it makes sense to follow this specific field of localised practices and logics by tracing the temporal scale through which these are operationalised, and also since it is a particular kind of futurity that is at stake and that validates these modes of governance.

The neoliberal values through which societal orders in Australia are lived and arranged not only operate through institutional modes of organisation, then, but also through specific modes of temporalisation. Even though neoliberalism is a heterogeneous term with diverse and contingent meanings, in the way I use it here—that is, taking from Aihwa Ong (2003, 2006: 4), in which "market-driven calculations are being introduced in the management of populations and the administration of special spaces"—neoliberalism not only operates at spatial and ideological scales to organise populations to fit institutional arrangements but also operates to organise populations to fit a particular temporal schema. The intent of neoliberal governing technologies is, according to Ong (2006: 4), to "optimize" the lives of individuals within a population in terms of their contribution to and participation within economic markets. But the idea of an optimised population implies a specific relationship between governed subjects and time: one based on a linear assumption of time as "process," which excludes ways of thinking about time outside of market-based modes of productivity (Hodges 2014).

In neoliberal rationalities, optimised time is that which is efficient and oriented towards maximising productive outputs. That is, neoliberal time can be thought of as a linear trajectory of seemingly infinite progress and advancement, which is measured in terms of economic market value. Rather than a focus on the near future as a source of material and existential comfort and satisfaction, neoliberal shapings of time force governed subjects to respond to the immediacy of their lives in relation to a longitudinal future horizon, creating anxiety and situations that Jane Guyer (2007: 417) terms "continual temporal arbitrage." Neoliberal governmentalities demand specific modes of temporalisation from governed subjects.

For the women I conducted fieldwork with, time is primarily experienced as circular. Theirs is a temporality of regenesis, marked as such by understandings of birth and death as well as regeneration and decomposition, not as origin and end points on a linear trajectory but as indicators of cyclic continuity. Temporal discordance results when these assumptions of circular time become undermined by the dominant temporal register of neoliberal time in Australia, producing an experience of cosmological friction.

Cosmological friction

The concept of "friction" has been theorised by Anna Tsing (2005) as an alternative way to characterise the process and effects through which disparate knowledge systems come to interact and produce more generalisable nodes of understanding and action. Scholars of globalisation have conventionally pulled out threads of difference to describe how cultures "clash" at global intersections. Tsing (2005), however, provides a new way to think about situations that force different global cultures together: not simply as conflicts but as friction through which these divergent understandings and misunderstandings converge, at times creating further dissonance and at other times being pulled together into mutually understandable systems of disparate but nonetheless workable logics.

The idea of friction is useful when considering how refugees from countries in Africa experience resettlement in Australia. The neoliberal imperatives of individualisation and economic productivity, which are associated with the kinds of existences that are valued in Australia, do not necessarily correspond to the ways in which refugees from Central Africa organise their lives following resettlement or to the activities that they themselves prioritise. The refugees I got to know focused primarily on securing the regenerative potentiality of their families, including both their immediate relations in Australia and those who remained in Africa. But maintaining this focus on social reproduction and family life is often made difficult by competing expectations that are placed on refugees by the services and programmes that they are connected with after being resettled and the new social orders that they are resettled into (Rousseau, Rufagari, Bagilishya, and Measham 2004). Over time, the disjunctures between expectations of everyday life and the lived reality of resettlement come to accumulate into a general sense of discordance between the logics of social regeneration that these Central African refugees value so highly and the contexts of individualisation into which they are settled. For refugees from Central Africa who prioritise sociality, these new contexts of economic essentialism and individualisation in Australia are not only difficult to navigate: they are a source of cosmological friction.

Motherhood was an arena in which experiences of cosmological friction came to be acutely realised and played out for women I conducted fieldwork with in Australia. The majority of women I got to know during fieldwork had become pregnant and had a child within the first two years of being resettled in Australia. The only women who did not have a child after being resettled in Australia were those who were, at that time, still teenagers and not yet married, outside of childbearing ages, or experiencing problems with fertility.

The imperative to bear a child upon being resettled in Australia can be understood in terms of the resettlement imaginary I outline in Chapter 5. The refugees I got to know in Uganda had told me that their problems with fertility would be resolved if they were resettled outside of Africa. They considered that the material and existential insecurity of life in Uganda was responsible for their being unable to generate new life and that, conversely, the imagined security of life in resettlement can be expressed through having children. When I asked women who had given birth to a baby in Australia why they had chosen to do so, most responses reflected that which was expressed by one of the women, Emmeline, who told me, "I needed to bring a baby in Australia. That is the life here, where you can do that. It was good to be here, and to bring a baby." Evidencing the possibility of new life through the birth of a child is a way for refugees to re-invigorate the regenerative potentiality of lives that had previously been made insecure and stagnant by the hardships of living in protracted asylum. For the women I conducted fieldwork with, having a child in Australia is a way to signal the regenerative potentiality of resettlement.

The desire to have children in Australia often eclipsed other, nonetheless salient, aspirations to participate in further education and pursue employment opportunities. One woman I got know during fieldwork, Beatrice, emphasised this when she told me that "a job can wait," meaning that she would prioritise conceiving and bearing a child over pursuing employment and the kinds of economic security that having a job would bring. Ironically, this topic of conversation with Beatrice first came up when I was visiting her home with an agenda to help her develop her resume as part of the process of looking for work. Although Beatrice and her family had been resettled in Australia for seven years, their financial situation was precarious. Beatrice had received an educational qualification in aged care, and her husband had received an undergraduate degree. Neither, however, had been able to find work in their fields. Beatrice was unemployed, and her husband worked at a local taxi agency. They relied on a fortnightly public benefit payment to get by and maintain rent on the house and food for the family, which at that time included six children.

The day Beatrice told me that "a job can wait," I sat with her in the dining room of her dilapidated rental house, watching as she teetered on the edge of a worn armchair with her stuck-out knees wrapped around a basket of clean washing. Beatrice was folding clothes that she had washed for her family that morning, and the space on the floor and furniture between us was covered in piles of neatly folded clean clothes, separated into piles that belonged to particular members of her family. As she continued to fold, we discussed a strategy for her to seek employment: develop a resume, get work experience, and directly approach local aged care facilities so that they could get to know her in person. Our topic of conversation rapidly changed, however, when Beatrice told me that her children had been anxiously pestering her over the past few weeks. She described to me how, "Every day the children come to me and say, 'Mama, we want another one!'" Smiling, Beatrice finished folding a worn pair of pants that clearly belonged to one of her younger sons. Gazing at the small pants and the piles of clothes already folded around her, she told me, with a seemingly bemused tone, "There are enough clothes here for another one: enough space, sure." Beatrice meant that she was experiencing both familial and personal pressure to conceive another child.

"Will you still look for a job if you become pregnant?" I asked Beatrice. I watched her expression shift into the same patient smile that she used to explain things to me that she herself considered to be obvious. To her, it seemed, bearing children and seeking a career were two separate processes not directly relevant to each other. "It would be nice, sure, to work," she told me. "But to have a baby? A job can wait."

The structure of support services to refugees who are resettled in Australia does not, however, reflect the idea that "a job can wait." The aim of the extensive specialised support that is provided to resettled refugees is predicated on precisely the opposite logic: that those services will prepare refugees to "equitably" contribute to Australian society as productive citizens. The services that are provided to refugees are administered in ways that, over time, guide them towards independence and self-reliance. For example, the Humanitarian Settlement Services (HSS) programme, which is provided to refugees after they first arrive in Australia, provides intensive casework to assist refugees in developing "the skills and knowledge to independently access services" (Department of Social Services 2017). When newly arrived refugees are eventually transitioned from the HSS programme 6–12 months after being resettled, it is expected that they will have the capacity to seek out and access services and support should they require them and to independently navigate the complex bureaucratic structuring of everyday life in Australia. This time-limited structure of the settlement services provided to refugees in Australia implies that the amount of time a person has lived in Australia, rather than empirical markers of independence, indicates self-reliance.

Temporal domination

Evidently, the services that provide support for refugees to settle in Australia operate from an assumption of linear time. Refugees from Central Africa, however, experience the temporality of everyday life from a contrasting assumption of circular time, in which acts of social regeneration, such as bearing children, are prioritised over activities that promote individual productivity, such as employment. Since this temporal register of circular time is counter-intuitive to the linearity that is embedded into the structure of the settlement services, refugees from Central Africa are not only situated as objects of institutional intervention upon being resettled in Australia: they also come to be approached through those agencies as problematic subjects whose transition into everyday life in Australia requires not only support, but domination.

The strictly time-limited provision of specialist services to refugees can be considered as what Javier Auyero (2012) describes as a "tempography of domination." Based on fieldwork with poor and marginalised populations in Argentina, Auyero (2012) describes how the organisation of time through bureaucratic encounters with public institutions serves to mould them into docile subjects, resigned to powerlessness. Auyero (2012) describes how, by being made to wait constantly without knowing when, or even whether, the services they require to survive will be made available to them, the poorest and most marginalised populations of Argentina are transformed into docile bodies by virtue of the temporal arrangement of their everyday lives' being organised by structures outside of their control.

In contrast to the arbitrariness of waiting—that is, the mechanisms through which control over time becomes a mechanism of domination in the research of Auyero (2012)—for the refugees I conducted fieldwork with it is a dynamic of speed and a temporal rigidity that serves as a technique of subjugation: it is the expectation that their sense of being settled in Australia will conform with a linear temporal trajectory. The services and programmes that are in place to support refugees who are resettled in Australia achieve this disciplining effect through accumulated instances of cosmological friction, which guide refugees to organise their time in ways that conform to a dominant temporal register of linearity. The system of refugee settlement in Australia requires refugees to focus on cultivating self-sufficiency rather than focusing on the activities of social regeneration that they themselves prioritise, leading to cosmological friction and, ultimately, to the protraction of existential displacement.

Illusions of refuge

The system of refugee settlement in Australia provides newly arrived refugees with a suite of specialist support and public services to assist them in transitioning into daily life in Australia. Providing services does not, however, automatically translate into the resolution of their displacement. Indeed, upon becoming incorporated into these programmes and services, refugees are often confronted with experiences of cosmological friction in which their assumptions about everyday life and human existence are refuted by the expectations imposed on them through the resettlement system, producing new and enduring experiences of existential displacement.

Differential experiences, perceptions, and arrangements of time are central to the ways in which the resettlement of refugees comes to reproduce enduring situations of cosmological friction and displacement. With the circular time of the refugees I conducted fieldwork with being refracted through, and refuted by, assumptions of linear time embedded in the trajectories of social welfare services in Australia, the different priorities of refugees, who focus on regenerating social life and expand family lineage, come to situate them, in encounters with these services, as incompetent and problematic subjects in need of intervention. These systems of public services and specialist refugee support services operate to incorporate refugees into new modes of governmentality based on individualising trajectories of linear time. As such, refugees, like the women I conducted fieldwork with, come to find that their lives in resettlement are characterised by ongoing instances of cosmological friction, in which the activities of regenerative continuity that they themselves prioritise are made difficult by new requirements placed on them by public institutions and settlement services.

Gradually, refugees come to realise that their prior imaginaries of resettlement as a context from which to generate new life are illusions. The security that is offered through resettlement is conditional on them internalising expectations of neoliberal governmentality that require them to move away from, and even give up, ways of living that had previously defined their entire sense of existential purpose. Although these new contexts of everyday life in Australia can develop into exciting possibilities, allowing women to fulfil aspirations for further education, employment, and increased independence, ultimately, these new potentialities of resettlement are part of a broader tempography of domination in which the value of their lives is measured in terms of economic productivity and self-reliance rather than sociality and acts of regeneration. Resettlement is, for these refugees, far from a setting of refuge.

Note

1 Centrelink is the national government public welfare agency.

References

Auyero, J. 2012. *Patients of the State: The Politics of Waiting in Argentina*. Durham, NC: Duke University Press.

Besteman, C. 2016. *Making Refuge: Somali Bantu Refugees and Lewiston, Maine*. Durham, NC: Duke University Press.

Department of Social Services. 2017. Humanitarian Settlement Services (HSS). Available at: www.dss.gov.au/our-responsibilities/settlement-and-multicultural-affairs/programs-policy/settlement-services/humanitarian-settlement-services-hss (Accessed 6 January 2017).

Dominelli, L. The Age of Austerity in Welfare Services: Impact Upon Social Work and Marginalized People. In *Participation, Marginalization, and Welfare Services: Concepts, Politics and Practices Across European Countries*. A. Matthies and L. Uggerhøj (Eds.), pp. 79–93. London; New York: Routledge.

Foucault, M. 1991. Governmentality. In *The Foucault Effect: Studies in Governmentality: With Two Lectures by and an Interview with Michel Foucault*. G. Burchell, C. Gordon, and P. Miller (Eds.), pp. 87–104. London: Harvester Wheatsheaf.

Foucault, M. 2008. *The Birth of Biopolitics: Lectures at the College de France, 1978–1979*. Translated by G. Burchell. London: Palgrave Macmillan.

Goldstein, D. 2012. Decolonialising 'Actually Existing Neoliberalism.' *Social Anthropology* 20(3): 304–309.

Graham, M. 2002. Emotional Bureaucracies: Emotions, Civil Servants, and Immigrants in the Swedish Welfare State. *Ethnos* 30(3): 199–226.

Guyer, J. 2007. Prophecy and the Near Future: Thoughts on Macroeconomic, Evangelical, and Punctuated Time. *American Ethnologist* 43(3): 409–421.

Hertzfeld, M. 1992. *The Social Production of Indifference*. Chicago, IL: University of Chicago Press.

Hilgers, M. 2012. The Historicity of the Neoliberal State. *Social Anthropology* 20(1): 8–94.

Hodges, M. 2014. Immanent Anthropology: A Comparative Study of 'Process' in Contemporary France. *Journal of the Royal Anthropological Institute* 20(S1): 33–51.

Jessop, B. 2013. Putting Neoliberalism in its Time and Place: A Response to the Debate. *Social Anthropology* 21(1): 65–74.

Ong, A. 2003. *Buddha is Hiding; Refugees, Citizenship, the New America*. Berkeley: University of California Press.

Ong, A. 2006. *Neoliberalism as Exception: Mutations in Citizenship*. Durham, NC: Duke University Press.

Peck, J. and Theodore, N. 2012. Reanimating Neoliberalism: Process Geographies of Neoliberalisation. *Social Anthropology* 20(2): 177–185.

Povinelli, E. 2011. *Economies of Abandonment: Social Belonging and Endurance in Late Liberalism*. London: Duke University Press.

Rousseau, C., Rufagari, M., Bagilishya, D., and Measham, T. 2004. Remaking Family Life: Strategies for Re-Establishing Continuity among Congolese Refugees during the Family Reunification Process. *Social Science & Medicine* 59(5): 1095–1108.

Thomson, M. 2012. Black Boxes of Bureaucracy: Transparency and Opacity in the Resettlement Process of Congolese Refugees. *Political and Legal Anthropology Review* 35(2): 186–205.

Tsing, A. 2005. *Friction: An Ethnography of Global Connection*. Princeton, NJ: Princeton University Press.

UNHCR. 2016. Australia: Country Chapter—UNHCR Resettlement Handbook. Available at: www.unhcr.org/en-au/protection/resettlement/3c5e542d4/unhcr-resettlement-handbook-country-chapter-australia.html(Accessed2February2017).

Wacquant, L. 2012. Three Steps to a Historical Anthropology of Actually Existing Neoliberalism. *Social Anthropology* 20(1): 66–79.

8 Refuge and shifted sociality

How do refugees resettled in Australia from Central Africa experience and create a sense of refuge? The settlement experiences that I have described in the previous two chapters depict a vision of resettlement in Australia as characterised by struggle and hardship, in which refugees are either racialised as unworthy citizens (Chapter 6) or problematised as objects of bureaucratic intervention and control (Chapter 7). Neither of these narratives is false, yet neither defines how refugees experience resettlement. These dynamics of unanticipated racialisation and the bureaucratisation of everyday life that were experienced by the refugees I conducted fieldwork with reflect what Michael Jackson (2008) terms the "shock of the new," that is, the experience of disorientation that follows migrants who settle in a vastly different country from that which they have left. But even within the disjuncture between resettlement imaginaries and settlement realities, the existential project of creating a "new life" continues to propel refugees to seek the possibility of refuge.

Refuge is a heterogeneous concept but one that is rarely distinctly defined when used in academic scholarship. Broadly, refuge is often used to describe a space of safety and security, "a private, often familial realm clearly differentiated from public space and removed from public scrutiny and surveillance" (Mallett 2004: 71). When considered in relation to asylum seekers, however, the concept of refuge often takes on a more political and juridical meaning, referring to the legal responsibility of states to host and provide temporary asylum to those seeking refugee status whose nation of origin is no longer safe for them to reside in (Hyndman and Mountz 2007). Indeed, this assumption of refuge as a politico-legal status of temporary or permanent protection is reflected in work with refugees more broadly, in which resettlement is largely depicted as a setting of refuge without significant critical analysis regarding whether this is how refugees themselves experience it.

Approaching refuge as an existential, rather than a politico-legal, condition of safety and security complicates the general tendency to conflate resettlement with refuge. This has been the focus of recent insightful work from Catherine Besteman (2016), based on the experiences of Somali Bantu refugees resettled in the US. Besteman (2016) emphasises that, as an affective and existential sense of security and belonging, refuge cannot be thought of as an automatic product of resettlement because the experience of becoming settled is itself, at least for those Somali Bantu refugees, conditioned by new struggles and hardships, which undermine connectedness to the host nation and the feeling of being secure there. Rather, Besteman (2016) characterises refuge as a process, and not a stable status: refuge is a feeling of belonging that requires "making," and which encompasses not only the efforts of refugees but the efforts of the host society in which they have been resettled. What emerges from Besteman's (2016) account is that refuge, while impacted by the political, sociocultural, and material contexts into which refugees seek to create new lives, is ultimately forged through complex intersections of sociality.

The refugees I conducted fieldwork with sought to make refuge through the same processes through which they experience cosmological continuity and locate existential purpose: that is, through the social and biological reproduction of children. This was why women I met described their desire to fall pregnant and have a child within the first few years of their settlement as crucial. By doing so, they were solidifying that, as one woman told me, "the life in Australia is good," and actualising, through the birth of a child, the regenerative potentiality of finally being secure and safe enough to bear and rear children. That reproduction is a crucial factor of migrant belonging for some women from Africa is also reflected in the work of Pamela Feldman-Savelsberg (2016). Based on research conducted with Cameroonian mothers in Berlin, Feldman-Savelsberg (2016) describes how these migrant women repurpose a customary valuing of motherhood and fertility to forge connectedness in the new and unfamiliar contexts of their everyday lives. Similarly, for the women I worked with, it was by feeling that they exist in a situation in which it is possible to bear and rear babies in safety and security that they come to experience a sense of refuge.

Yet the domestic spheres in which children are raised in resettlement are not neutral havens, immune from the impacts of settling in a new and unfamiliar country. New pressures of everyday life in resettlement can cause domestic strain and tension, forcing previously taken-for-granted arrangements of family life and assumptions about ways of living to be reconfigured. As I describe in this chapter, these new household orders can throw the very possibility of creating refuge in Australia into jeopardy.

Securing futures

That the refugees I conducted fieldwork with locate the process of making refuge through securing the futurity of their children was emphasised to me on an afternoon that I spent with Jeanette. We sat together on her patio on a warm autumn afternoon, watching her youngest children and some of their friends playing in the yard after they had returned home from school. The setting was idyllic in many ways. We alternated between drinking from glasses of cold ice water and cups of warm sweet tea, discussing all sorts of topics, while her husband occasionally joined us, alternating between ducking in and out of the house to receive phone calls from friends and chatting with us. The banter of the children filtered up to us on the patio: chatter of imagination and play strategies, with nothing more serious to be concerned over than who would take on what role in whatever game they happened to be playing in that moment. With her gaze fixed on the children, Jeanette told me that resettlement in Australia had made her children "well again."

"Were they sick in Africa?" I asked her.

"We were all sick in Africa," she responded. "People, I don't know who, had poisoned us in the camp. One day I was cooking dinner, inside the house, and I fed my children with that food. But that night, my youngest got sick, vomiting, headache ... Then the next ... All of us. We could not eat. We could not sleep. The poison was there. It could not be fixed. The poison was stuck in us."

"What did you do?" I asked her. "How did you fix it?"

"Georgina," Jeanette replied, shaking her head. "Poison is very hard. We were sick. No treatment worked. Only when we got to Australia did the poison leave us. My children became well again."

"Was it medicine in Australia?" I asked her. Jeanette shook her head again.

"No," she responded, "it is not the kind that can be treated with medicine. It is because, in Australia, the life is good."

When I asked Jeanette to clarify what she meant by saying "the life is good," she told me that in Australia, she and her family were able to access resources that are necessary for life without the hardship and struggle that these had presented as a refugee in Africa: that is, steady income, secure housing, good medical and health care, and education. In Australia, Jeanette felt that the possibility of a good life for her children was secure.

The primacy of motherhood as a thread of existential continuity and the possibility of making refuge was emphasised to me again when I traced the experiences of Beatrice. For many months, Beatrice had been attempting to get a job in an aged care facility, so that the precarious financial situation that she and her husband were facing could be eased by a second income. I found out, with some initial disbelief and frustration, that after I had supported her to apply for work for some time Beatrice had been made a job offer, but had refused it after a quick deliberation on the employment conditions. After I asked her why she did not take the job, she told me that the hours did not suit her life. Explaining what she meant, Beatrice told me that she required a job that would allow her to be off between the hours of 2 p.m. and 5 p.m. most days. When I asked her why, she told me that those were the hours in which she cooked the main meal for her family. This was an act of care that she was not willing to forfeit, even for the lure of a job and financial security.

Even in the most pressured and seemingly inconvenient of moments, women sought to insert themselves into the regenerative potentiality of circular time by prioritising and engaging in acts of caring for their children. This was a thread of existential continuity that women held onto and nurtured and through which they sought to create refuge. However, many women I conducted fieldwork with in Australia found making refuge in their lives through attention to family and caring for children difficult. It seemed that the "shock of the new" (Jackson 2008) resonated deeply across, and required reconfigurations of, the most fundamental basis of existential purpose for these women: family. For many women I got to know during fieldwork seeking refuge in the futurity of children was complicated by the rupture of family life itself.

Isolation

Settling in Australia was, for most of the women I conducted fieldwork with, a profoundly, and somewhat unexpectedly, isolating experience. The overwhelming majority of refugees who are selected for resettlement to Australia are settled as a nuclear family because the migration system prioritises family groups who are connected through direct genetic relatedness, such as biological parents and offspring (Wilmsen 2011). Being resettled generally means, then, that refugees are separated from extended family and friends.

To resolve the isolating effects of resettlement, many of the refugees I got to know during fieldwork sought to create new social networks by joining churches, creating community groups based on national and ethnic background, and spending time in local migrant community centres. Although most of the women had developed a significant network of social relations through participating in such organisations, this did not necessarily translate into the development of close friendships. For them, intimate sociality is developed over time through mutually visiting friends at home and especially through sharing food together. Domestic intimacy was especially difficult to achieve with locally born Australians, however, because of different social norms around friendship. "They ask me what day and what time I will come to see them," one woman told me. She then added, sounding deeply offended, "It is like I am booking an appointment. And when I turn up, it is just tea."

But even developing close friendships with other resettled refugees who share similar social norms proved problematic for refugees, especially those in their first years of arrival. Most of the women I conducted fieldwork with were living in cheap rental accommodation in the sprawling outer suburbs of large Australian cities, with limited access to public transport. Maintaining the intimacy of everyday relatedness with new friends was made difficult by this lack of physical proximity. Only after getting access to personal modes of transport did most refugees come to develop close friendships.

Within these newly isolating social landscapes, many refugees lost the more expansive sociality that had characterised their lives prior to their being resettled to Australia. Subsequently, they began to rely more intensively on the immediate relatedness between husband and wife as well as between parent and offspring in ways that they never did in Africa. As one woman told me:

> [h]ere, people just have their family. I just have my husband and children. My other family, my sisters and their children, they are not here. The life, here, it is not like Africa. There, every day, I have people coming to my house. Talking together. Eating food together. Here ... it is hard.

This unfamiliar dependency on immediate domestic relations created new tensions that, for some, erupted into violence and family breakdown.

Interdependence and gender complementarity

Prior to being resettled, the refugees I conducted fieldwork with had been part of domestic arrangements ordered by gender and age hierarchies as well as other extended family dynamics. In those contexts, I was told, upon becoming a husband or partner and having a child, men were generally positioned as household heads and expected to provide material security for their family. As one woman told me, "The woman is the manager of the house, looking after the children and the food," and the men are "out looking for money." Although the women described this gendered ordering of households as being pervasive in Africa broadly, it was not a defining arrangement nor was it an indication that African women are treated as inherently inferior to men. The women also told me that they would often work and, if it could be afforded, pursue education. Then, upon becoming a wife or partner and having a child, women would generally take on the additional, and much respected, responsibility of overseeing the practical functioning of the household (Amadiume 1987; Oyewumi 2000), including, in some cases, doing the bulk of childcare, preparing meals, and dealing with domestic chores.

This kind of gender complementarity of household roles is recognised as common in numerous social groups across continental Africa (Devisch 1993; Feldman-Savelsberg 1999, 2016; Moore 1986; Moore, Sanders, and Kaare 1999). It can be interpreted as a gendered ordering of existence that constructs and reinforces specific domains of female power or as a vertical hierarchy of patriarchal power in which men maintain control over crucial domains of power, such as finances and property (Moore 1986). Recognising, however, that in many African social settings, children are the most prized sources of power, recognition (Oyewumi 2000), and status, the largely feminised role of caring for and socialising children in the immediacy of their growing lives can be seen as complementary with, rather than inferior to, the primarily masculinised role of providing financial and material security for a family.

With the refugees I got to know during fieldwork viewing parenthood as a fundamental basis of existential purpose, the primacy that is placed on women providing care to children cannot be simplistically viewed as a constraining effect of patriarchy. Regardless, importing what are essentially Eurocentric models of gender and patriarchal subjugation into analyses of the lives of people in Africa reproduces a kind of academic imperialism that ignores how local experience and perceptions shape gendered relations of power (Amadiume 1987; Oyewumi 1997, 2000, 2002). It is especially tenuous to apply seemingly universal analyses of patriarchy to the ordering of family life in African contexts, according to Oyeronke Oyewumi (2002), because so much feminist theorisation of domestic gender inequality is derived from a distinctly Western assumption of the nuclear family and the primacy of the male "husband" and female "wife" relationship that, for many people across diverse African contexts, is not a similarly foundational category of experience.

Rather, the sociality that is produced through motherhood is a central ordering factor of domestic life across many sociocultural contexts in Africa and a much revered and respected social role (Amadiume 1987: 191; Oyewumi 2002). Reading the domestic arrangements of peoples from Africa through Eurocentric categories of gender and patriarchy can overlook the ways in which African women attain status and power as mothers in ways that are distinct from their positions as wives: these women are not only known in relation to men, as is often the case in Euro-American sociocultural contexts (Amadiume 1987). To have the status and purpose that is attached to motherhood recognised and validated requires, however, a context of everyday life in which more expansive forms of sociality, beyond conjugal relatedness, are valued.

But, in Australia, the organisation of everyday life through public institutions continues to reflect and validate a distinctly patriarchal nuclear family model in which men, and specifically heterosexual men, continue overall to be the default locus through which household power and control is directed (Gorman-Murray 2008). Within this context, refugees who resettle from Africa to Australia come to rely more intensively, in both economic and emotional terms, on the immediacy of conjugal relatedness. Rather than being seen foremost as mothers, their lives come to be defined in relation to their male partners and vice versa. This new sociocultural context of everyday life in Australia following resettlement can lead to immense strain and pressure on domestic relationships.

Reconfigured gender roles

Domestic life in Australia is, broadly, far from equal in terms of gender. When taking into account socioeconomic background, racialisation, sexuality, and disability, the prosperity of family livelihoods and distribution of family resources is even more stratified (Korpi, Ferrarini, and Englund 2013; Morley and MacFarlane 2008). The societal gender order (Connell 1987) in Australia generally continues to reward men and disadvantage women, and household orders in which men generally have more mobility and less domestic responsibilities than women are not exactly exceptional (Bamberry and Homsey 2013; Organa, Head, and Waitt 2013). Despite the persistence of gender inequality across many areas of everyday life in Australia, however, economic participation and striving for self-sufficiency seem to be incorporated at an institutional level as an expectation for all, regardless of gender (McDonald 2000). It is difficult for anyone to be unemployed and dependent on the public benefit system in Australia for long periods of time. The payments are often insubstantial for the cost of living, and recipients who are designated as able to work must meet often strenuous employment-seeking criteria in order to continue receiving payments, including either being enrolled as a full-time student or attending frequent appointments at private sector employment offices that operate to link unemployed people with available jobs. It is an expectation of the Australian government that both men and women participate in the labour market in Australia, or nonetheless maintain a self-sustaining livelihood if not.

But securing meaningful and well-paid employment was generally difficult for the resettled refugees I got to know in Australia. The lack of employment opportunity was a source of acute distress for them. Many of the men had entered Australia with previous educational qualifications and experience that would have allowed them to be employed as a skilled worker, except that these were not recognised as equivalent in Australia. This meant that many men were forced to work in low-skill and low-paying work, even as they tried to regain educational qualifications and professional skills to mobilise themselves out of those jobs. Many of the husbands of women I conducted fieldwork with were employed in a local chicken-processing factory, where they worked long shifts at all hours of the day and night. Others worked as taxi drivers, again working late nights and dealing with the stress of often inebriated passengers. I rarely saw husbands or male partners during my fieldwork, in fact, because they would often come home in the early hours of the morning, exhausted from the work, sleep a few hours, then leave during the daylight hours to attend classes and study, with the aspiration of getting qualifications that would enable them to find better work.

But even when they did get those qualifications and experience, better and higher-paying jobs were not always available. The husband of one of the women I was very close to during my fieldwork, for example, was one of the few who was fortunate enough to gain work at a local migrant settlement agency, but the pay was small and the requirements of the job—to support and provide casework for other refugees—created stress and tension with people he considered friends. He left the job to drive a taxi, where he was able to earn more money. He kept looking for another job in the community service sector because he had gained a university qualification in that area. Despite applying for many jobs however, he was never successful in his attempts: at least, not during the period I was conducting fieldwork.

The difficulties that men faced in securing work created tension in the households of the refugee families I became familiar with during my fieldwork. Subsisting on public benefit payments or taking up low-paying, menial jobs not only created financial insecurity but also displaced the role of these men as the customary economic provider for their family. Although I did not have extensive interaction with men specifically, other researchers describe how this reconfiguration of established gender roles creates intense shame and emotion distress for them (Correa-Velez and Onsando 2009, 2013; Correa-Velez, Spaaij, and Upham 2013; Marlowe 2011; Muchoki 2013). For the refugees I conducted fieldwork with, this distress seemed to be exacerbated when women began taking up work and, in some cases, went on to become the primarily financial provider for their families. Many women I got to know pursued educational qualifications in fields related to nursing, aged care, and childcare, among others. Although they, too, often found it difficult to gain employment, these caring industries often had a high turnover staff, which meant that, often, women were able to secure employment more easily than their husbands or male partners who were often seeking work in the highly competitive community service sector. Even when women did not work, however, the structure of public benefit payments in Australia meant that most women had an individual bank account separate from their husbands', meaning that they had access to financial resources and economic independence in a way that most did not when living in Africa.

Generally, the refugees I got to know in Australia, including men and women, embraced that women were able to find work and earn an independent income, especially when the increasing flow of finance was seen not only as an individual gain but as a resource for the entire family of women. For many, however, the increased access to individual streams of income also meant that women could be more financially, and as a result socially, independent from their husbands, a situation that was generally welcomed by women I worked with but did not seem to be similarly welcomed by their husbands or male partners. As one woman told me, in reference to the increased economic independence of women following resettlement, "In Australia, we have our own pockets."

The inversion of conventional gender roles and the increased independence of women seemed to compound the feelings of inadequacy that men experienced when they were unable to be the primary financial provider for their families (Fisher 2013; James 2010; Marlowe 2011). With women taking up increased financial responsibility for their families, and often then becoming increasingly economically and socially independent from their husbands, it was not uncommon for men from refugee backgrounds to feel that they had not only lost control of their roles as providers, but that they have lost control of their roles and significance within their families overall.

These new household dynamics often created severe tension for the refugees I conducted fieldwork with. During my fieldwork, I became aware of four situations in which these tensions escalated from general frustration and anger to accusations of physical violence: one committed by a husband against his wife and their children, another committed by a husband against his wife, another committed by a wife against her husband, and another committed by both parents and an older sibling against an adolescent child.

Despite experiencing often severe household tension and occasional outbreaks of family violence, physical violence in and of itself was rarely a cause of family breakdown and separation. In the only one case of spousal violence I was made aware of, the coupled separated but that separation was complicated by other factors related to the custody and care of children. In reference to refugees who experience family violence in Australia, Kerrie James (2010: 280) describes situations in which refugees "just want the violence to stop" rather than to "abandon their families and cultures." With refugees generally being aware of the potentially serious legal repercussions of committing physical violence, when such instances did occur and become known by other friends and support people, these were seen as points of intervention and relationship-building rather than points of breakdown and separation. The tension between men and women, husbands and wives, was not the only source of family conflict, however.

Parenting children

Parenting was a significant area of anxiety for women I conducted fieldwork with. The women told me that, prior to being resettled, parenting was approached with a kind of casual naturalness: they had generally been surrounded by infants and children their entire lives, throughout their own childhood and adolescent years, and into early adulthood. But in Australia, as in other Western contexts, parenting is approached as a technical skill that can be mastered, whereby children themselves are imagined as docile subjects who, with the "correct" parenting, can be moulded into model citizens (Rose 1990). From the viewpoint of public institutions in Australia, parenting is also a locus of anxiety in which refugee families are considered to be especially vulnerable to caregiving issues because difficulties of settlement compound with pre-migration experiences of trauma and different methods of care (Lewig, Arney, Salveron 2010). Given that parenting is a site in which national anxieties are played out (Anderson 2012; Dever 2005; Luibhéad 2002, 2004; Shandy 2008), it was no surprise that the cultural orientation sessions, provided to these women in the pre-departure phase of their resettlement following the early weeks of their arrival, had included information about the kinds of parenting skills that are expected in Australia. From those sessions, and other from other social welfare interventions, they learned that many of the normal ways they parented children, from the use of sibling caregiving to physical disciplining, were not only socially unacceptable in Australia: in many cases, those parenting practices were also illegal.

For many of these refugees, family life and household orders in Africa had been arranged not only by gendered differences but also by age hierarchies. Children were taught from a young age to respect the authority of people older than them, especially their parents. As one woman told me, "Even if they were raised in a hard way, the child always looks after their parent." But for these refugees, parenting in Australia turned out to be more complex and difficult than they had previously imagined possible.

Resettlement is not only difficult for adult refugees. It poses specific challenges to refugees who resettle in Australia as children and adolescents. These refugee youth often "long to belong" within the new social settings in which they have come to settle (Correa-Velez, Gifford, and Barnett 2010), but they are confronted with numerous hardships, as the significant corpus of literature focusing on experiences of adolescent refugee resettlement in Australia emphasises (Buchanan, Abu-Rayya, Kashima, and Paxton 2016; Gifford, Bakopanos, Kaplan, and Correa-Velez 2007; McMichael, Gifford, and Correa-Velez 2010; Nunn, McMichael, Gifford, and Correa-Velez 2014; Sampson and Gifford 2010). Refugee youth sometimes experience racialisation and assumptions of cultural difference, which can make them feel inherently different from their peers. The expectation that they follow the cultural scripts of interdependency set for them by parents and other relatives can often come into conflict with the cultural backgrounds of their peers at school. Many also suffer in terms of their educational experience because they are only provided with six months of intensive English language tuition before they are moved into a class based on their age rather than their ability, meaning that some, who may have had patchy and interrupted schooling in which they gained little familiarity with English literacy, end up being placed in senior high school classes with no concept of the material being taught to them. This is a system that often sets refugee youth up to fail. Educational failure was extremely distressing to many refugee youth I got to know during fieldwork because, a lot of the time, they felt immense pressure from their parents and other relations to achieve educational success (Atwell, Gifford, McDonald-Wilmsen 2009). Children were often held up by the refugees I met as representing a future of prosperity in which educational failure was not an option. In addition, many refugee youth are also managing the trauma of pasts that have been punctuated by violence and insecurity.

Feeling ostracised from their peers, inadequate in their schooling, and at times dealing with trauma from their pasts, it appeared that many of the adolescent children in the families of the refugees I conducted fieldwork with felt disenfranchised after being resettled. Some turned to what are seen as anti-social and destructive behaviours by their parents, such as joining gangs, drinking alcohol, and doing drugs. These situations created immense family conflict. What was most distressing to women I worked with was that, when they attempted to take control of the situation and guide their children into what they saw as better opportunities, their authority as parents and elders was not respected. Indeed, this lack of respect for an age-based hierarchy, ingrained in a legal system that provides children with autonomous rights that outweigh the authority of parents, was the dominant explanation that these women attributed to the unexpected difficulties of raising teenagers in Australia.

After the adolescent child of one woman stopped coming home at night, instead spending time with his friends and hanging out with them on the streets, she came to me, crying and said, "What can I do? This is the problem of Australia. He is free. He is free to do what he wants." "In Australia," another woman asked me, angrily, "why do the police not give respect to parents, not even one per cent?" She had made contact with the police after her son, then fifteen, refused to attend school and had begun going missing at night. She had asked the police to come and discipline him, since she, apparently, could not. The police gave her a referral to a youth worker and told her there was nothing she could do: he was a young adult who was making his own decisions. If she felt concerned and angry towards him, she was advised to "just walk away." Never before had these women had to contemplate a situation in which they would walk away from a child.

The contestation of parental authority represented a broader social transformation that was taking place in the younger generations of resettled refugees: namely, a turn towards individualisation. One woman described this process by telling me how her oldest child is an "African man." She said:

> He came here when he was fourteen. He grew up in Africa and knows that he must respect his parents. For the other children, it is different. They are Australian people now. They go to school here, and they learn about disrespecting their parents, they do not think about their family.

These women talked about the sociality between parent and child as if it was an innate relationship that is corrupted by the normalisation of individualism in Australia.

The disjuncture between parental authority and child autonomy was a significant source of distress for these women, as is recognised elsewhere (Deng and Marlowe 2013; Levi 2014), but not just because it created family conflict. Because it was through the futurity of children that these women located a sense of cosmological continuity, what they saw as the descent of their children into ways of living that are incompatible with a cosmology of regeneration came to mean that these experiences produced an acute sense of existential displacement. As a result, despite having access to more resources for physical security and social mobility, it was not uncommon that women felt insecure and unsafe about the future of their family in resettlement. As Nyomanda told me, crying from frustration and anxiety one afternoon, "This is not supposed to be the life here. They are supposed to be safe. But what can I do?" She felt she had lost her connection to her most precious and fundamental thread of existential continuity: her children.

Reproductive insecurity

That displacement endures as an existential condition in Australia, through which it is the lives of children and the possible futures that they signify that are at stake, was a reoccurring theme amongst the refugees I conducted fieldwork with. It was not just through the disintegration of child–parent relations that this experience of displacement came to be wrought, however. It was also through experiences of reproductive insecurity, a theme that I outlined previously in relation to the ways in which refugees in protracted asylum in Uganda experience and express a sense of being displaced (Chapter 4). Those refugees imagined that life in Australia would resolve reproductive insecurity because Australia is generally understood to be a place in which the conditions to maintain a pregnancy and rear children are better resourced: that is, the political, economic, and medical conditions of child birth and rearing are more secure. But refugees in Uganda also, it seems, underestimate how affective aspects of everyday life create "reproductive insecurity" (Feldman-Savelsberg 2016: 8).

The enduring displacement of refugees in Australia, as embodied and expressed at the most intimate scales of reproductive insecurity, was acutely emphasised to me during an emotional encounter with Solange, one of the women I got to know well during my fieldwork.

At 7 a.m. on a humid autumn morning, I received a panicked phone call from Solange. In her alarmed state, I was unable to understand much of what she was saying. I could only ascertain that she had been admitted to the local hospital. When I asked why she was there, Solange could only sob in response.

After arriving at the hospital, I was directed to a recovery ward. Solange was sitting up in a hospital bed, gazing at a strip of sunlight streaming in from a nearby window. She appeared to be calmer than when I had spoken with her on the phone. I went to her bedside, but we did not speak for some time. Eventually, Solange told me, quietly but emphatically, "I have lost another baby here."

Solange was recovering from an emergency dilation and cutterage procedure following an unexpected and difficult miscarriage. Sitting together in the ward, she told me how, the previous afternoon, she had begun to experience unexpected bleeding. Her husband had driven her to the hospital immediately, but after being consulted there, they were informed that the pregnancy had miscarried.

Although in many such cases, a woman might be told to return home and wait for the miscarriage to finish without medical intervention, the visible distress displayed by Solange in response to this news had prompted the medical practitioners to hasten the miscarriage through a medical procedure and for them to encourage her to remain, sedated, in the hospital overnight. That morning, prior to being released, Solange spoke with me in a slow drawl. She was still mildly sedated, both to manage the pain of the procedure and to calm her emotional response to it. There was a protracted silence before, again, she began to speak.

"This problem," she said, "it never happened to me before coming here."

"What do you mean?" I asked her.

"In Africa I was bringing babies with no problem," she responded. "But since coming here, since being around these problems here, I have had troubles. This is the second time..." Solange trailed off, unable to finish her sentence. "It is the problem of the life here," she continued, eventually. "Coming here, to Australia, it is too hard to make a life."

When I asked Solange, a few days after the miscarriage, what she had meant by it being "too hard to make a life" in Australia, she first told me that it was the general "pressure" of everyday existence that made it too stressful for her to successfully maintain a pregnancy. She went on to say, however, that she had been visited by a social worker at home on the afternoon of the miscarriage, who had asked her invasive questions about her family life, parenting, and housekeeping. Solange had been deeply offended by the assumptions of deficiency implied by the scrutiny. However, she had also been anxious about what the eventual purpose of the visit from the social worker would serve. Hours after the visit, the miscarriage had begun. Solange directly linked the social worker's visit, which she saw as an indicator of the potential hostility, danger, and pressure of everyday life in Australia, as an existential explanatory factor for the failed pregnancy. To her, the miscarriage was not simply a devastating biological accident. The miscarriage was a cosmological indicator that she was living in a state of existential impossibility, where the future is uncertain and controlled by external, and seemingly hostile, forces that throw the circularity of existence into chaos.

The concept of reproductive insecurity (Feldman-Savelsberg 2016: 8) can be used more broadly than just in relation to physiological pregnancy, however. Reproductive insecurity can also be considered as a way to characterise the broader states of existential displacement experienced by women I conducted fieldwork with, in which the possibility of a future of regenerative potentiality is undermined. Although primarily, the concept of reproductive insecurity refers to the inability to physiologically conceive and bear children to term, Feldman-Savelsberg (2016: 8) also points out that insecurity about reproducing particular forms of "social organization and a sense of cultural distinctiveness" are crucial components of anxiety over reproduction. When the women I conducted fieldwork with see the norms and beliefs of their children transforming in ways that do not correspond to their own values, the result is a kind of reproductive insecurity: not in terms of physiological uncertainty about the physical ability to conceive and bear a child, but in regard to the possibility of rearing and raising children who reflect the continuity of their own beliefs and values.

The temporalisation of refuge

For the refugees I conducted fieldwork with, resettlement in Australia is far from an automatic setting of refuge. Although, generally, they are able to experience increased physical security and opportunities for social mobility through education and employment in Australia than that which they may have had as refugees in Africa, these dynamics of civic life do not translate into an immediate existential sense of safety, belonging, and refuge (Fozdar and Hartley 2013; Ndhlovu 2011). Because they experience refuge as a condition of existential security, what these refugees are searching for is a context of everyday life in which they feel that the futurity of their children is safe. Since resettlement often results in experiences of isolation, individualisation, and transformation of customary household orders based on gender differentiations and age hierarchies, these dimensions of cosmological friction resonate across intimate dimensions of family life and throw the possibility of refuge and secure futures into jeopardy.

If the temporal dynamics of refuge are taken into account, however, then the picture of resettlement in Australia as a setting of refuge is not as grim as it emerged in those moments of acute desperation and reproductive insecurity that I witnessed during my fieldwork. Over time, the "shock of the new" (Jackson 2008) dissipates somewhat into familiarity with ways of living in Australia, creating new ways to think about personal and collective futures and identities in which cosmological frictions can be reconciled into ways of being. The processes through which refugees and other migrants come to adjust to ways of living in a new country is often described in terms of place-making, encompassing both material and affective dimensions (Hage 1997; Larsen 2011; Lems 2016; Sampson and Gifford 2010). Referring to the experiences of migrants from Lebanon in Australia, Ghassan Hage (1997: 102) describes how the ability to feel settled depends not only on finding physical shelter to live in but on making the materiality of that shelter into a "home" by building a sense of connection to it with "affective building blocks" that create feelings of security, familiarity, community, and, importantly, a sense of possibility.

Locating the possibility of refuge within the stability and materiality of a safe place and home, however, attaches a temporal staticity to the idea of refuge: as if it is a distinct event or outcome on a linear trajectory of lived experience. As Catherine Besteman (2016) suggests, however, refuge is not a feeling that can be achieved: it is processual and requires "making." For the refugees I conducted fieldwork with, refuge is not a temporal state of stability that is achieved through creating affective and material connections to place. Rather, for them, refuge is constituted in the temporal dynamism of growth and regeneration and experienced through sociality rather than materiality. Ultimately, it was by feeling secure in the futurity of their children that the possibility of refuge could be realised.

Subsequently, although dynamics of resettlement could certainly obstruct the possibility of refuge, it was rare that such friction would foreclose that possibility entirely since the temporal dynamism of refuge meant that new ways of nurturing the futurity of children were being continuously sought and created. I observed that, after being settled in Australia for a few years, refugees had become familiar enough with the context and cosmological frictions of everyday life in resettlement to attempt to create new ways to nurture futures of regenerative potentiality. Friendships and social networks were forged between refugees, preventing the isolation of resettlement from becoming overwhelming. From these formations of communality, refugees would attempt to manage what were recognised to be pervasive problems of adjusting to life in resettlement, including the disenfranchisement of men and the destructive behaviours of teenagers. Outreach from local schools and community organisations with these groups resulted in the creation of a number of different initiatives that attempted to celebrate, preserve, and regenerate the cultural distinctiveness of these refugees and make this a point of pride for their children: music and dance groups for children and teenagers became a popular outlet, and sports, especially football, were another point of collective identity building. Eventually, Solange managed to carry a baby to term.

As such, it was through re-configuring and creating new forms of sociality that the futurity of children and the possibility of refuge came to be realised for refugees in resettlement. However, as Ghassan Hage points out in an interview with Mary Zournazi (2002), the idea of possibility, and the related idea of hope, is never stable. Drawing on Pierre Bourdieu (2006), Hage (in Zournazi 2002: 151) considers that hope and possibility are often tied in with a general *illusio* of existential purpose: possibility implies the idea of an "existence of something to live for, what gives life meaning..." For the women I conducted fieldwork with, bearing and raising children was understood to be the fundamental reason to exist. Being a mother was the antithesis of social death. When seeking to secure the futures of their children in resettlement, these women were working from the assumption that the connection between mother and child cannot be severed. This, it was to turn out, was an inaccurate assumption.

References

Amadiume, I. 1987. *Male Daughter, Female Husbands: Gender and Sex in an African Society*. London; New Jersey: Zed Books Ltd.

Anderson, Z. 2012. Borders, Babies, and 'Good Refugees': Australian Representations of 'Illegal' Migration, 1979. *Journal of Australian Studies* 36(4): 499–514.

Atwell, R., Gifford, S., and McDonald-Wilmsen, B. 2009. Resettled Refugee Families and Their Children's Futures: Coherence, Hope, and Support. *Journal of Comparative Family Studies* 40(5): 677–697.

Bamberry, L. and Homsey, C. 2013. Household Gender Regimes—What Can We Learn from Census Income Data? Presented at the *Australian Sociological Association Conference*, 2013. Available at: www.tasa.org.au/wp-content/uploads/2013/11/Bamberry.pdf (Accessed 4 February 2017).

Besteman, C. 2016. *Making Refuge: Somali Bantu Refugees and Lewiston, Maine*. Durham, NC: Duke University Press.

Bourdieu, P. 2006. *Pascalian Meditations*. Translated by R. Nice. Oxford: Polity Press.

Buchanan, Z.E., Abu-Rayya, H., Kashima, E., and Paxton, S. 2016. The Interconnection between Acculturation and Subjective and Social Wellbeing among Refugee Youth in Australia. *Journal of Refugee Studies*. doi:10.1093/jrs/few040.

Connell, R. 1987. *Gender and Power: Society, the Person, and Sexual Politics*. Cambridge: Polity Press.

Correa-Velez, I. and Onsando, G. 2009. Educational and Occupational Outcomes amongst African Men from Refugee Backgrounds Living in Urban and Regional Southeast Queensland. *Australasian Review of African Studies* 30(2): 114–127.

Correa-Velez, I. and Onsando, G. 2013. Longitudinal Evidence on Educational and Occupational Outcomes amongst South Sudanese Men from Refugee Backgrounds Living in Urban and Regional Southeast Queensland. In *South Sudanese Diaspora in Australia and New Zealand: Reconciling the Past with the Present*. J. Marlowe, A. Harris, and T. Lyons (Eds.), pp. 129–143. Newcastle upon Tyne: Cambridge Scholars Publishing.

Correa-Velez, I., Gifford, S., and Barnett, A. 2010. Longing to Belong: Social Inclusion and Wellbeing among Youth with Refugee Backgrounds in the First Three Years in Melbourne, Australia. *Social Science & Medicine* 71(8): 1399–1408.

Correa-Velez, I., Spaaij, R., and Upham, S. 2013. 'We Are Not Here to Claim Better Services Than Any Other': Social Exclusion among Men from Refugee Backgrounds in Urban and Regional Australia. *Journal of Refugee Studies* 26(2): 163–186.

Deng, S. and Marlowe, J. 2013. Refugee Resettlement and Parenting in a Different Context. *Journal of Immigrant and Refugee Studies* 11(4): 416–430.

Dever, M. 2005. Baby Talk: The Howard Government, Families, and the Politics of Difference. *Hecate* 31(2): 45–61.

Devisch, R. 1993. *Weaving the Threads of Life: The Khita gyn-eco-logical Healing Cult among the Yaka*. London: The University of Chicago Press.

Feldman-Savelsberg, P. 1999. *Plundered Kitchens, Empty Wombs: Threatened Reproduction and Identity in the Cameroon Grasslands*. Ann Arbor: The University of Michigan Press.

Feldman-Savelsberg, P. 2016. *Mothers on the Move: Reproducing Belonging between African and Europe*. Chicago, IL: University of Chicago Press.

Fisher, C. 2013. Changed and Changing Gender and Family Roles and Domestic Violence in African Refugee Background Communities Post-Settlement in Perth, Australia. *Violence against Women* 19(7): 833–847.

Fozdar, F. and Hartley, L. 2013. Civic and Ethno Belonging among Recent Refugees to Australia. *Journal of Refugee Studies* 27(1): 126–144.

Gifford, S., Bakopanos, C., Kaplan, I., and Correa-Velez, I. 2007. Meaning or Measurement? Researching the Social Contexts of Health and Settlement among Newly-Arrived Refugee Youth in Melbourne Australia. *Journal of Refugee Studies* 20(3): 414–440.

Gorman-Murray, A. 2008. Masculinity and the Home: A Critical Review and Conceptual Framework. *Australian Geographer* 39(3): 367–379.

Hage, G. 1997. At Home in the Entrails of the West: Multiculturalism, Ethnic Food and Migrant Home-Building. In *Home/world: Space, Community and Marginality in Sydney's West*. Grace, H., Hage, G., Johnson, L., Langsworth, J. and Symonds, M. (Eds.), pp. 99–153. Annandale, NSW: Pluto Press.

Hyndman, J. and Mountz, A. 2007. Refuge or Refusal. In *Violent Geographies: Fear, Terror, and Political Violence*. D. Gregory and A. Pred (Eds.), pp. 77–91. New York: Routledge.

Jackson, M. 2008. The Shock of the New: On Migrant Imaginaries and Critical Transitions. *Ethnos: Journal of Anthropology* 73(1): 57–72.

James, K. 2010. Domestic Violence within Refugee Families: Intersecting Patriarchal Culture and the Refugee Experience. *Australian & New Zealand Journal of Family Therapy* 31(3): 275–284.

Korpi, W., Ferrarini, T., and Englund, S. 2013. Women's Opportunities under Different Family Policy Constellations: Gender, Class, and Inequality Tradeoffs in Western Countries Re-Examined. *Social Politics* 20(1): 1–40.

Larsen, B.R. 2011. Drawing Back the Curtains: The Role of Domestic Space in the Social Inclusion of Refugees in Rural Denmark. *Social Analysis* 55(2): 142–158.

Lems, A. 2016. Placing Displacement: Place-Making in a World of Movement. *Ethnos* 81(2): 315–337.

Levi, M. 2014. Mothering in Transition: The Experiences of Sudanese Refugee Women Raising Teenagers in Australia. *Transcultural Psychiatry* 51(4): 479–498.

Lewig, K., Arney, F., and Salveron, M. 2010. Challenges to Parenting in a New Culture: Implications for Child and Family Welfare. *Evaluation and Program Planning* 33(3): 324–332.

Luibhéad, E. 2002. *Entry Denied: Controlling Sexuality at the Border*. Minneapolis: University of Minnesota Press.

Luibhéad, E. 2004. Childbearing against the State? Asylum Seeker Women in the Irish Republic. *Women's Studies International Forum* 27(4): 335–349.

Mallett, S. 2004. Understanding Home: A Critical Review of the Literature. *The Sociological Review* 52(1): 62–89.

Marlowe, J. 2011. 'Walking the Line': Southern Sudanese Masculinities and Reconciling One's Past with the Present. *Ethnicities* 12(1): 50–66.

McDonald, P. 2000. Gender Equity, Social Institutions and the Future of Fertility. *Journal of the Australian Population Association* 17(1): 1–16.

McMichael, C., Gifford, S., and Correa-Velez, I. 2010. Negotiating Family, Navigating Resettlement: Family Connectedness amongst Resettled Youth with Refugee Backgrounds Living in Melbourne. *Journal of Youth Studies* 14(2): 179–195.

Moore, H. 1986. *Space, Text, and Gender: An Anthropological Study of the Marakwet of Kenya*. Cambridge: Cambridge University Press.

Moore, H., Sanders, T., and Kaare, B. (Eds.). 1999. *Those Who Play With Fire: Gender, Fertility, and Transformation in East and Southern Africa*. London: Bloomsbury.

Morley, C. and MacFarlane, S. 2008. The Continued Importance of a Feminist Analysis; Making Gendered Inequalities Visible through a Critique of Howard Government Policy on Domestic Violence. *Just Policy: A Journal of Australian Social Policy* 47: 31–38.

Muchoki, S.M. 2013. '[In Australia] What Comes First Are the Women, then Children, Cats, Dogs, Followed by Men': Exploring Accounts of Gender Relations by Men from the Horn of Africa. *Australasian Review of African Studies* 34(2): 78–98.

Ndhlovu, F. 2011. Post-Refugee African Australians' Perceptions About Language and Becoming Australian: Language, Discourse and Participation. *African Identities* 9(4): 435–453.

Nunn, C., McMichael, C., Gifford, S., and Correa-Velez, I. 2014. 'I Came to this Country for a Better Life': Factors Mediating Employment Trajectories among Young People Who Migrated to Australia as Refugees during Adolescence. *Journal of Youth Studies* 17(9): 1205–1220.

Organa, V., Head, L., and Waitt, G. 2012. Who Does the Work in Sustainable Households? A Time and Gender Analysis in New South Wales, Australia. *Gender, Place & Culture: A Journal of Feminist Geography* 20(5): 559–577.

Oyewumi, O. 1997. *The Invention of Women: Making an African Sense of Western Gender Discourses*. Minneapolis: University of Minnesota Press.

Oyewumi, O. 2000. Family Bonds/Conceptual Binds: African Notes on Feminist Epistemologies. *Signs* 25(4): 1093–1098.

Oyewumi, O. 2002. Conceptualizing Gender: The Eurocentric Foundations of Feminist Concepts and the Challenges of African Epistemologies. *Jenda: A Journal of Culture and African Women Studies* 2(1): 1–9.

Rose, N. 1990. *Governing the Soul: The Shaping of the Private Self*. London: Taylor and Frances and Routledge.

Sampson, R. and Gifford, S. 2010. Place-making, Settlement, and Well-Being: The Therapeutic Landscapes of Recently Arrived Youth with Refugee Backgrounds. *Health & Place* 16(1): 116–131.

Shandy, D. 2008. Irish Babies, African Mothers: Rites of Passage and Rights in Citizenship in Post-Millennial Ireland. *Anthropological Quarterly* 81(4): 803–831.

Wilmsen, B. 2011. Family Separation: The Policies, Procedures, and Consequences for Refugee Background Families. *Refugee Survey Quarterly* 30(1): 44–64.

Zournazi, M. 2002. *Hope: New Philosophies for Change*. Annandale: Pluto Press.

9 Thresholds and being dead

Motherhood and caring for children was a fundamental locus of existential purpose and cosmological continuity for women I conducted fieldwork with. For them, displacement cannot be essentialised to a politico-legal category of statelessness: it is an experience that derives from having their cosmological logics of regeneration and temporal sense of circular time made precarious by external forces. It was when the possibility of bearing and rearing became either targeted through acts of violence in conflict or affected by the insecurity of protracted asylum that these women especially came to experience a sense of displacement. Conversely, it was having the capacity to bear and rear children restored through resettlement that caused them to feel that their displacement could be resolved. What happens, however, when bearing and rearing children itself is made precarious in resettlement? When the very connectedness between mother and child is severed?

Three of the women I conducted fieldwork with in Australia had their children unexpectedly forcibly removed from their care as a result of an intervention from a government-operated child welfare institution. Three may not seem a substantial number, but these are only women I directly worked with out of a small sample. Regardless, even one instance of forced child removal sends ripples of terror across the entire network of resettled refugees in a specific local area and probably beyond.

Many of the women I conducted fieldwork with who did not directly experience the removal of their children acutely feared such processes. Often knowing families who had been affected, they saw little difference between themselves and those who had been the target of a child welfare intervention. "They were a good family, with good children," one woman told me. "If it can happen to them, it can happen to us."

Forced child removal produces a seemingly unparalleled experience of displacement for those women and families who live it: even though these are women who have survived the extreme violence of war and conflict, who have fled their homes to protect the lives of their family, and who have endured the physical insecurity and existential uncertainty of life as a refugee in protracted asylum. If, as I propose, displacement is an existential experience of having cosmological trajectories of the world made precarious, then forced child removal represents, for Central African women whose sense of existential continuity depends on regenerating the circularity of time through motherhood, a threshold experience: that is, an experience of displacement so extreme that it no longer manifests as a sense of cosmological friction but as the rupturing of entire worlds and ways of being. It is through motherhood that these women locate their sense of future possibility. When the possibility of motherhood itself is severed, then those futures are not only challenged and transformed: they are annihilated.

An unimaginable possibility

Before being resettled in Australia, it was incomprehensible for the refugees I conducted fieldwork with that a government could remove children from the care of parents. I had direct insight into the ways in which, prior to resettlement, the idea of forced child removal is unimaginable for refugees in Africa. One morning in Uganda, I was sitting on the steps of the apartment where I lived in Kampala. Elena and Pulani joined me. We sat together, surrounded by buckets and clothes in various states of being washed. Both in their late teens and, at that time, unmarried, Elena and Pulani were intensely curious about my life in Australia. As I dipped my hands into the sudsy water to scrub and wring my dirty laundry, I tried to give them a realistic portrayal of life in Australia and what it is like to be resettled. Our discussion soon turned towards having children in Australia. I said, offhandedly, "You do realise the Australian government can take a mother's children away?"

Both Elena and Pulani turned to each other, then laughed in response. They continued their washing unconcernedly.

"No, seriously," I continued. "The government in Australia has the right to take children away from their parents if they think the parent is not doing a good job." Still, it seemed, Elena and Pulani did not believe me.

"You are joking," Elena said, slapping my leg with a wet hand. "They could not do that," Pulani added, "When you are a parent, you are a parent."

"Well they do, seriously," I continued. "They take some children, and put them with other families. It happens."

"But Africans are good," Elena said. "We are good parents."

"Yes," I respond. "But the government decides that. I know some women who have had their babies taken away in Australia."

Finally, both Elena and Pulani looked at me with serious expressions, seeming to grasp the gravity of what I was explaining. Still, they were unable to fully accept the idea of forced child removal as a reality. The notion that a government would forcibly intervene into the parenting of children was incomprehensible to them. "No, that is not good," Elena said. "That could not happen." Except, as the women I conducted fieldwork with in Australia found out, such experiences do happen. Forced child removal is a devastating, but nonetheless real, possibility in resettlement.

The mandate of child protection

The mandate to protect the welfare of children in Australia is the responsibility of individual state and territory governments rather than a federated system. Nonetheless, child welfare interventions follow a similar general structure across state- and territory-level scales of operation, which makes it possible to talk about the child protection system in Australia as an overarching institution despite its being guided by different legislation at state and territory levels (AIHW 2014: 2). Across Australia, institutions of family welfare and child protection follow similar procedures for receiving and assessing reports of suspected abuse, which follow the general structure I describe here. Once a report has been made in regard to a child or children, workers from the child welfare institution assess the severity of the notification and investigate it, a complex process that can include the use of standardised risk assessment instruments along with consensus-based assessment tools (Child, Family, and Community Australia 2017). In doing so, they determine whether the child or children are at a risk of significant harm. If it is determined that the risk of harm to a child or children outweighs protective factors, the child is removed into temporary foster care. After a removal, the care environment from which the welfare institution removed the child or children is evaluated. Based on these evaluations, child protection workers develop a "care" or "stability" plan, which recommends to the court whether the risk of harm to the child can or cannot be outweighed by increased protective factors longitudinally, ultimately deciding whether to recommend that the removed children be restored to their family or, alternatively, be placed in the permanent guardianship of the state. It is a magistrate who then considers these evaluations, often in addition to arguments made by legal representatives of the parents and an independent lawyer for the children, to make a final determination as to whether the state or parents are to be provided with guardianship over the children.

It is estimated that children from an African refugee background are over-represented in the child welfare system in Australia (Losoncz 2015: 416). The dominant explanation for this heightened vulnerability is that African refugees find it challenging to adapt to expectations of parenting in Australia (Lewig, Arney, and Salveron 2010; Renzaho and Vignjevic 2011). This explanation is consistent with observations I made during my fieldwork, in which I could recognise that particular expectations around parenting in Australia were difficult for parents I got to know. These challenges did not stem from intrinsic parental deficiency but from the ways in which conditions of everyday life in resettlement make their conventional styles of caregiving more difficult. For example, some women described to me how, before coming to Australia, it was easy to leave children alone because there was generally always an older sibling or adult nearby to watch them. But in Australia, these refugees are isolated from friends and family who would normally support them to supervise children. Trying to adjust to these differences was not easy. However, putting the causality of child welfare interventions directly onto their caregiving practices risks overlooking the ways in which assumptions of difference based on racialisations may make refugees more visible to institutions of child protection, more vulnerable to intervention, and make assessments of their parenting more critical (Walter, Taylor, and Habibis 2011).

The procedures that are in place to identify and assess risk of significant harm to children in child welfare institutions are aimed towards objectivity. But these processes are nonetheless initiated by and operated through people, and people inevitably bring subjectivity. Although child welfare assessment procedures in Australia and elsewhere increasingly rely on actuarial tools that minimise the potential influence of individual worker bias, it is, nonetheless, individual workers who engage with those families and who determine, based on subjective understandings, what dynamics of parenting are problematic. This means that experiences of child welfare interventions continue to vary depending on individual workers assigned to cases despite the increased use of actuarial assessment tools (Scherz 2011).

Becoming the subject of a child welfare intervention is also a cause of intense fear for highly visible black African people in Australia, who often feel frustrated at what they see as "over attention" being drawn to them from government agencies and public services, including through the child welfare system (Losoncz 2015; Wickramaarachchi and Burns 2016: 88). Because allegations of abuse that are reported to the child welfare agency are generally made by people from educational institutions, health and medical settings, social welfare organisations, and even the local public, it follows that attention to highly visible refugee families and initial evaluations of their parenting will be conditioned by subjectivities, including those based on stereotypes and biases. For example, one of the women I got to know during fieldwork described how she had become the subject of a child protection intervention after neighbours in her block of public housing apartments made a report about her young adolescent son, who was seen by the neighbours walking outside the apartments at around 8pm at night. It was the first day of school holidays and the boy had been walking through the public housing complex to stay overnight at the house of a friend. "They probably think he is in a gang," she told me. Even if these reports do seem superficial, they can accumulate and nonetheless serve to bring refugees into the analytical frame of the child welfare system. This makes them vulnerable to more serious interventions, such as the forced removal of children from parental care.

During my fieldwork, I became close to three women whose lives had been drastically transformed through interventions from the child welfare agency. Specificities of each case mean that direct comparisons are problematic, and providing extensive details can risk identifying those involved. In each case, the removal of a child or children was initiated following allegations of physical violence. Even when the perpetrators of the violence were removed from the family context, however, the procedure of the child welfare agency to examine the overall caregiving context of the home before determining whether to recommend restoring the child or children to parental care or placing them under the permanent guardianship of the state meant that the caregiving behaviours of the women themselves came to be under scrutiny. Observations of, and evaluations about, caregiving often arose based on interactions that took place during visitations between women and their removed children during the period in which the care plan for their family future was being drawn up by the child welfare agency.

I attended many supervised visitations between African refugee mothers and their children who had been placed into foster care. Although these visitations took place in a variety of settings, many seemed, at least to me, to be wildly inappropriate for the sensitive and emotional situation of a mother meeting with children forcibly removed from her care: some visits took place in the building of the child welfare agency in which the mothers had spent hours attempting, unsuccessfully, to negotiate the return of their children, some took place in the more calming settings of a local community centre or park, and many I attended took place in the dining rooms of fast food restaurants. The often unfamiliar and alienating setting of the contact visitations was also exacerbated by the presence of a worker who had been assigned to supervise the visit and take notes: they could often be seen conspicuously writing in a notebook, recording activities and discussion. It was also common for an interpreter to be included in these supervised visits, meaning that all of the conversations between women and their children could be effectively surveilled. It was within those settings that women were expected to demonstrate effective caregiving practices.

This often created a context of visitation between mother and children that felt uncomfortable and hostile to the women I conducted fieldwork with. On one occasion, in which I was accompanying Camille on a visitation with her children, I witnessed the extent of this surveillance when a worker, who seemed visibly panicked, asked me to "watch" the children. The worker had been instructed to followed and observe Camille at all times and that included following her into the bathroom to watch her change the soiled nappy of one the children. After the incident, Camille told me that she felt humiliated. "Like I cannot change a nappy," she said. "They make me feel like I am not a mother."

The impossible possibility of severing maternal connectedness

The forced removal of children is devastating for parents who become involved in a child welfare intervention. But for women I conducted fieldwork with, such interventions resonate beyond the violence of separating parents from children. The ability of the Australian government to remove children from the care of parents creates a new possibility of existence that was previously incomprehensible: that in which the connectedness between mother and child, previously understood to be immutable, can be severed.

The disjuncture between the immutability of maternal relatedness and the possibility of severing that connectedness was most acutely emphasised during my fieldwork in an encounter between Sophia, one of the women whose children were removed from her care, and workers from a child welfare agency. At the beginning of this particular meeting, Sophia held a toothpick in one hand while picking nervously at her fingernail cuticles on the other, unable to meet the eyes of the workers from the child welfare agency that sat opposite her. She had been called into the meeting that day to ascertain her availability to have visitation meetings with her children. These visitations were to occur once per month for two hours and would be supervised by a contracted welfare agency. Workers funded by the state had been appointed as case managers to oversee the foster care experience of the children, and the workers were also responsible for organising visitation meetings. They sat across from Sophia with a printed-out calendar and asked her to circle dates on it when she would be available to do visitations with the children.

This process immediately confused Sophia. The workers were asking her to pick out dates over a 12-month period. She told me, later, that the idea of organising meetings with her children in this way was extremely offensive to her, "like booking an appointment" with her own offspring. Sensing that Sophia was confused, one of the workers began explaining to her, again, in a slow and patronising tone, what they were trying to achieve.

"We would like to organise dates for visitation now," the woman directly opposite Sophia said. "It means that all of us will be able to set them up well in advance and never miss any." She gave what appeared to be a sympathetic nod toward Sophia. She then added, "It is very important that you are able to maintain a relationship with your children. We do not want you to lose your relationship with them."

There was a moment of silence following this spiel. Then Sophia stood up abruptly from her chair and directed an uncharacteristically forceful outburst at the workers across the table.

"I am a mother," she said. "Those children grew here," she added with her hand splayed over her belly, "in my stomach." The workers stared at Sophia, seeming to be unable to comprehend the meaning of her outburst. "They are my children," Sophia continued. "They grew inside me. They will always know me. I will always know them. We are always connected." She then turned and promptly left the room.

The child welfare system, and those individuals who are embedded as operational actors within it, clearly work from the assumption that maternal relatedness is nonessential and transmutable. For Central African women like Sophia, however, the idea that connectedness between mother and child is able to be severed is impossible. Over time, however, I was to witness how the seeming impossibility of severed maternal relatedness comes to be not only a possibility for resettled Central African refugees but a lived reality, specifically for those who experience it.

As the period of time in which the children were in foster care lengthened, the interpersonal connectedness between mother and children became greater. During fieldwork, I once picked up Sophia following a contact visit with the children to find her crying uncontrollably outside of a train station. I had initially thought that the tears were an emotional reaction to saying goodbye to her children and watching them get driven away to their foster care home in some anonymous location she was not privy to. Sophia often cried after visiting the children. This time, however, her sadness at leaving them was interwoven with a new kind of loss. Sophia told me that, on that day, she had attempted to talk with the children in their first language, but they had been unable to understand her. At some points during the visit she had been unable to communicate with her children.

Months later, I went to visit Sophia at home. Where previously Sophia had made a point of maintaining a well-kept garden filled with various plant foods, including beans and maize, the garden was now laid to waste, overgrown, and wild. Inside the house was not much better. What had previously been an orderly and well-organised home was now a mess of unwashed dishes, dirty carpets, and piles and piles of paperwork. After walking through the garden into the house and mechanically exchanging the usual pleasantries, Sophia and I sat down together on the sofa in her living room. Strangely, she offered no beverage or food, something that always accompanied a visit with other Central African women. Sophia only stared blankly ahead and explained that she could not sleep: she was resorting to sleeping pills, prescribed by a doctor, to rest. Then she mentioned that she would no longer be visiting the children. When I asked her why, she simply said that it was "too hard."

Having children forcibly removed from her care produced a situation in which Sophia was no longer able to exist in the world as a mother or to engage in all of the everyday practices of care that are encompassed within that role as a specific ontology of "feeding," as I describe in Chapter 2, which involves cultivating gardens, preparing and cooking food, and bearing and rearing children. Being made to feel as if they are "not a mother," as Camille described it, means that women who experience forced child removal are pushed beyond an existential threshold. They are women whose sense of meaningful existence has not only been made precarious through instances of cosmological friction but has been acutely ruptured. They continue nonetheless to exist but do so in a condition of existential displacement and temporal discordance in which their lives are suspended in the immediacy of the present towards an impossible future. The women described this experience of being ejected from the temporal rhythms of circular time and the cosmological cycle of regenerative possibility as a state of being "dead."

Being dead

Sitting with Camille in her apartment on an August afternoon in 2013, the silence that surrounded us emphasised the lack of children in her home. On the coffee table in front of us was a tattered photo album turned to a photograph depicting a newborn baby, her youngest child, wrapped in a hospital blanket. "Three months since I have seen him," she continued. "My boy. He is walking very well now, talking too. But just in English." Poring through the photo album with me, Camille reflected on how, as a refugee in Africa, she was able to protect her children within circumstances of extreme violence.

"The soldiers came to my village at night," she told me:

> I tried to hide in my home, but people were running everywhere and I knew I could not be safe that way. I had only been married a year, and John [her oldest child] was still a very small baby. My husband, he had left in the night to find some information about what was happening, and he never came back. I had to run, you see? So I left the house with Jon strapped across my chest. But the soldiers, they began shooting at me.

Camille then lifted her foot and touched the centre where a twisted scar puckered the skin. Pointing to the old wound, she told me:

> They shot me, and somehow the bullet hit me, here. I fell. I was bleeding a lot, so I wiped that blood across my body and lay there, for hours. John was still tied across my chest, and I had to lay there, face down. He was only a small baby, and he was crying. I used my body to hide his screams. I pretended to be dead so we could survive.

In Australia, however, she was judged as incapable of protecting her children from harm. This paradox was incomprehensible to Camille:

> When they told me I would be going to Australia, I thought, 'This is good! My children will have a life!' But here they took all of my children ... they came at night and took them out of their beds. I didn't get to hug them; I didn't know what was happening. And my smallest baby, he was still on the breast. They took them, even though I protected them in Africa. I kept them safe. I wish I could take them back there, to Africa. Or I wish we had all died there, and not come here. I am dead now.

That was not the first time Camille had referred to herself as dead nor was it to be the last. When she describes herself as dead, Camille is not referring to death in a biological sense. Rather, she is referring to a sense of social death: that is, an enduring state of existential displacement in which she physiologically lives but, because she has no fundamental identity and status of motherhood from which to be recognised through and to exist as, has ceased to have anything to live for.

The concept of social death was theorised by Orlando Patterson (1982) as a way to characterise the lives of people who have ceased to exist to others and within their everyday environment in a socially meaningful way. The concept was used by Patterson (1982) to characterise the lives of enslaved peoples from diverse historical contexts, with the general sense of slavery being described in reference to those peoples whose lives have come to be defined entirely by a master–slave relationship, who are thereby concurrently integral actors within a social context of everyday life but utterly excluded from social meaning within it. Although the theorisation put forward by Patterson (1982) can be critiqued on the basis that it does not take critical account of the ways in which enslaved peoples themselves create sociality, meaning, and community even in the experience of slavery (Scott 1990), the idea of social death is still a useful way to describe, more broadly, how lives can come to be lived without existential purpose.

The women I conducted fieldwork with whose children were removed from their care can be considered as subjects who have come to exist in such a state of social death. Orlando Patterson (1982) differentiates between two different modes of social death: intrusive and extrusive. Intrusive social death is caused by bringing an outsider into a social situation and excluding them from the opportunity to become socially meaningful. Extrusive social death refers to the experience when a person who already existed as part of a social milieu becomes excluded from it, so that they exist as an "insider who had fallen, one who ceased to belong and had been expelled from normal participation in the community because of a failure to meet certain minimal legal or socioeconomic norms of behaviour" (Patterson 1982: 41).

In the social worlds of the refugees I conducted fieldwork with, women who cease to exist as mothers occupy the extrusive category of social death. They are people who are expelled from everyday ways of being and contexts of social life because they no longer possess the fundamental status of motherhood from which their sociality and existential purpose is realised. Although these women generally elicited sympathy from other refugees around them, the ambiguity of their status as mothers made it nonetheless difficult to incorporate them into social contexts. It was as if they had become living examples of matter out of place (Douglas 1966): that is, subjects who could not be distinctly categorised. These were women who occupied the ambiguous status of being, concurrently, mothers who had borne children but also not-mothers because they no longer had children with them, whose motherhood had been contested by the state. They could not be easily categorised and, as peoples embodying matter out of place, had come to signify ambiguity, awkwardness, and even danger to existing social orders.

I observed the effects of this ambiguity most distinctly when Sophia came to me in tears one day, explaining that she had been ejected from an English language class that was exclusively set up for mothers, who were allowed to bring their children into class in order to breastfeed. Since Sophia no longer had a child following the child welfare intervention, she had eventually been asked to join the general English language class. Although the other refugee women around her were sympathetic, they also agreed that the change was necessary. More broadly, I observed that women who had their children removed were generally ejected from the social circles in which they had previously been integral members. The ambiguity of their social status was one reason for this exclusion, but other refugee women also feared that associating with those who had their children removed might also make them more visible to the child protection agency. The removal of children had created a situation in which these women had extrusive social death forced on them. Where once they had occupied a distinct social status, their lives became, overnight, void of social meaning.

Re-thinking thresholds of displacement

That refugees come to exist in diminished states of being has become a trope in refugee studies. Often, the idea that refugees epitomise a state of "bare life," as theorised by Giorgio Agamben (1998), has been used to describe the empirical lives of refugees in situations of protracted asylum. The concept of bare life, as theorised by Agamben (1998), derives from an ancient Greek division between citizens and exiles, in which those subjects whose lives had political significance were understood to have *zoe*, political life, and those whose lives were excluded from civic value had only *bios*, bare life, or life that is reduced to purely physiological existence without social or political value. Those whose lives are defined by bare life, according to Agamben (1998), occupy a condition in which they are able to be killed by the state or governing body because they have biological existence but are not able to be sacrificed because their lives have no political value.

The figure of the refugee, according to Agamben (1998), epitomises a contemporary status of bare life. Refugees are stateless subjects who exist without being able to be included in the operations of a state as citizens but still occupy a physiological presence within states, making them subjects whose physical presence makes them able to be controlled and killed by state actors but whose lack of civic status makes their lives and deaths lack political meaning or repercussion. Despite the persistence of this trope of refugees as the embodiment of bare life in scholarly depictions, particularly of those living in camps (Stratton 2011), the characterisation is limited: it does not take into account the numerous and nuanced ways in which refugees seek and exert agency, even in the most desperate of circumstances (Fassin 2012). But even if refugee lives could be reduced to a state of bare life or some other form of extreme diminishment, the Agamben (1998) conceptualisation of this condition is one in which the bare life of refugees is essentialised to their status of statelessness: their exclusion from the polis is always understood in relation to, and at the boundaries of, their politico-legal status. It is from such conflations of the politico-legal ambiguity of refugees with a status of fundamentally diminished life and reduced agency that the idea of displacement comes to be predominantly understood in relation to the statelessness of refugees, which can be resolved by re-inserting them back into a framework of national identity and citizenship (Malkki 1992, 1995b), rather than as an existential condition.

But if the diminishment of refugee lives endures even after their politico-legal status as stateless peoples has been resolved, as is the case for refugees in resettlement, then the idea that they can experience social death in those contexts requires thinking about the possibility of displacement as an existential condition that can be realised not only through politico-legal exclusion but also through temporal control. When women whose children are removed from their care by the Australian government have their status of mothers made ambiguous, this state of cosmological rupture produces an experience of social death that is not realised through their politico-legal status, but which is made possible through having their ways of being and assumptions about the future totalistically subordinated to the interests and agendas of state actors. Thinking about how the displacement of refugees endures, and is indeed realised, in contexts of resettlement opens up new ways to conceptualise displacement as a condition that is not defined by the politico-legal borders of statelessness and citizenship, as it is conventionally understood across academic scholarship, governments, and humanitarian bodies, but which is also realised as an existential condition that is wrought through temporal control and constraint.

The concept of the threshold is a useful way to understand this distinction. Conventionally, the forced migration experience has been characterised as a linear trajectory from exodus to exile to eventual solution. The thresholds of displacement and refuge embedded in that reading of forced migration are those that are realised at politico-legal boundaries of statelessness: at which displacement is realised upon refugees becoming stateless peoples and from which displacement is resolved when they are re-inserted back into a recognisable status of citizenship. But if the thresholds of displacement are understood to be realised through temporal dynamics, then the experience of displacement emerges when the futures of refugees, and perhaps other actors more broadly, is made precarious. Conversely, a sense of refuge is realised when futures of possibility are able to be not only imagined but lived. What this means is that when assumptions of futurity are not only made precarious, but destroyed, by processes of forced child removal, resettled refugees are not only crossing into a state of enduring displacement: they have transcended a temporal threshold of existential impossibility in which they are not only living as displaced peoples but as peoples who exist in the present towards a seemingly impossible future.

Impossible futures and necropolitics of social death

With the children placed in permanent foster care until they turn 18 years old, the pain of visiting them and seeing the distance grow between them had become too much for Camille to stand. Eventually, she stopped participating in visitations. With no children, the public benefit payments she received were drastically reduced, meaning she had to move out of the house she had been living in. It had been difficult trying to find another rental house alone, and, besides, the city where she had lived with the children was now haunted by painful memories. By the time my fieldwork was drawing to a close, Camille was living a transient existence earning money by picking fruit for growers along the Eastern coast of Australia. I drove up the coast to visit her in that situation. That evening, we sat together in the tent she was living in: the third tent she had been through that month because tropical storms had damaged the others. Without electricity, we sat in the tent under the light of an oil lamp and spoke of the violences she had experience in Australia:

> "There, in that tent in the refugee camp, life was hard." Camille rubbed her back and sides, as she said, "But, there I had my children. Here," she indicated her stomach. "And here," she said, pointing to her back.
>
> "In Australia," she continued, "I am back in the tent. But here, I have no children. None. Australia has killed me."

The ways in which Camille and other women I conducted fieldwork with describe life as a resettled refugee in Australia as "too hard to make a life," a context in which they are "dead," or as an experience in which they have been "killed," opens up new ways to consider how necropolitics operates to govern and control populations. The concept of necropolitics is theorised by Achille Mbembe (2003: 14) as "the generalised instrumentalisation of human existence and the material destruction of human bodies and populations." What we see in the experiences of the refugees I conducted fieldwork with, who have either experienced forced child removal or who live in acute fear of it as a previously unimaginable and yet very real possibility, is a kind of necropolitics of social death (Ramsay 2017a) in which control of populations is mobilised, not through the threat of destroying physical life, but through destroying fundamental bases of humanity and, consequently, ways of future building. For women I got to know during fieldwork, this destruction is levelled at the possibilities of life that are embodied in the futurity of their children.

It may seem extreme to characterise the lives of women who have had their children removed from their care as lives that are lived in a state of social death. These are extreme cases, however, precisely because these women have surpassed a threshold from the possibility of a viable future to the reality of an impossible future. Describing how existential purpose is maintained even in desperate situations, Michael Jackson (2013a: 212) considers that "[t]o be subdued by circumstances one cannot change, acted upon yet powerless to act, may be bearable if there is the hope or promise of some reward." Through all of the hardships, struggles, and devastations of conflict and war, asylum and encampment, and resettlement and cosmological friction, the women I conducted fieldwork with were able to maintain a thread of hope and possibility of regenerating futures live that could be worth living because these possible futures were embodied by the survival of their children. The forced removal of children by the Australian government severs the parental connectedness necessary to this process of social reproduction, making those women who experience such devastation feel that they are "dead" because the very future itself has been made impossible.

The idea of "possibility" is generally utilised in anthropological research in ways that imply optimism: "[O]nly rarely does peril move explicitly into sharp focus under its aegis" (Guyer 2009: 364). But as Jane Guyer (2009) points out, in reference to the work of Anna Tsing (2005) on global friction, it is necessary to consider that futures are horizons of possibility in which both hope and despair intersect, making it necessary to consider possibility beyond the exclusivity of optimism and to recognise the courage and struggle it takes to forge life out of possibility in conditions of control and constraint. Resettlement emerged from my fieldwork as one such situation in which the possibility of a future is simultaneously intertwined with the possibility of destruction.

References

Agamben, G. 1998. *Homo Sacer: Sovereign Power and Bare Life*. Translated by Daniel Heller-Roazen. Stanford, CA: Stanford University Press.

Australian Institute of Health and Welfare [AIHW]. 2014. Child Protection in Australia: 2012–2013. Available at: www.aihw.gov.au/WorkArea/DownloadAsset.aspx?id=60129548164 (Accessed 26 December 2014).

Child, Family, Community Australia. 2017. Risk Assessment Instruments in Child Protection: CFCA Resource Sheet—June 2016. Available at: https://aifs.gov.au/cfca/publications/risk-assessment-child-protection (Accessed 16 January 2017).

Douglas, M. 1966. *Purity and Danger: An Analysis of Concepts of Pollution and Taboo*. London; New York: Routledge.

Fassin, D. 2012. *Humanitarian Reason: A Moral History of the Present*. Berkeley: University of California Press.

Guyer, J. 2009. A Response to 'How Is Anthropology Going?' *Anthropological Theory* 9(4): 355–370.

Jackson, M. 2013a. *The Wherewithal of Life: Ethics Migration, and the Question of Well-Being*. Berkeley: University of California Press.

Lewig, K., Arney, F., and Salveron, M. 2009. Challenges to Parenting in a New Culture: Implications for Child and Family Welfare. *Evaluation and Program Planning* 33(3): 324–332.

Losoncz, I. 2015. 'The Government Just Stops Parents Parenting'—Finding Better Ways to Build Safety Around Children in Families From a Refugee Background.

Child Abuse and Neglect. RegNet Research Page 76. Available at: https://poseidon01.ssrn.com/delivery.php?ID=589112090009122100127006091123065064031038028079005001126105084005088009068025072031100048097039026028033106100064091028095117017001002076092010083101126117082118080054048004021017118006005069095123090026011116079010025082026089071065004070068003117125&EXT=pdf (Accessed 29 January 2017).

Malkki, L. 1992. National Geographic: The Rooting of Peoples and the Territorialization of National Identity among Scholars and Refugees. *Cultural Anthropology* 7(1): 24–44.

Malkki, L. 1995b. Refugees and Exile: From 'Refugee Studies' to the National Order of Things. *Annual Review of Anthropology* 24: 495–523.

Mbembe, A. 2003. Necropolitics. *Public Culture* 15(1): 11–40.

Patterson, O. 1982. *Slavery and Social Death: A Comparative Study*. Cambridge, MA: Harvard University Press.

Ramsay, G. 2017a. Incommensurable Futures and Displaced Lives: Sovereignty as Control over Time. *Public Culture* 29(3): 515–538.

Renzaho, A. and Vignjevic, S. 2011. The Impact of a Parenting Intervention in Australia among Migrants and Refugees from Liberia, Sierra Leone, Congo, and Burundi: Results from the African Migrant Parenting Program. *Journal of Family Studies* 17: 71–79.

Scherz, C. 2011. Protecting Children, Preserving Families: Moral Conflict and Actuarial Science in a Problem of Contemporary Governance. *PoLAR: Political and Legal Anthropology Review* 34(1): 33–50.

Scott, J. 1990. *Domination and the Arts of Resistance: Hidden Transcripts*. New Haven, CT; London: Yale University Press.

Stratton, J. 2011. Zombie Trouble: Zombie Texts, Bare Life, and Displaced People. *European Journal of Cultural Studies* 14(3): 265–281.

Tsing, A. 2005. *Friction: An Ethnography of Global Connection*. Princeton, NJ: Princeton University Press.

Walter, M., Taylor, S., and Habibis, D. 2011. How White is Social Work in Australia? *Australian Social Work* 64(1): 6–19.

Wickramaarachchi, N. and Burns, E. 2016. Sudanese Humanitarian Migrants in Australian Refereed Journals. *Australasian Review of African Studies* 37(2): 80–106.

10 Sovereignty and incommensurable futures

When they told me I would be going to Australia, I thought, 'This is good! My children will have a life!' But here they took all of my children … they came at night and took them out of their beds. I didn't get to hug them. I didn't know what was happening. And my smallest baby, he was still on the breast. They took them, even though I protected them in Africa. I kept them safe. I wish I could take them back there, to Africa. Or I wish we had all died there, and not come here. I am dead now.

I return to these words, spoken by Camille following the removal of her children from her care through the child protection system, because they reflect the primary paradox that I encountered during my research. After being resettled, refugees can be confronted with new—and for some, like Camille, more devastating—experiences of displacement. When the hardships of protracted asylum in Africa, and even death, are preferable to being resettled in Australia, it is evident that the assumptions of benevolence that are attached to the resettlement of refugees conceal enduring formations of power.

Because the displacement that is experienced by refugees is conventionally conflated with the ambiguity of their statelessness, it is often assumed that displacement is resolved once they are resettled and able to be politically and legally recognised as belonging to and incorporated within a nation state. From fieldwork I conducted with refugees in Australia, however, it is clear that resettlement does not resolve displacement. Rather, resettlement puts refugees into new contexts of ambiguity in which it is not their politico-legal status that is problematised, but the futures that they, as subjects who are marked by assumptions of difference and inferiority, represent to the agenda and interests of the host state in which they have been settled. Recognising that the control and constraint of refugee lives as threats to nationhood continues even after resettlement opens up new ways to think about how sovereignty is realised through temporal domination.

Sovereignty is a term that refers to the contentious dynamic between individual autonomy and political organisation, that is, the complex "locus and nature of the agency that constitutes a political system" (Strong 2005: xi). Sovereignty is approached analytically in two primary ways (Hansen and Stepputat 2006): as a direct force of population control whereby power is realised through the determination of legal categories of recognition and exclusion, or as a decentralised force whereby populations reproduce the hegemonic horizons through which their regulation is normalised. In the former vein, sovereignty originates through direct and unilateral power relations, and is produced through the instrumentalisation of law. In the latter, sovereignty is the effect of power relations through which forms of governmentality are produced and normalised.

When sovereignty is approached as a form of power that is realised at horizons of law, the category of citizenship, and other forms of national identification and permanent residency, becomes crucial to the reproduction of sovereign power because it is through these classifications that jurisdiction of absolute authority and population control is organised. In a world system in which the organisation of populations depends on what Liisa Malkki (1992) calls a "national order of things," the legal figure of the refugee, who contests the seemingly natural conflation between person and citizen through which national sovereignty, population control, and the world order is premised, is a distinct problem: a category and figure of "exception" to the rule of politico-legal systems of order. According to Carl Schmitt (1985: 5), it is, in fact, through the differentiation of populations as either subject to the rule of law or as exceptions to it that the authority of sovereign power is realised for "Sovereign is he who decides on the exception." Extending on Schmitt (1985), Giorgio Agamben (1998) has argued that the figure of the refugee epitomises the contemporary state of exception because the determination of refugee status is a determination of legal statelessness. According to Agamben (1998), it is through determining those who occupy this fundamental state of exception that the condition of "bare life" is produced, and sovereignty is realised. Examining the treatment of refugees, and especially how populations of refugees are controlled and constrained by the nations that host them, is a way to trace how sovereign power is exerted and imposed.

But the state of exception is not so totalistic in reducing subjects to bare life as the Agamben (1998) conceptualisation presents it (Fassin 2012). The image of the state of exception that is offered by Giorgio Agamben (1998) is one that, following Carl Schmitt (1985), locates the production of sovereign power entirely within the legal process of determining which populations are subject to the rule of law and which are exceptions to it. However, the contingency of the exception state is especially evident when the sovereign power that constrains the agency of those relegated to the exception state is recognised as a decentralised and dynamic force rather than a mode of power that is exclusively realised at the boundaries of law. Because sovereignty works to include and exclude peoples from political recognition and national protection in "aleatory" (Dunn and Cons 2013) and "graduated" (Ong 2006) ways, it is possible to consider, as well, that the state of exception similarly cuts across a continuum of agentic possibility and constraint.

The exclusion and inclusion of subjects from or into the rule of law is contingent: and, at times, the classification of populations within the rule-exception dynamic is used strategically by states to meet market interests that intersect with, but also exist in isolation from, the authority of sovereign states (Ong 2006). In the same way that populations who might conventionally be understood as citizens subject to the rule of law can be strategically excluded from it in order to meet market interests, refugees, who are supposed to epitomise the exception state, can also be brought into the rule of law, depending on the national context. For example, the Ugandan government allows refugees to have similar rights to those of its citizens, including rights to residency, freedom of movement, and employment, which complicates how they can be understood as categorical figures of exception. As Aihwa Ong (2006) similarly recognises, the ways in which this exception state is graduated often reveals intersecting formations of power and population governance between the sovereignty of nation states and the market interests of global capitalism. When the Ugandan government includes refugees into civic life by offering them legal rights to work and residency, then, this is not necessarily the product of humanitarian sentiment intended to collapse the dichotomy between citizen and refugee. These processes of supposed civic integration also reflect the ways in which the lives of refugees, and others, can be defined in terms of market logics and their value measured in regard to economic productivity as much as in politico-legal terms.

The state of exception can, then, be considered as a "graduated" status (Upton 2014) that is not totalistically realised at, and reducible to, horizons of politico-legal inclusion and exclusion. But if peoples who are legally recognised as stateless refugees in Uganda can nonetheless be incorporated into civic rules of law because the logics of capitalist markets operate alongside, and in intersections with, sovereign power, then, conversely, it can be considered that those refugees, whose legal status of statelessness is resolved upon being resettled, may also continue to experience a state of exception that transcends being realised at legal horizons. When resettled refugees in Australia are identified as problematic civic actors because their value within the market logics of neoliberal capitalism is ambiguous, they come to exist in a state of exception that is graduated depending on their economic participation rather than the (non)recognition of their civic status. The kind of sovereignty that is realised through this graduated state of exception is decentralised and produced through processes of temporal domination in which the control of everyday life in the present by institutions that reinforce both state interests and market logics work from a temporal orientation to produce particular kinds of futurity and deny others. "Pitiless in its punishment of those who fail to perform or those who fall behind" (Hansen and Stepputat 2006: 304), it is through control over time and, consequently, the kinds of futures that are able to be imagined and lived, that such decentralised forms of sovereignty are imposed (Ramsay 2017a).

Stolen lives

Assuming that sovereignty is realised through the legal determination of the exception status would mean that contemporary acts of forced child removal, which operate according to a government mandate to protect all children that transcends specific legal categories of civic recognition, are wholly benevolent and do not reproduce conditions of state control. But contemporary instances of forced child removal that are experienced by women from Central African refugee backgrounds in Australia suggest that sovereignty is not exclusively realised through legal determinations of the rule and the exception, but is decentralised and embedded into the structuring of ordinary life. Focused on the reproduction of particular ways of living through the socialisation of children, the sovereignty that is imposed through interventions of forced child removal operates, specifically, as a control on temporality: as the prevention and destruction of particular kinds of futures.

"Stolen" was the term used by women I conducted fieldwork with to describe this experience of having an anticipated future destroyed by acts of forced child removal. "The Australian government has stolen my children," I was told by one woman, Camille, after the removal of her children. Her choice of the word "stolen" is pertinent. It describes not only her personal experience of forced child removal but also echoes the experiences of Aboriginal peoples in Australia who, from at least 1869 to 1969, were the subject of practices of systematic forced child removal in which it was legal for government authorities to remove children from the care of Aboriginal families by virtue of their racialisation alone (Van Krieken 1999). Those Aboriginal children who were removed during that period are referred to in public discourse in Australia as the "Stolen Generations" (Cuthbert and Quartly 2013). Exact numbers of children affected by these policies are unknown, but estimates suggest that between 1 and 3 and 1 in 10 Aboriginal children were removed from the care of their Aboriginal families and placed into state-run institutional care homes or adopted by white Australian families during the 100 years of forced removal (Commonwealth of Australia 1997). Those generations of Aboriginal children were indeed "stolen" in both a physical sense of being absent from their families and in temporal sense in which their futures were determined not by their own agency, but by the state (Ramsay 2017a). The purpose of these policies was, ostensibly, to "protect" children from the damaging effects of Aboriginal culture. The result was that an entire generation of Aboriginal children grew up without connection to their family or culture, leading to intense intergenerational trauma.

The child welfare system no longer removes children from the care of their family exclusively on the basis of race. The dynamic between power, othering, protection, and children continues, however, to be salient. For example, in 2001, the Australian government alleged that asylum seekers upon the

Tampa IV boat, which had begun to sink en route to Australia, had attempted to throw children overboard as a way to get attention from naval authorities. In a public interview, the then-Prime Minister, John Howard, claimed, "[We] do not want in Australia people who would throw their own children into the sea" (Four Corners 2002). These allegations were later proven to be false. It was found that, instead of trying to murder their children for the sake of protection, the asylum seekers had held the infants in the air to emphasise the vulnerability of their situation and attempt to hasten their rescue from the sinking boat. Nonetheless, the immediate effect of this dehumanisation was a legitimatisation in public opinion of the need for the Australian government to protect the sovereignty of national borders from asylum seekers (Hugo 2002; Pickering and Lambert 2002): an attitude that has since become solidified in the bi-partisan government policy of mandatorily detaining people seeking asylum in Australia by boat. The protection of asylum seeker lives, especially those of children, is regularly cited in Australian politics as the purpose of this dehumanising policy (Gale 2004; Millbank 2009), even though it is widely recognised that children within the detention facilities suffer from intense medical and mental health issues (AHRC 2014). The solidification of sovereign borders is being played out in Australia through contestations over the best way to protect the lives of children.

Another example of sovereignty being played out through the imagery of children in need of protection occurred in 2007 when the Australian government launched an operation in the Northern Territory of the country that used military intervention to control what was depicted as a "crisis" of child sexual abuse in geographically remote Aboriginal communities. The suspension of the Anti-Discrimination Act that allowed this intervention to occur on the basis of "racial" descent, and the restrictions on welfare payments that followed, have been condemned as having little to do with the protection of children and much to do with the Australian government seeking to solidify control in those areas, especially in relation to land use and the introduction of "leases" on land that had previously been considered in relation to Aboriginal sovereignty (Lattas and Morris 2010). The protection of children continues to be utilised in Australia as a way to exert and legitimise sovereign power. The effect of doing so is an alignment of population lifestyles towards the creation of particular kinds of futures that meet the interests and agendas of the state.

These dynamics of protection, racialisation, and power also shape the lives of refugees resettled in Australia from Africa. It was not only Camille who recognised parallels between the contemporary removal of children from the families of African refugees and the historical removal of children from the families of Aboriginal people in Australia. One evening during my fieldwork, I was sitting in the back seat of a van, listening to Miriam excitedly update her friend, Louise, on events that had occurred in Australia whilst Louise had been away visiting family in Africa. It was after midnight, and we were making the long drive back to the regional city we lived in after picking Louise up from the international airport in Sydney earlier in the evening. I became directly involved in the conversation when Miriam turned to me to say, "Tell her that it is true. That family—you know who I mean—their children were taken by the government."

I confirmed that the story was true. I watched Louise silently stare out of the passenger seat window. She appeared to be in shock from the realisation that the Australian government had dismantled another family of refugees from Africa. Miriam, however, did not remain silent. "Isn't this what the government did with the Aboriginal people?" Visibly angered, she went on, "Didn't they get all of their children taken away?"

Recognising that there is a parallel between interventions of the child welfare system that are experienced by resettled refugees now and the systematic removal of Aboriginal children historically opens up new ways to think about sovereignty in temporal terms. The historical removal of Aboriginal children was justified for decades by consecutive governments who claimed that doing so was in the best interests of those children, themselves. Such spurious and paternalistic justifications reflect a kind of sovereignty that is realised through the determination of rule of law and exception, since those policies only affected Aboriginal people who, as non-citizens at the time, had extremely restricted legal rights through which they could attempt to push back against government policy. But the continuing vulnerability of Central African refugee families to interventions from the child welfare system contests the idea that it is through politico-legal status, exclusively, that formations of sovereignty are realised and imposed. Rather, it is through the very incorporation of these women into civic life through resettlement that they come to experience the direct and absolute authority of sovereign power to reduce them to a graduated state of exception because their marginalisation and de-legitimisation as citizens who are marked as problematic and deficient makes it difficult for them to then exert political agency. The sovereignty that produces this exception state, in which these women exist outside of conventions of civic order, is that which is imposed through decentralised modes of control and grounded in a temporal orientation to produce, through population controls, particular kinds of futures that align with state interests.

Policing the family

It is through governmentality that particular kinds of futures that align with state interests are made possible. The concept of governmentality refers to the ways in which states produce self-governing populations who have internalised dominant state interests and thereby come to assume that ways of living that align with those interests are normal and good and that ways of living that deviate from those are bad and in need of intervention (Foucault 1991, 2008). In Australia, as elsewhere, it is behaviours that affirm and reproduce market logics and economic participation that are valued: prioritising work and productivity, individualisation, and the accumulation of commodities to produce societal hierarchies. But how are such self-governing populations produced and such logics internalised as normal?

The family is a crucial institution through which techniques of self-governance and the interests of the state are internalised and reproduced. Family life is a microcosm of societal values and possible futures. As Nikolas Rose (1990: 151) points out, "'the family' has come to operate as a social mechanism for producing and regulating the subjective capacities of future citizens." When particular populations within a society are marked as potentially problematic to the interests of the state, then it is through institutional interventions into family life that they are brought into alignment with dominant modes of governmentality. The policing of the family by government institutions is not arbitrary or neutral but, rather, represents a form of social control through which states seek to develop and confirm the "quality" of the national body and the citizens it is comprised of (Donzelot 1979). I observed such processes while working with women whose children were removed from their care and observing the ways in which the attempt to promote the welfare of children and families also works as a technique of disciplining refugees.

The disciplining imperative of the child welfare system to reproduce particular models of governmentality became especially apparent from reports made about the parental care behaviours of women I conducted fieldwork with, following supervised visitations between mothers and the children who had been removed from their care. For example, one of the women I conducted fieldwork with whose children have been removed was evaluated as lacking "attachment" to her children because, during such visitations, she did not overtly "play" with her children, despite having access to toys and games. Being labelled as lacking attachment to her children was a way to characterise the caregiving of that mother as deficient because attachment is a term used in early childhood professions in Western contexts to describe the intensity of connection between caregivers and offspring, and which is considered to be a crucial indicator of the potential of a caregiver to provide for the care, safety, and protection needs of children. But the demonstration of attachment is not universal (LeVine and Norman 2001): care and connectedness to children follows cultural norms. For women I conducted fieldwork with, playing with children is not a conventional way to interact with them: it is an activity that is generally reserved for older siblings. But these contingencies of attachment were not taken into account in the case of that mother, who was instead labelled as a deficient parent. In another case, a woman was reprimanded because her children exhibited what were termed "parentified" behaviours, that is, older siblings were actively involved in caring for younger siblings, and this was taken to be an indicator of negligent parenting. These are behaviours that deviate from the overarching aim of parental care in Western contexts, which is, according to Angela McRobbie (2013), to produce citizens whose "potential" for economic participation has been maximised.

Caregiving practices were not the only dynamics of family life problematised for women who had their children removed from their care. The care plans that were developed by the child protection agency, which set out the conditions under which children could be feasibly returned to parental care, often required women to attempt to make drastic changes to their lives in ways that would solidify them as productive citizens. During fieldwork, I observed situations in which, as part of the care plan, one mother was instructed to continue attending English language classes, attempt to find employment, acquire more suitable housing arrangements, attend parenting classes, and maintain health and medical care appointments, including regular visits to a psychologist, all at the same time. Taking into account that, like the other refugees I conducted fieldwork with, this woman was simultaneously still becoming proficient in English, had to rely on often unreliable public transport systems, was living in poverty, and was trying to deal with the emotional trauma of having her children forcibly and unexpectedly removed from her care, it was not surprising to me when she subsequently "failed" to meet the expectations of the child welfare agency and had the care of her children permanently transferred to the guardianship of the state. Her supposedly incompetent parenting stemmed less from an intrinsic deficiency of her caregiving and more from her inability to demonstrate good neoliberal citizenship: and, subsequently, her ability to socialise those values into her children and the possible futures that they embody. The intervention of the child welfare system into the lives of women I conducted fieldwork served as much to govern and discipline them into internalising and reproducing neoliberal values as a dominant mode of governmentality as it did to protect the welfare of children.

The removal of children is not, then, simply a technique of producing governmentality through the family. It is a method of "punitive governance" (Lancaster 2010). According to Roger Lancaster (2010), punitive governance is a way to describe how maintaining conditions of governmentality is achieved through the normalisation of violence from the state onto citizens as a technique of producing social order. Punitive governance is, according to Lancaster (2010: 74), the "real cultural logic of neoliberalism" because it creates the conditions in which the precarity of daily life under neoliberalism becomes projected onto those who are othered by poverty or racialisation (Ortner 2016): making state violence that is imposed on them seem necessary because they are not able to govern and regulate themselves toward the same disciplinary methods as others. The forced removal of children is not, then, just a method of protecting the welfare of children and families. It is the endpoint of a more extensive regime of punitive governance in which those who, like resettled refugees, become marked as other to the agenda and interests of the neoliberal Australian state are not simply forced into alignment with state agendas, but have their entire ways of being annihilated.

Who does this protection of children benefit, then? Forcibly removing children from their family not only serves as a way to protect them from a risk of significant harm. It also means that other aspects of their lives, like cultural identity, familial connections, and linguistic background, become diminished and incorporated into the hegemonic order of society. Writing about the experiences of Aboriginal people in Australia, Elizabeth Povinelli (2009, 2011) describes how the systematic removal of children from the care of Aboriginal parents and other interventionist modes of control into the lives of Aboriginal people serve, both historically and contemporaneously, to destroy aspects of Aboriginal ways of being that do not align with the interests of the state. The violence of cultural domination and annihilation through intervention into the family life of marginalised peoples in Australia is justified as normal and, indeed, made routine through a central political locus of sacrifice (Povinelli 2011). The Australian political system and public have come to accept that the suffering and destruction of particular aspects of Aboriginal cultures are necessary if doing so means that the future of the broader society, oriented towards prosperity measured in economic terms, is protected. This is what Povinelli (2011) terms an "economy of abandonment," in which the destruction of particular populations in a society, physically or culturally, is accepted as necessary and routine. The ways in which the child welfare system in Australia operates to not only protect the lives of children but to inculcate particular formations of family life and remove the parental rights of those who do not conform can be usefully considered through this framework as an economy of abandonment. Removing children is a way to enforce particular ways of being—and, subsequently, particular projected futures—by sacrificing those ways of living that may not necessarily present objective harm to children, but which represent deviations from state interests.

Incommensurable futures

Sovereignty is realised through temporal orientations, not only through determinations of politico-legal in- and exclusion from the national order. The temporal dynamic of sovereignty operates as a decentralised force of governmentality, regulating action in the present toward an aspirational future horizon that is assumed to be shared by all. But some lives can be viewed by dominant governing bodies as incommensurable to and with the hegemonic futures that are projected by the state. Those lives become marked as the exception: the populations whose ways of living are not protected by the rule of law in the same ways as the dominant population and who are, then, more vulnerable to violence instituted through the very rule of law that is in place to both govern and protect them. These are people who occupy a state of exception that is not realised through determinations of their politico-legal status but is graduated across various modes of civic exclusion that work to specifically impose and normalise methods of control onto lives like theirs, which have less value to state interests. This temporal context of sovereignty is constructed around an implicit societal hierarchy in which "the futures of some, or the hopes that they have for their future, can never be a *future* ... they can only drag others into the past" (Povinelli 2011: 28, emphasis in original). Such assumptions of temporal incommensurability serve to justify processes of systematic marginalisation through which interventions of the state and institutions that reflect state interests slowly suffocate ways of living that do not conform with neoliberal governmentalities, and which become, subsequently, untenable. The threshold between lives lived in a state of exception and lives made unliveable is temporal. When futures become not only precarious but impossible, the work of sovereign power is realised and complete.

The removal of children is an intensification of this process of producing hegemonic futures because it is an act that acutely severs the social reproduction of one type of future in order for the futures embodied by children to be re-oriented toward another. The policing of caregiving behaviours in the child welfare system as part of the mandate of child protection forces parents to conform to hegemonic orders of familial care that will, ostensibly, benefit their growing children and the future populace as a whole. Ultimately, however, all refugees resettled in Australia from Central Africa become incorporated into this process of temporal dominance. The system of refugee settlement in Australia is designed in a way that a priori problematises them. Refugee settlement systems not only provide support to the welfare of newly resettling refugees, but also organise their lives in ways that mostly align with neoliberal objectives that reflect state interests.

As temporalised subjects whose futures are imagined to represent a problem to those that make up the normative horizon of the society in which they are living, the lives of refugees are a contested temporal domain. But rather than simply "let die"—the conventional understanding of sovereignty as a supreme and top-down exertion of state power to determine the life and death of those within a particular polity (Hansen and Stepputat 2006)—the problem that these refugees represent to the hegemonic futures of the society in which they are living are controlled and constrained in temporal terms. The domination and subjugation of their futures through techniques of governmentality and, for some, direct intervention represents the exertion of a kind of sovereignty that circulates across and beyond the spatial and politico-legal borders of the nation state: that is, sovereignty as control and constraint over time.

References

Agamben, G. 1998. *Homo Sacer: Sovereign Power and Bare Life*. Translated by Daniel Heller-Roazen. Stanford, CA: Stanford University Press.

AHRC. 2014. The Forgotten Children: National Inquiry into Children in Immigration Detention. Available at: www.humanrights.gov.au/sites/default/files/document/publication/forgotten_children_2014.pdf (Accessed 3 October 2016).

Commonwealth of Australia. 1997. Bringing Them Home Report: National Inquiry into the Separation of Aboriginal and Torres Strait Islander Children from Their Families. Available at: www.humanrights.gov.au/sites/default/files/content/pdf/social_justice/bringing_them_home_report.pdf (Accessed 26 December 2014).

Cuthbert, D. and Quartly, M. 2013. Forced Child Removal and the Politics of National Apologies in Australia. *The American Indian Quarterly* 37(1): 178–202.

Donzelot, J. 1979. *The Policing of Families*. New York: Pantheon Books.

Dunn, E. and Cons, J. 2013. Aleatory Sovereignty and the Rule of Sensitive Spaces. *Antipode* 46(1): 92–109.

Fassin, D. 2012. *Humanitarian Reason: A Moral History of the Present*. Berkeley: University of California Press.

Foucault, M. 1991. Governmentality. In *The Foucault Effect: Studies in Governmentality: with Two Lectures by and an Interview with Michel Foucault*. G. Burchell, C. Gordon, and P. Miller (Eds.), pp. 87–104. London: Harvester Wheatsheaf.

Foucault, M. 2008. *The Birth of Biopolitics: Lectures at the College de France, 1978–1979*. Translated by G. Burchell. London: Palgrave Macmillan.

Four Corners. 2002. To Deter or Deny. Available at: www.abc.net.au/4corners/stories/s531993.htm (Accessed 1 January 2016).

Gale, P. 2004. The Refugee Crisis and Fear: Populist Politics and Media Discourse. *Journal of Sociology* 40(4): 321–340.

Hansen, T. and Stepputat, F. 2006. Sovereignty Revisited. *Annual Review of Anthropology* 35: 295–315.

Hugo, G. 2002. Australian Immigration Policy: The Significance of the Events of September 11. *International Migration Review* 36(1): 37–40.

Lancaster, R. 2010. Republic of Fear: The Rise of Punitive Governance in America. In *The Insecure American: How We Got Here and What We Should Do About It*. H. Gusterson and C. Besteman (Eds.), pp. 63–76. Berkeley: University of California Press.

Lattas, A. and Morris, B. 2010. Embedded Anthropology and the Intervention. *Arena Magazine* 107: 15–20.

LeVine, R. and Norman, K. 2001. The Infant's Acquisition of Culture: Early Attachment Reexamined in Anthropological Perspective. In *The Psychology of Cultural Experience*. C. Moore and H. Mathews (Eds.), pp. 83–103. Cambridge: Cambridge University Press.

Malkki, L. 1992. National Geographic: The Rooting of Peoples and the Territorialization of National Identity among Scholars and Refugees. *Cultural Anthropology* 7(1): 24–44.

McRobbie, Angela. 2013. Feminism, the Family, and the New 'Mediated' Maternalism. *New Formations* 80–81: 119–137.

Millbank, A. 2009. Kind or Cruel?: Labor's Boat People Policies. *People and Place* 17(4): 8–17.

Ong, A. 2006. *Neoliberalism as Exception: Mutations in Citizenship and Sovereignty*. Durham, NC; London: Duke University Press.

Ortner, S. 2016. Dark Anthropology and Its Others: Theory since the Eighties. *HAU: Journal of Ethnographic Theory* 6(1): 47–73.

Pickering, S. and Lambert, C. 2002. Deterrence: Australia's Refugee Policy. *Current Issues in Criminal Justice* 14(1): 65–86.

Povinelli, E. 2009. Beyond Good and Evil, Whither Liberal Sacrificial Love? *Public Culture*. 21(1): 77–100.

Povinelli, E. 2011. *Economies of Abandonment: Social Belonging and Endurance in Late Liberalism*. Durham, NC and London: Duke University Press.

Ramsay, G. 2017a. Incommensurable Futures and Displaced Lives: Sovereignty as Control over Time. *Public Culture* 29(3): 515–538.

Rose, N. 1990. *Governing the Soul: The Shaping of the Private Self*. Florence, KY: Taylor & Francis / Routledge.

Schmitt, C. 1985. *Political Theology: Four Chapters on the Concept of Sovereignty*. Cambridge, MA: MIT Press.

Strong, T. 2005. Forward. In *Political Theology: Four Chapters on the Concept of Sovereignty*. C. Schmitt (Ed.). pp. vii–xxxvi. Chicago, IL: University of Chicago Press.

Upton, J.C. 2014. Guantánamo Bay, Anthropologists, and the State of Exception. *Finalist Paper*, Association for Political and Legal Anthropology 2014 Graduate Student Paper Prize.

Van Krieken, R. 1999. The Stolen Generations' and Cultural Genocide: The Forced Removal of Australian Indigenous Children from their Families and its Implications for the Sociology of Childhood. *Childhood* 6(3): 297–311.

Conclusion

"This is violence. What they are doing to us here, now. This is violence."

I return to these words spoken by Helen because the experiences and stories recounted in previous chapters have illuminated the context of her claim that violence endures in the lives of refugees even following resettlement. Resettlement is not an automatic and durable solution to the displacement of refugees. For some, it is no solution at all.

If resettlement is not necessarily a solution to the displacement of refugees, then what could be? Is it even possible to identify a solution to displacement as a distinct, stable, and absolute condition of refuge? What is at stake when being critical about resettlement given that, for so many refugees, it may provide the only possible means to alleviate situations of extreme physical insecurity in camps and urban asylum across the world? These questions haunted me in the months and years after I conducted my fieldwork. The only response to them that I feel encapsulates a departure from conventional ways of approaching refugees requires turning toward what is always at the centre of the lives of women I conducted research with: connection.

When I refer to connection, I mean an attempt to recognise shared dimensions of the human condition. I do not mean to apply optimistic possibility to the recognition and celebration of difference. Indeed, it is often the case, especially in Australia, that supporting the development of a "multicultural" society in which difference is celebrated means homogenising and reifying marginalised populations in ways that benefit dominant groups (Hage 1998; Povinelli 2002). Rather, when I speak about connectedness, I mean nurturing the opportunity for, and possibility of, intersubjective reciprocity between displaced peoples and those they encounter across multiple scales of forced migration experience, so that categories such as "refugee," and the assumptions of difference embedded within those and other labels, cease to be salient and are eclipsed by the possibility of connection.

The lives and livelihoods of millions of displaced peoples are clearly at stake in attempts to create solutions that can address the displacement of refugees. These are not just theoretical meanderings about how to best approach an abstract problem: these are real lives being played out through global politics at a mass scale. And yet the rush to label these people and processes reproduces divisions that obscure the lived experiences of refugees. Terms like "crisis," "flows," and "mass displacement" speak to the scale of experience (Leach 2003), but not to the experience itself. Perhaps it is the focus on the solution as a distinct and definable object that is the central impasse through which the problem of refugees continues to be reproduced, and which makes this supposed problem seem impossible to resolve.

A turn to connection when attempting to both theorise and address these emergent conditions of global precarity and forced migration means recognising that the lives of those labelled as refugees or other kinds of displaced and marginalised peoples are not exclusive but are intimately bound together with dominant populations in a shared future horizon. Connecting shared dimensions of the human condition is, however, only possible when the focus of dialogues about precarity and migration, across local, national, and global levels, shifts from talking about refugees to recognising people and the possibility of shared futures.

Unsettling the humanitarian benevolence of resettlement

Even though the programme of resettlement in Australia is optimistically called the "Humanitarian Programme," it seems impossible to characterise the resettlement of refugees to Australia as a humanitarian solution to displacement because the refuge that it offers to refugees is so clearly conditional. Humanitarianism is a general ethic to "do good," that is, to alleviate human suffering and improve aspects of the human condition. This ethic becomes expressed across a number of different fields involving numerous actors from different backgrounds and contexts: as a cluster of sentiments, through laws and policy, and as itself a form of government (Ticktin 2014). The paradox of humanitarianism that has fascinated many anthropologists is that even though the humanitarian ethic implies providing care for the intrinsic good of the recipient without the expectation of return or reward, the instrumentalisation of humanitarian sentiment, especially through systems of transnational humanitarianism, is embedded within power relations that implicitly, if not explicitly, impose conditions, and often violence, on those who receive care (Beckett 2017; Harrell-Bond 1986; Harrell-Bond, Voutira, and Leopold 1992; James 2012), or require their suffering to take a particular form in order to be recognised as valid (Fassin 2012; Fiddian-Qasmiyeh 2011; Malkki 1996; Ticktin 2011; Timmer 2010). Humanitarianism can be thought of, then, as a "gift" in the sense described by Marcel Mauss (1969): that is, as a form of sociality that connects the self-interest of the giver with care for others, making the conditions under which humanitarianism can be repressive possible. In the Mauss (1969) perspective of a gift, it is impossible to isolate the intent of providing care without recognising that doing so stems from, and produces implications for, the self-interests in the donor. Although Mauss (1969) recognises social welfare programmes as one area in which the gift of care may become an arena of developing mutual moral sentiment, forms of giving that seem intrinsically altruistic are not isolated from this dynamic of giver and receiver, meaning that the gift can be tyrannical as much as beneficial to the recipient (Scheper-Hughes 2007).

The settlement of asylum seekers and refugees is one area in which the humanitarian sentiment of providing care to a suffering population evokes a hierarchical dynamic between giver and receiver. The settlement of refugees and asylum seekers in a host nation of refuge is so often conditional on their performing particular roles of victimhood, and demonstrating suffering, subservience, and gratefulness (Fassin 2011: 250–251; Jackson 2013b: 95). For the refugees I conducted fieldwork with, however, it was not just that resettled refugees were expected to perform subservience. The structure of the programme of refugee settlement in Australia is one in which the lives of newly settling refugees are organised to meet implicit expectations of social homogeneity and neoliberal logics of individualisation and self-sufficiency. These refugees are not only expected to be subservient but to dissolve the apparent burden of their resettlement to Australia by becoming a particular kind of citizen whose value is measured through economic productivity and whose differences must be subsumed into the dominant culture, rather than embraced. When refugees cannot conform to these expectations of resettlement in Australia, their lives, being unable to fit into a dominant aspirational future horizon, are slowly suffocated through institutional constraints. The project of refugee resettlement is humanitarian only in so far as the settlement of refugees does not challenge existing nationhood projects and the hegemonic futures towards which these are oriented. Resettlement in Australia is conditional refuge.

Displacing categories

More than 30 years ago, Liisa Malkki (1992, 1995a, 1995b) urged researchers to be critical about the ways in which they reproduce the "refugee" as an exceptional category of person who exists outside of what is taken to be a natural conflation between persons and citizenship. When the "refugee" is taken to be the parameters of an exceptional category of existence, then not only are the lives of those displaced peoples essentialised to their politico-legal status: when applying such labels uncritically researchers also risk reproducing the seeming naturalness of nationhood as a central organising factor of the world order and conceal the violences that attempting to maintain national interests produce. Malkki (1995a) pointed to the ways in which, in contexts where there are less institutional constraints in place to manage and control refugees, the layers of their displacement become less salient as they strive towards, and create, futures of their own making, meaning that the "refugee" category is not always so essentialising as it can seem when presented as the defining factor of displaced peoples' lives. However, research continues to focus on the ways in which the lives of refugees are diminished by constraints related to their politico-legal status or the ways in which they seek to exert agency despite those constraints. There is little recognition that the lives of refugees or those who have been displaced are constrained in ways that are not defined by or reducible to the politico-legal status of statelessness, which the more expansive perspective on displacement put forward by Liisa Malkki (1992, 1995a) began to unravel.

The "refugee" figure has been theorised by Zygmunt Bauman (2004) as a potential lens through which to think about the increasingly generalised condition of precarity and uprootedness that has proliferated under neoliberal capitalism. Few, however, have taken up this idea and applied it to empirical settings as a way to consider that it is possible to exist as a refugee across diverse global settings, and that the term can more expansively be applied to those who do not fit the conventional idea of a refugee as a person who is forcibly and physically dislocated from one country to seek refuge and protection in another. Recognising that the "refugee" concept cannot be essentialised to the international legal parameters of statelessness, Anne Allison (2012) connects the idea of the "refugee," as a generalised sense of a deterritorialised subject, to the experiences of youth in contemporary Japan. Living with seemingly unresolvable precarity, these youth have become "refugees" because the state is not able to provide them with security. Although Allison (2012) points to the expansive potentiality of the "refugee" concept to other populations of displaced peoples as "ordinary refugees," I would consider that it is the experience of existential displacement itself—as a sense of existing in the present towards an uncertain or seemingly impossible future—rather than the categorical condition of refugeeness that is the locus of these shared dimensions of experience that transcend politico-legal classifications. As Allison (2012) recognises, conventional modes of thinking about refugees are a basis from which to connect the experiences of broad populations of people whose lives have been similarly trapped in a state of temporal incommensurability.

If, as the experiences of women who have been resettled as refugees in Australia suggest, displacement endures as an existential condition beyond the politico-legal status of existing as a "refugee," then it is possible to think about what it means to be displaced in a way that goes beyond defining displacement as a dislocation of national identity that is realised at the borders of nation states and resolved upon being re-inserted within those borders as a recognised resident or citizen. Rather, displacement is also an existential condition that is realised through shifts in the temporalisation of everyday life: that is, when the predictability of the present and assumptions about the future are jeopardised and made precarious.

That displacement resonates at a temporal level for refugees and asylum seekers is increasingly recognised in anthropological literature (Brun 2015; El-Shaarawi 2015; Griffiths 2014; Ramadan 2013; Rotter 2016). There continues, however, to be a tendency to conflate the politico-legal ambiguity of statelessness with a dynamic of temporal suspension. Focusing on the ways in which refugees and asylum seekers spend long periods of time attempting to order and arrange their lives while waiting within insecure temporalities and existing towards uncertain futures is important. However, approaching displacement as an experience of liminality is limiting in some ways. Liminality implies a linear structure of existence in which it is possible to resolve temporal suspension through ritual reincorporation. In the case of asylum seekers and refugees, the ritual aspect relates to those processes through which asylum seekers and refugees become re-inserted back into a framework of national identity, by either being expatriated back to a country of origin or being given permission to settle in a host nation of refuge. But, as we have seen, displacement endures beyond the parameters of national identity.

The problem with this linear model of forced migration is that it is not necessarily how refugees themselves live and experience displacement and refuge, as if these are two distinct categories of existence that can be mapped onto a linear temporal trajectory. Characterising displacement as a temporal condition of liminality, in which refugees and other irregular migrants are suspended in a kind of temporal and politico-legal limbo between categories of nationhood and the stability of claiming nationhood, may inadvertently reproduce their otherness. The "refugee," "asylum seeker," and "irregular migrant" have come to represent a kind of displacement that is not only defined by politico-legal ambiguity within the national order of things, but which is conflated with a seemingly essential condition of temporal otherness: of being outside the time rhythms of ordinary life. By characterising politico-legal ambiguity as concurrent with an experience of temporal otherness, deploying the refugee category can serve, then, to reduce the object of anthropological inquiry as being of another time (Fabian 1983): a denial of coevalness that reproduces and essentialises that category of person. Using that category as a basis from which to develop solutions to displacement as a liminal temporal experience that intertwines statelessness and suspended time rhythms means automatically assuming that incorporating refugees into the national order is a way to bring them into normal rhythms of time: thereby implicitly normalising logics of linear and neoliberal time.

It is not that those situations of stasis and precarity that so often emerge in the experiences of migrants do not produce displacement and uncertain temporal rhythms and future horizons. Rather, the experience of being displaced cannot be exclusively understood as a product of those physical migrations and politico-legal dislocations because, when considered as an existential experience, displacement is a fundamentally human condition that can confront any person who is seeking to create a life worth living within contexts of constraint (Jackson 2013a). Thinking about the temporal uncertainty of refugees and other irregular migrants as related, instead, to displacement as an existential experience rather than defined by their condition of ambiguous citizenship, is a way to think about how regimes of temporal incommensurability operate more expansively to dominate marginalised populations across multiple layers of societal populations. Doing so displaces politico-legal categories of citizenship and statelessness as the fundamental locus through which domination and sovereignty are produced. Connecting the experiences of those labelled as refugees with other marginalised groups can be a way to trace how displacement is experienced more broadly, and how displacement is produced through de-centralised techniques of sovereignty that resonate across diverse populations that are marked and encoded with temporal incommensurability.

Forward momentum

How might this turn to connection take form, empirically and theoretically, when attempting to address the displacement of refugees and other displaced peoples? More poignantly, perhaps, is connectedness, that is, the recognition of shared human reciprocity and potential for empathetic engagement, even possible under current systems of responding to and providing refuge for those who are displaced? Based on research observing how humanitarian actors interact with refugees in contexts of protracted asylum, Catherine Brun (2016: 405) argues for an "ethics of care" in which "tending to relationships between people becomes the core" as a way to resolve the problem of humanitarian intervention into the lives of refugees, which so often forces them into suspended temporalities. The ethics of care brought forward by Brun (2016: 405) is premised on feminist ideals about the necessity of connection, "in which social relationships of mutuality and trust rather than dependence are foregrounded." It is only through making the former stranger and other into a relation that humanitarianism can work towards a future, rather than suspend refugees as objects to be governed into a temporal impasse.

I agree with Brun (2016) in that it is only by foregrounding refugees as people that a sense of temporal continuity and forward momentum is able to be imagined and made possible. The ethic of care, however, is, as Brun (2016) acknowledges, a basis of connection that can nonetheless reproduce, at least at first, hierarchical relations based on giver and recipient. At a local scale, as Brun (2016) suggests, these hierarchies can be mediated over time by humanitarian actors and recipients of aid sharing experiences together, which is a basis from which to develop reciprocal empathy and to shift refugees from being an unknown other to being a personal relation. But can these local possibilities for connectedness be incorporated into at a broader scale, at the level of national and international humanitarian regimes? At those scales, humanitarian intervention often works from the assumption that being displaced means being ejected from a national order, and that, therefore, restoring politico-legal rights is the best basis from which to resolve displacement. Undoubtedly, rights are very important to the possibility of living a good life. Yet at those scales of humanitarian intervention the ethic of care is not oriented at the level of interpersonal connectedness, but is a discourse of benevolence that conceals how the organisation of refugee lives through the global humanitarian system and host nations that provide them with refuge can inflict and impose harm as much as protect and restore security.

As it stands, it seems that enabling connectedness would require an overhaul, not only of the international systems of responding to refugees and forced migration but of the very organising logics of neoliberal capitalist societal frameworks, themselves. Formal institutions of responding to populations of asylum seekers and refugees, in particular, operate in ways that immediately create divisions between them and locals. Conventionally, this division has been codified in spatial terms, through the containment of refugees in camps located in the host nation of asylum (Agier 2008, 2011). Now, even this technique of containment is being pre-empted by the construction of increasingly dangerous barriers and fortifications to stop the physical movement of migrants and populations more broadly (Andersson 2014; Fassin 2011; Hyndman 1999; Reeves 2014; Sur 2013). But even in settings where the local integration of refugees is supposed to be taking place, such as in Uganda and countries of resettlement, like Australia, the overriding neoliberal logics of self-sufficiency and individualisation through which lives in refuge are organised means that the opportunity for deep and meaningful connection with others is limited. Indeed, the precariousness of life under states and systems that prioritise neoliberal interests produces a situation in which it is necessary to create division and hierarchy between societal groups as a way to justify what might otherwise be seen as punitive modes of governance (Ortner 2016).

Toward the possibility of connection

By describing how assumptions of benevolence that are attached to the resettlement of refugees across academic, humanitarian, public, and political discourses obscure and conceal the significant violences that are imposed on refugees through processes of becoming settled and summing up these findings into the two simple words of "impossible refuge," my research and findings seem firmly situated within what Sherry Ortner (2016) refers to as "dark anthropology" and what Joel Robbins (2013) describes as the "suffering slot." That is, from my fieldwork and analysis, I have produced an ethnography of violence that is somewhat typical of anthropology: of lives disrupted and controlled, constrained and diminished, and of women who have been given the opportunity to have the cruel optimism of aspiring to be resettled made possible only to be further victimised and made vulnerable when that imaginary is finally realised.

In a critical reflexive analysis of the discipline of anthropology, Joel Robbins (2013) describes how early anthropological research was grounded in a premise of radical difference by situating objects of anthropological inquiry into the "savage slot." In contemporary anthropological research, the tendency to other remains, according to Robbins (2013), except that the mode of reification has transitioned from the "savage slot" to the "suffering slot." Because trauma creates a sense of shared humanity and an imperative to action, the "suffering slot" has become a trope in contemporary anthropology because it seemingly affirms the relevance of the discipline. Robbins (2013) advocates for a turn to an "anthropology of the good" as a way to transcend the risk of reproducing the anthropological other as the suffering subject.

Attention to cultural models of time is one way to open up this possibility of encountering the good because the ways in which people experience and invest their time in specific ways often reveals the possibility of happiness in both moments of temporal immediacy and aspirational future horizons (Robbins 2013, 2015). However, as Sherry Ortner (2016: 50) points out, for so many people, life under neoliberalism does become organised in ways that produce suffering and violence, meaning that the "dark anthropology" that is the focus of Robbins' (2013) critique is not only another disciplinary mode of othering but also reflects the "increasingly problematic conditions of the real world under neoliberalism."

Can the imperative to document the reality of lived suffering be reconciled with recognition of the good life or aspirations toward it? Jane Guyer (2009) draws attention to the idea of "possibility" as a way to direct anthropological inquiry towards future horizons that transcend both the false imperative of crisis and the anxiety of projected futures that have come to dominate how anthropological research, whether "dark" or "good," is situated in time. The framework of "possibility" is a way to consider the temporal immediacy of processes through which horizons of hope and suffering are longitudinally created.

Refuge is always going to be an impossible endeavour for refugees when it is imagined, or assumed, to be a temporally stable point of experience on a linear trajectory of forced migration that is realised through politico-legal incorporation into a host society. I have described in this book the conditions under which the possibility of refuge as a stable and absolute solution to displacement is made impossible. But when refuge is taken to be a process rather than a distinct "solution," it becomes a possibility. Attention to connection is a theoretical and empirical orientation that captures the intersubjective dynamics of future-building, which are so often the basis of both hope and despair in the present. It was through the possibility of connection that refugees sought to create the conditions of refuge in their lives, and it is through attention to the possibility of connection, rather than the fortification and renewal of borders and boundaries of difference and otherness, that global systems of responding to forced migration may work towards shared, rather than incommensurable, futures.

References

Agier, M. 2008. *On the Margins of the World: The Refugee Experience Today.* Cambridge: Polity Press.

Agier, M. 2011. *Managing the Undesirables: Refugee Camps and Humanitarian Government.* Cambridge: Polity Press.

Allison, A. 2012. Ordinary Refugees: Social Precarity and Soul in 21st Century Japan. *Anthropological Quarterly* 85(2): 345–370.

Andersson, R. 2014. Hunter and Prey: Patrolling Clandestine Migration in the Euro-African Borderlands. *Anthropological Quarterly* 87(1): 119–150.

Bauman, Z. 2004. *Wasted Lives: Modernity and its Outcasts.* Cambridge: Polity Press.

Beckett, G. 2017. A Dog's Life: Suffering Humanitarianism in Port-au-Prince, Haiti. *American Anthropologist* 119(1): 35–45.

Brun, C. 2015. Active Waiting and Changing Hopes: Toward a Time Perspective on Protracted Displacement. *Social Analysis* 59(1): 19–37.

Brun, C. 2016. There is No Future in Humanitarianism: Emergency, Temporality and Protracted Displacement. *History and Anthropology* 27(4): 393–410.

El-Shaarawi, N. 2015. Living in an Uncertain Future: Temporality, Uncertainty, and Well-Being among Iraqi Refugees in Egypt. *Social Analysis* 59(1): 38–56.

Fabian, J. 1983. *Time and the Other: How Anthropology Makes Its Object.* New York: Columbia University Press.

Fassin, D. 2011. Policing Borders, Producing Boundaries: The Governmentality of Immigration in Dark Times. *Annual Review of Anthropology* 40: 213–226.

Fassin, D. 2012. *Humanitarian Reason: A Moral History of the Present.* Berkeley: University of California Press.

Fiddian-Qasmiyeh, E. 2011. The Pragmatics of Performance: Putting 'Faith' in Aid in the Sahrawi Refugee Camps. *Journal of Refugee Studies* 24(3): 533–547.

Griffiths, M. 2014. Out of Time: The Temporal Uncertainties of Refuges Asylum Seekers and Immigration Detainees. *Journal of Ethnic and Migration Studies* 40(12): 1991–2009.

Guyer, J. 2009. On 'Possibility': A Response to 'How is Anthropology Going?' *Anthropological Theory* 9(4): 355–370.

Hage, G. 1998. *White Nation: Fantasies of White Supremacy in a Multicultural Society.* Annandale, NSW: Pluto Press.

Harrell-Bond, B. 1986. *Imposing Aid: Emergency Assistance to Refugees.* Oxford: Oxford University Press.

Harrell-Bond, B., Voutira, E., and Leopold, M. 1992. Counting the Refugees Gifts, Givers, Patrons, and Clients. *Journal of Refugee Studies* 5(3–4): 205–225.

Hyndman, J. 1999. A Post-Cold War Geography of Forced Migration in Kenya and Somalia. *The Professional Geographer* 51(1): 104–114.

Jackson, M. 2013a. *The Wherewithal of Life: Ethics Migration, and the Question of Well-Being.* Berkeley: University of California Press.

Jackson, M. 2013b. *The Politics of Storytelling: Variations on a Theme by Hannah Arendt.* 2nd Edition. Copenhagen: Museum Tusculanum Press.

James, E. 2012. Witchcraft, Bureaucraft, and the Social Life of (US)Aid in Haiti. *Cultural Anthropology* 27(1): 50–75.

Leach, M. 2003. Disturbing Practices: Dehumanizing Asylum Seekers in the Refugee "Crisis" in Australia, 2001–2002. *Refuge* 21(3): 25–33.

Malkki, L. 1992. National Geographic: The Rooting of Peoples and the Territorialization of National Identity among Scholars and Refugees. *Cultural Anthropology* 7(1): 24–44.

Malkki, L. 1995a. *Purity and Exile: Violence, Memory, and National Cosmology among Hutu Refugees in Tanzania*. Chicago, IL: University of Chicago Press.

Malkki, L. 1995b. Refugees and Exile: From 'Refugee Studies' to the National Order of Things. *Annual Review of Anthropology* 24: 495–523.

Malkki, L. 1996. Speechless Emissaries: Refugees, Humanitarianism, and Dehistoricization. *Cultural Anthropology* 11(3): 377–404.Mauss, M. 1969. *The Gift: Forms and Functions of Exchange in Archaic Societies*. London: Cohen & West.

Ortner, S. 2016. Dark Anthropology and Its Others: Theory since the Eighties. *HAU: Journal of Ethnographic Theory* 6(1): 47–73.

Povinelli, E. 2002. *The Cunning of Recognition: Indigenous Alterities and the Making of Australian Multiculturalism*. Durham: Duke University Press.

Ramadan, A. 2013. Spatialising the Refugee Camp. *Transactions* 38(1): 65–77.

Reeves, M. 2014. *Border Work: Spatial Lives of the State in Rural Central Asia*. Ithaca, NY: Cornell University Press.

Robbins, J. 2013. Beyond the Suffering Subject: Toward an Anthropology of the Good. *Journal of the Royal Anthropological Institute* 19: 447–462.

Robbins, J. 2015. On Happiness, Values, and Time: The Long and Short of It. *HAU: Journal of Ethnographic Theory* 5(3): 215–233.

Rotter, R. 2015. Waiting in the Asylum Determination Process: Just an Empty Interlude? *Time & Society* 25(1): 80–101.

Scheper-Hughes, N. 2007. The Tyranny of the Gift: Sacrificial Violence in Living Donor Transplants. *American Journal of Transplantation* 7(3): 507–511.

Sur, M. 2013. Through Metal Fences: Material Mobility and the Politics of Transnationality at Borders. *Mobilities* 8(1): 70–89.

Ticktin, M. 2011. The Gendered Human of Humanitarianism: Medicalising and Politicising Sexual Violence. *Gender & History* 23(2): 250–265.

Ticktin, M. 2014. Transnational Humanitarianism. *The Annual Review of Anthropology* 43: 273–289.

Timmer, A. 2010. Constructing the "Needy Subject": NGO Discourses of Roma Need. *Political and Legal Anthropology Review* 33(2): 264–281.

Index